Lecture Notes in Computer Science 13800

Founding Editors

Gerhard Goos
  Karlsruhe Institute of Technology, Karlsruhe, Germany

Juris Hartmanis
  Cornell University, Ithaca, NY, USA

Editorial Board Members

Elisa Bertino
  Purdue University, West Lafayette, IN, USA

Wen Gao
  Peking University, Beijing, China

Bernhard Steffen ⓘ
  TU Dortmund University, Dortmund, Germany

Moti Yung ⓘ
  Columbia University, New York, NY, USA

More information about this series at https://link.springer.com/bookseries/558

Akash Lal · Stefano Tonetta (Eds.)

Verified Software

Theories, Tools and Experiments

14th International Conference, VSTTE 2022
Trento, Italy, October 17–18, 2022
Revised Selected Papers

 Springer

Editors
Akash Lal
Microsoft Research
Karnataka, India

Stefano Tonetta ⓘD
Fondazione Bruno Kessler
Trento, Italy

ISSN 0302-9743   ISSN 1611-3349 (electronic)
Lecture Notes in Computer Science
ISBN 978-3-031-25802-2   ISBN 978-3-031-25803-9 (eBook)
https://doi.org/10.1007/978-3-031-25803-9

Preface

This volume contains the contributed papers presented at VSTTE 2022, the 14th Working Conference on Verified Software: Theories, Tools and Experiments held on October 17–18, 2022 in Trento, Italy. The working conference was co-located with the 22nd International Conference on Formal Methods in Computer-Aided Design (FMCAD 2022).

The Verified Software Initiative (VSI), spearheaded by Tony Hoare and Jayadev Misra, is an ambitious research program for making large-scale verified software a practical reality. VSTTE is the main forum for advancing the initiative. VSTTE brings together experts spanning the spectrum of software verification in order to foster international collaboration on the critical research challenges.

There were 20 submissions to VSTTE 2022, with authors from 14 countries. The Program Committee consisted of 27 distinguished computer scientists from all over the world. Each submission was reviewed by at least three Program Committee members in a single-blind mode. In order to ensure that topic-specific expert reviews were obtained, help was also sought from five sub-reviewers. After a comprehensive discussion on the strengths and weaknesses of papers, the committee decided to accept nine papers. The technical program also included two invited talks by Aws Albarghouthi (University of Wisconsin, Madison, USA) and Cezara Dragoi (Amazon, France), as well as an invited tutorial by Sanjit Seshia (University of California, Berkeley, USA) that was held jointly with FMCAD 2022.

We greatly acknowledge the help of the FMCAD 2022 Organizing Committee as well as Natarajan Shankar with all logistical matters in running VSTTE 2022. We are also thankful to EasyChair for providing an easy and efficient mechanism for submission of papers, management of reviews, and eventually in the generation of this volume.

December 2022
Supratik Chakraborty
Akash Lal
Stefano Tonetta

Preface

Organization

General Chair

Supratik Chakraborty   IIT Bombay, India

Program Chairs

Akash Lal   Microsoft Research, India
Stefano Tonetta   FBK, Italy

Program Committee

Christel Baier	TU Dresden, Germany
Nikolaj Bjorner	Microsoft Research, USA
Roderick Bloem	Graz University of Technology, Austria
Borzoo Bonakdarpour	Michigan State University, USA
Supratik Chakraborty	IIT Bombay, India
Chih-Hong Cheng	Fraunhofer IKS, Germany
Grigory Fedyukovich	Florida State University, USA
Bernd Finkbeiner	CISPA Helmholtz Center for Information Security, Germany
Carlo A. Furia	Università della Svizzera Italiana, Switzerland
Rajeev Joshi	AWS, USA
Zachary Kincaid	Princeton University, USA
Akash Lal	Microsoft Research, India
Thierry Lecomte	ClearSy, France
Sergio Mover	Ecole Polytechnique, France
Kartik Nagar	IIT Madras, India
Aina Niemetz	Stanford University, USA
Gennaro Parlato	University of Molise, Italy
Kristin Yvonne Rozier	Iowa State University, USA
Natarajan Shankar	SRI International, USA
Stefano Tonetta	FBK, Italy
Elena Troubitsyna	KTH, Sweden
Hiroshi Unno	University of Tsukuba, Japan
Jyothi Vedurada	IIT Hyderabad, India
Yakir Vizel	Technion-Israel Institute of Technology, Israel
Yuepeng Wang	Simon Fraser University, Canada

Chao Wang   University of Southern California, USA
Kirsten Winter   University of Queensland, Australia

Additional Reviewers

Hsu, Tzu-Han
Larrauri, Alberto
Lee, Juneyoung
Momtaz, Anik
Passing, Noemi
Wu, Haoze

Contents

Compositional Safety LTL Synthesis

Suguman Bansal[1], Giuseppe De Giacomo[2], Antonio Di Stasio[2], Yong Li[3],

Moshe Y. Vardi[4], and Shufang Zhu[2(✉)]

[1] University of Pennsylvania, Philadelphia, PA, USA
[2] Sapienza University of Rome, Rome, Italy
zhu@diag.uniroma1.it
[3] SKLCS, Institute of Software, CAS, Beijing, China
[4] Rice University, Houston, TX, USA

Abstract. Reactive synthesis holds the promise of generating automatically a verifiably correct program from a high-level specification. A popular such specification language is Linear Temporal Logic (LTL). Unfortunately, synthesizing programs from *general* LTL formulas, which relies on first constructing a game arena and then solving the game, does not scale to large instances. The specifications from practical applications are usually large conjunctions of smaller LTL formulas, which inspires existing compositional synthesis approaches to take advantage of this structural information. The main challenge here is that they solve the game only after obtaining the game arena, the most computationally expensive part in the procedure. In this work, we propose a compositional synthesis technique to tackle this difficulty by synthesizing a program for each small conjunct separately and composing them one by one. While this approach does not work for general LTL formulas, we show here that it does work for *Safety* LTL formulas, a popular and important fragment of LTL. While we have to compose all the programs of small conjuncts in the worst case, we can prune the intermediate programs to make later compositions easier and immediately conclude unrealizable as soon as some part of the specification is found unrealizable. By comparing our compositional approach with a portfolio of all other approaches, we observed that our approach was able to solve a notable number of instances not solved by others. In particular, experiments on scalable conjunctive benchmarks showed that our approach scale well and significantly outperform current Safety LTL synthesis techniques. We conclude that our compositional approach is an important contribution to the algorithmic portfolio of Safety LTL synthesis.

1 Introduction

Reactive synthesis is the automated construction, from a high-level description of its desired behavior, of a reactive system that continuously interacts with an uncontrollable external environment [7]. By describing a system in terms of what it should do, instead of how it should do it, this declarative paradigm holds the promise of correct-by-construction philosophy of program design [26,32]. We believe that reactive synthesis will be a viable way to create verified software. A popular language for specifying properties that systems should satisfy is Linear Temporal Logic (LTL) [25].

In the last decade, there have been extensive breakthroughs in the study of LTL synthesis [4,22,33]. A natural next step is to consider large scale synthesis instances. Many practical specifications, by and large, are conjunctions of complex but smaller (shorter) *inner* temporal specifications. While the development of techniques for reactive synthesis for these inner formulas remains an active area of research [5,11,13,22,23], It is fair to combat large-scale practical specifications starting with developing synthesis algorithms for large conjunctions of (inner) temporal formulas.

Previously, large conjunctions, such as strong fairness properties, have been handled successfully in the context of model-checking [1]. One of the cornerstones of scalable model-checking is to represent the model by a *partitioned transition relation*, i.e., the transition relation of the model is represented as a product of smaller transition relations. In model-checking, this representation has been a boon to scale to very large systems. In reactive synthesis, however, this representation has been shown to be a bane to scalability. More specifically, [31] attempts to solve synthesis of large conjunctions by representing the state-space of the final game automaton as a product of the state-space of the game automaton of every inner formula. The issue is that by doing so, the state space of the final game may grow very large, since the algorithm loses the ability to perform fast minimization of the game automaton [35].

On the other hand, compositional approaches have shown promise in synthesis of large conjunctions. Theoretical compositional approaches are well known [12,19] and implementations that handle large conjunction have been emerging [2,5,9,22]. For example, Lisa [2] successfully scales synthesis to large conjunctions of LTL formulas over finite traces or LTL_f [17] for short. This approach has been further extended to handle large disjunctions in Lydia [9]. Yet, a challenge in these approaches is that the inner formulas cannot be synthesized one after another separately to generate a program for the large conjunction [19]. This is because having correct programs for all inner formulas does not necessarily indicate the existence of a correct program of the large conjunction. To this end, compositional approaches have been deployed to generate the game automaton only, and not to solve the game. The game is solved only after the generation of the complete game arena, which is the main difficulty of synthesis for formulas with large lengths [26,34].

In this work, we tackle this difficulty by looking into *specialized* compositional synthesis techniques for *Safety* LTL formulas, which is a popular and important fragment of LTL [20,24,28]. The key observation is that, for a Safety LTL formula, instead of utilizing its exact game arena when being conjuncted with other formulas, we only need to approximate the partial game arena to ensure the satisfaction of it under all circumstances, hence reducing the state space for subsequent operations. We note that recently, another safety fragment of LTL called *extended bounded response* (EBR) LTL [8] has been shown to be expressively equivalent to Safety LTL, but differs in the syntax of Safety LTL. The conversion from Safety LTL to EBR-LTL may incur blow-up of formula lengths [8], so we only consider Safety LTL here.

The synthesis instances we consider are Safety LTL formulas given in the form of $\varphi = \varphi_1 \wedge \varphi_2 \wedge \ldots \wedge \varphi_n$. The Safety LTL fragment and the conjunctive instances together form a special structure, which naturally enables us to develop a more advanced compositional synthesis approach. Indeed, our compositional synthesis technique can apply at two decomposition levels. To begin with, the specification-level decomposition breaks φ into the set of conjuncts $\{\varphi_1, \varphi_2, \ldots, \varphi_n\}$ and constructs the *deterministic safety automaton* (DSA) of each conjunct $\varphi_i, 1 \leqslant i \leqslant n$. Meanwhile, inspired by [33], we observe that one can directly consider the negation of Safety LTL φ_i in *negation normal form* (NNF) as an LTL_f formula, a finite-trace variant of LTL that has the same expressiveness power as first-order logic over finite traces [17]. This allows us to utilize LTL_f-to-DFA construction tools integrated with compositional techniques [2,9], which have been proven outperforming MONA, to obtain the DFA of the bad prefixes of each φ_i, which is simply the dual of the DSA of φ_i. Furthermore, instead of utilizing the partitioned transition relation, which nullifies the benefits of automata minimization, we keep the explicit-state symbolic-transition representation of each DSA to take the maximal advantage of automata minimization, as in [2,9]. As a result, our compositional approach avoids the straightforward DSA construction from the whole formula φ and performs the DSA construction for each conjunct φ_i separately.

Beyond that, before composing the DSAs to construct the ultimate one, the game-level decomposition splits each DSA into winning part and losing part by conducting a safety game. More specifically, we propose two decomposition versions, that are state-based game-level decomposition and strategy-based game-level decomposition. The state-based decomposition considers the winning part as the set of winning states. It thus trims the DSA by clustering all losing states into a single one and minimizes the resulting DSA. The strategy-based decomposition, instead, considers the winning part as the maximally permissive strategy of the safety game, e.g., a finite-state transducer, that encompasses all the necessary information to ensure the satisfaction of the conjunct under all circumstances [3]. Thereby, it trims the DSA by clustering all states and also *transitions* that do not belong to this strategy. The trimmed DSA is also minimized for subsequent computation. In addition, minimization is applied during every round of composing two DSAs into a product automaton.

We have implemented our compositional synthesis algorithms in a prototype tool called Gelato. To demonstrate the efficiency of our algorithms, we perform an empirical evaluation by comparing Gelato with the monolithic approach, i.e., not leveraging the proposed compositional synthesis technique, and Strix [22], the state-of-the-art LTL synthesis tool. By comparing our compositional approach with a portfolio of other approaches, we observed that our approach was able to solve a notable number of instances that were not solved by others. In particular, experiments on scalable conjunctive benchmarks showed that our approach scale well and significantly outperform current Safety LTL synthesis techniques. We are convinced that our compositional approach is a valuable and important contribution to the current portfolio of Safety LTL synthesis algorithms.

Related Works. There have been several theoretical compositional synthesis approaches and implementations proposed for LTL formulas of the form $\varphi = \varphi_1 \wedge \cdots \wedge \varphi_n$. In [19], a Safraless compositional approach, inspired by [21], uses generalized co-Büchi *tree* automata to avoid the determinization of Büchi automata and parity condition for obtaining the game arena. This compositional approach checks the realizability of $\varphi = \varphi_1 \wedge \cdots \wedge \varphi_n$ by first checking the realizability of each sub-formula φ_i with the structure of tree automata rather than DSAs that we use in this work; they try to reuse the result of each conjunct φ_i when checking $\varphi = \varphi_1 \wedge \cdots \wedge \varphi_n$. To the best of our knowledge, there is no implementation for this approach. This may partially be because tree automata are not as easy and well studied as word automata, especially in terms of tool support. We note that current practical synthesis tools [5, 11, 13, 23] are all based on *word* automata, just as our algorithm is here.

To make use of word automata, in [14], the authors proposed an algorithm that treats the tree automaton for each conjunct φ_i as a universal co-Büchi word automaton, the game on which can then be solved by a reduction to solving a safety game, based on a given bound of the length of words. When composing the synthesized programs for the conjuncts to obtain a program for the whole formula φ, this algorithm also relies on the computation of the maximally permissive strategy for each safety game as we do in this work; they have implemented the algorithm in the tool Acacia+ [5]. In fact, our strategy-based decomposition variant is inspired by this approach. The difference is that we do not need a given bound for building the safety game, since we focus on Safety LTL formulas, while their algorithm can be incomplete if the given bound is not large enough. Another key difference is that we construct the safety game based on the construction of automata on finite words, while their algorithm builds a universal co-Büchi automaton for each conjunct. This allows us to leverage advanced compositional DFA construction in literature [2, 9], a key to make our algorithm outperform the state of the arts (cf. Sect. 4).

Another compositional synthesis approach, presented in [29], constructs compositionally a parity game from an LTL formula of the form $\varphi = \varphi_1 \wedge \cdots \wedge \varphi_n$ based on a variant of Safra's determinization. In addition, this approach tries to detect local parity games that are equivalent to safety games to improve efficiency. As aforementioned, we construct automata on finite words, which is different from the algorithm in [29].

The compositional approach proposed in [15] is based on decomposing the LTL formula into sub-formulas that are independent, such that completely separate synthesis tasks can be performed for them. The approach from [16] first splits the system into components and then proceeds in an incremental fashion such that each component can already assume a particular strategy for the synthesized components. The implementations of both approaches above are not, however, publicly available. We remark that there is a compositional construction of the game arena from LTL formulas [12], which is not involved with the synthesis task.

2   Preliminaries

2.1   LTL/LTL$_f$

Linear Temporal Logic (LTL) [25] is one of the most popular logics for temporal properties. Given a set $\mathcal{P}$ of propositions, the syntax of LTL formulas is defined as:

$$\varphi ::= \; true \mid false \mid p \mid (\neg p) \mid (\varphi_1 \wedge \varphi_2) \mid (\varphi_1 \vee \varphi_2) \mid (\bigcirc \varphi) \mid (\varphi_1 \, \mathcal{U} \, \varphi_2)$$

$$\mid (\varphi_1 \, \mathcal{W} \, \varphi_2) \mid (\varphi_1 \, \mathcal{M} \, \varphi_2) \mid (\varphi_1 \, \mathcal{R} \, \varphi_2).$$

where $p \in \mathcal{P}$ is an *atom*. $\bigcirc$ (Next), $\mathcal{U}$ (Until), $\mathcal{W}$ (Weak Until), $\mathcal{M}$ (Release) and $\mathcal{R}$ (Weak Release) are temporal connectives. We use the abbreviations $\Diamond\varphi \equiv true\,\mathcal{U}\,\varphi$ and $\Box\varphi \equiv false\,\mathcal{M}\,\varphi$, for temporal connectives $\Diamond$ (Eventually) and $\Box$ (Always).

A *trace* $\pi = \pi_0\pi_1\ldots$ is a sequence of propositional interpretations (sets), where $\pi_m \in 2^{\mathcal{P}}$ ($m \geqslant 0$) is the m-th interpretation of π, and $|\pi|$ represents the length of π. Trace π is an *infinite* trace if $|\pi| = \infty$, which is formally denoted as $\pi \in (2^{\mathcal{P}})^{\omega}$. Otherwise π is a *finite* trace, denoted as $\pi \in (2^{\mathcal{P}})^*$. LTL formulas are interpreted over infinite traces. Given an infinite trace π and an LTL formula φ, we inductively define when φ is *true* in π at instant i ($i \geqslant 0$), written $\pi, i \models \varphi$, as follows:

- $\pi, i \models true$ and $\pi, i \not\models false$;
- $\pi, i \models a$ iff $a \in \pi_i$ and $\pi, i \models \neg a$ iff $a \notin \pi_i$;
- $\pi, i \models \varphi_1 \wedge \varphi_2$, iff $\pi, i \models \varphi_1$ and $\pi, i \models \varphi_2$;
- $\pi, i \models \varphi_1 \vee \varphi_2$, iff $\pi, i \models \varphi_1$ or $\pi, i \models \varphi_2$;
- $\pi, i \models \bigcirc\varphi$, iff $\pi, i+1 \models \varphi$;
- $\pi, i \models \varphi_1 \mathcal{U} \varphi_2$, iff $\exists k.k \geqslant i$ such that $\pi, k \models \varphi_2$, and $\forall j.i \leqslant j < k, \pi, j \models \varphi_1$.
- $\pi, i \models \varphi_1 \mathcal{W} \varphi_2$, iff either $\exists k.k \geqslant i$ such that $\pi, k \models \varphi_2$, and $\forall j.i \leqslant j < k$, we have $\pi, j \models \varphi_1$, or $\forall k.k \geqslant i$ we have $\pi, k \models \varphi_1$.
- $\pi, i \models \varphi_1 \mathcal{M} \varphi_2$ iff $\exists k.k \geqslant i$ such that $\pi, k \models \varphi_1$, and $\forall j.i \leqslant j \leqslant k, \pi, j \models \varphi_1$.
- $\pi, i \models \varphi_1 \mathcal{R} \varphi_2$, iff $\exists k.k \geqslant i$ such that $\pi, k \models \varphi_1$, and $\forall j.i \leqslant j \leqslant k, \pi, j \models \varphi_2$, or $\forall k.k \geqslant i$ we have $\pi, k \models \varphi_2$.

LTL$_f$ is a variant of LTL interpreted over *finite traces* instead of infinite traces [17]. The syntax of LTL$_f$ is exactly the same to the syntax of LTL. We define $\pi, i \models \varphi$, stating that φ holds at position i, as for LTL, except that for the temporal operators:

- $\pi, i \models \bigcirc\varphi$ iff $i < last(\pi)$ and $\pi, i+1 \models \varphi$;
- $\pi, i \models \varphi_1 \mathcal{U} \varphi_2$ iff $\exists j.i \leq j \leq last(\pi)$ and $\pi, j \models \varphi_2$, and $\forall k.i \leq k < j$ we have $\pi, k \models \varphi_1$.
- $\pi, i \models \varphi_1 \mathcal{W} \varphi_2$, iff either $\exists k.i \leq k \leq last(\pi)$ such that $\pi, k \models \varphi_2$, and $\forall j.i \leq j < k$, we have $\pi, j \models \varphi_1$, or $\forall k.i \leq k \leq last(\pi)$ we have $\pi, k \models \varphi_1$.
- $\pi, i \models \varphi_1 \mathcal{M} \varphi_2$ iff $\exists k.i \leq k \leq last(\pi)$ such that $\pi, k \models \varphi_1$, and $\forall j.i \leq j \leq k$, $\pi, j \models \varphi_1$.
- $\pi, i \models \varphi_1 \mathcal{R} \varphi_2$, iff $\exists k.i \leq k \leq last(\pi)$ such that $\pi, k \models \varphi_1$, and $\forall j.i \leq j \leq k$, $\pi, j \models \varphi_2$, or $\forall k.i \leq k \leq last(\pi)$ we have $\pi, k \models \varphi_2$.

where we denote the last position in the finite trace π by $last(\pi)$. In addition we define the *weak next* operator $\bullet$ as abbreviation of $\bullet\varphi \equiv \neg\bigcirc\neg\varphi$. Note that, over finite traces, $\neg\bigcirc\varphi \not\equiv \bigcirc\neg\varphi$, instead $\neg\bigcirc\varphi \equiv \bullet\neg\varphi$. We say that a trace *satisfies* an LTL$_f$ formula φ, written $\pi \models \varphi$, if $\pi, 0 \models \varphi$.

Without loss of generality, assume the input LTL formulas in Negation Normal Form (NNF), which requires negations only occurring in front of atomic propositions.

2.2 Safety/Co-safety LTL

Intuitively, a *safety* formula rejects traces whose "badness" follows from a finite prefix. Dually, a *co-safety* formula accepts traces whose "goodness" follows from a finite prefix. We formally refer to these prefixes as bad/good prefixes accordingly. Consider a language $\mathcal{L} \subseteq (2^{\mathcal{P}})^{\omega}$ of infinite traces $\mathcal{P}$. A finite trace $h \in (2^{\mathcal{P}})^*$ is a *bad (resp., good)* prefix for $\mathcal{L}$ iff for all infinite traces $\pi \in (2^{\mathcal{P}})^{\omega}$, we have that $h \cdot \pi \notin \mathcal{L}$ (resp., $h \cdot \pi \in \mathcal{L}$). A language $\mathcal{L}$ is a *safety language* iff every trace that violates (resp., satisfies) φ has a bad (resp., good) prefix. We say that an LTL formula is a safety (co-safety) formula iff $||\varphi||$, i.e., the set of infinite traces that satisfy φ, is a safety (co-safety) language.

We now introduce a fragment of LTL, where safety (resp., for co-safety) is expressed as a syntactical feature, by restricting the occurrences of temporal connectives.

Definition 1 ([6,27]). *Safety LTL (resp. Co-Safety LTL) formulas are LTL formulas in NNF containing only temporal operators such as* $\bigcirc$, $\mathcal{R}$, *and* $\mathcal{W}$ *(resp.* $\bigcirc$, $\mathcal{M}$, *and* $\mathcal{U}$*).*

Theorem 1 ([6,27]). *Every safety (resp., co-safety) formula is equivalent to a formula in Safety LTL (resp., Co-Safety LTL).*

Note that, the syntactic fragment of Safety (resp. Co-Safety) LTL in Definition 1 is equivalent to the one defined in [33], which requires that the $\mathcal{U}$ (resp. $\mathcal{R}$) connective does not occur. Specifically, since $\varphi_1 \mathcal{W} \varphi_2 \equiv ((\bigcirc \varphi_2) \mathcal{R} \varphi_1) \vee \varphi_2$, and $\varphi_1 \mathcal{M} \varphi_2 \equiv \varphi_2 \mathcal{U} (\varphi_1 \wedge \varphi_2)$, every occurrence of $\mathcal{W}$ can be replaced by $\mathcal{R}$ and $\bigcirc$, and every occurrence of $\mathcal{M}$ can be replaced by $\mathcal{U}$, without introducing any extra negations. Thus, every safe (resp., co-safe) formula is equivalent to a Safety (resp., Co-Safety) LTL formula φ.

2.3 Safety LTL Synthesis

Reactive synthesis concerns constructing the behaviors of an *agent* that satisfy a given property while interacting with its *environment* [26]. Formally, a reactive synthesis problem is described as a tuple $\mathcal{P} = \langle \mathcal{X}, \mathcal{Y}, \varphi \rangle$, where $\mathcal{X}$ and $\mathcal{Y}$ are two disjoint sets of variables controlled by the *environment* and the *agent*, respectively, and φ is a linear temporal formula over $\mathcal{X} \cup \mathcal{Y}$ expressing desired properties. A *deterministic* agent strategy is a function $\sigma : (2^{\mathcal{X}})^* \rightarrow 2^{\mathcal{Y}}$. A *trace* is an infinite sequence $\pi = (X_0 \cup Y_0)(X_1 \cup Y_1) \ldots \in (2^{\mathcal{X} \cup \mathcal{Y}})^{\omega}$ over the alphabet $2^{\mathcal{X} \cup \mathcal{Y}}$. A trace π is *compatible* with an agent strategy σ, if $\sigma(\epsilon) = Y_0$ and $\sigma(X_0 X_1 \ldots X_i) = Y_{i+1}$ for every $i \geqslant 0$, where ϵ denotes empty trace. Analogously, finite prefix $\pi^k = (X_0 \cup Y_0)(X_1 \cup Y_1) \ldots (X_k \cup Y_k)$ is *compatible* with σ if $\sigma(X_0 X_1 \ldots X_i) = Y_{i+1}$ for every $0 \leqslant i < k$. Given a synthesis problem $\mathcal{P} = \langle \mathcal{X}, \mathcal{Y}, \varphi \rangle$, an agent strategy σ *realizes* φ if every trace π that is compatible with σ satisfies φ. There are two versions of reactive synthesis, depending on the first player. Here we consider the case where the *agent* moves first; the variant where the environment moves first can be obtained with a minor modification.

In this paper, we focus on the problem of *Safety LTL Synthesis*.

Definition 2 (Safety LTL Synthesis). *The problem of Safety LTL synthesis is described as a tuple* $\mathcal{P} = \langle \mathcal{X}, \mathcal{Y}, \varphi \rangle$, *where* φ *is a Safety LTL formula over* $\mathcal{X} \cup \mathcal{Y}$. *Computing an agent strategy* σ *that realizes* φ *if one exists, is called the Safety LTL synthesis problem.*

The problem of Safety LTL synthesis can be solved by a reduction to *safety games*, which is a two-player game over a so-called *deterministic safety automaton* [33].

Deterministic Safety Automata. A *deterministic safety automaton* (DSA) is a tuple $\mathcal{D} = (2^{\mathcal{P}}, S, s_0, \delta)$, where $2^{\mathcal{P}}$ is the alphabet, S is a finite set of states with s_0 as the initial state, and $\delta : S \times 2^{\mathcal{P}} \rightharpoonup S$ is a partial transition function. Given an infinite trace $\pi \in (2^{\mathcal{P}})^{\omega}$, the run r of $\mathcal{D}$ on π, denoted by $r = \mathsf{Run}(\mathcal{D}, \pi)$, is a sequence of states $r = s_0 s_1 s_2 \ldots$ such that $s_{i+1} = \delta(s_i, \pi_i)$ for every $i \geqslant 0$. π is accepted by $\mathcal{D}$ if $r = \mathsf{Run}(\mathcal{D}, \pi)$ is well defined. Note that, δ is a partial function, meaning that given $s \in S$ and $a \in 2^{\mathcal{P}}$, $\delta(s, a)$ can either return a state $s' \in S$ or be undefined. Thus, $r = \mathsf{Run}(\mathcal{D}, \pi)$ may not be an infinite sequence due to the possibility of $\delta(s_i, \pi_i)$ being undefined for some $(s_i, \pi_i) \in S \times 2^{\mathcal{P}}$.

Symbolic DSA. The *symbolic-state* representation of a DSA $\mathcal{D} = (2^{\mathcal{P}}, S, s_0, \delta)$ is a tuple $\mathcal{A} = (\mathcal{S}(\mathcal{Z}), \mathcal{K}(\mathcal{Z}, \mathcal{P}, \mathcal{Z}'))$, where $\mathcal{Z} = \{z_1, \ldots z_n\}$ are propositions encoding the state space S, with $n = \lceil \log |S| \rceil$, and their primed counterparts $\mathcal{Z}' = \{z'_1, \ldots z'_n\}$ encode the next state. Each state $s \in S$ corresponds to an interpretation $Z \in 2^{\mathcal{Z}}$ over propositions $\mathcal{Z}$. When representing the next state of the transition function, the same encoding is used for an interpretation Z' over $\mathcal{Z}'$. Then, $\mathcal{S}$ and $\mathcal{K}$ are Boolean formulas representing s_0 and δ, respectively. $\mathcal{S}(\mathcal{Z})$ is satisfied only by the interpretation of the initial state s_0 over $\mathcal{Z}$. $\mathcal{K}(\mathcal{Z}, \mathcal{P}, \mathcal{Z}')$ is satisfied by interpretations $Z \in 2^{\mathcal{Z}}$, $P \in 2^{\mathcal{P}}$ and $Z' \in 2^{\mathcal{Z}'}$ iff $\delta(s, P) = s'$, where s and s' are the states corresponding to Z and Z'.

Safety Games. A safety game is defined as a tuple $\mathcal{G} = (\mathcal{X}, \mathcal{Y}, \mathcal{D})$, where $\mathcal{D} = (2^{\mathcal{X} \cup \mathcal{Y}}, S, s_0, \delta)$ is a DSA, and $\mathcal{X}$ and $\mathcal{Y}$ are two disjoint sets of variables, controlled by the environment, and the agent, respectively. A trace $\pi \in (2^{\mathcal{X} \cup \mathcal{Y}})^{\omega}$ is *winning* for the agent if $r = \mathsf{Run}(\mathcal{D}, \pi)$ is accepted by $\mathcal{D}$. An agent strategy σ is winning if every trace π that is compatible with σ is a winning play. *Solving a DSA game* aims to computing an agent winning strategy if one exists. A state $s \in S$ is *winning* for the agent if there exists an agent strategy such that all traces beginning in s are winning for the agent. The winning set of a DSA is the set of all winning states of the agent. To compute the winning set of $\mathcal{G}$, we perform the fixpoint computation as follows:

$$\mathsf{Win}_0 = S;$$
$$\mathsf{Win}_{i+1} = \mathsf{Win}_i \cap \{s \in S \mid \exists Y \forall X. \delta(s, X \cup Y) \in \mathsf{Win}_i\}.$$

Clearly, a safety game $\mathcal{G}$ can be analyzed by checking whether the initial state s_0 is a winning state, in which case we say that $\mathcal{G}$ is *realizable*. Next, we see that for safety games there exists *maximally permissive strategies* [3].

Maximally Permissive Strategies. Different definitions of maximally permissive strategies exist. In this work we refer to the definition in [3], where strategies are compared by looking at inclusion of the behaviors/outcomes they allow.

Definition 3 (Non-Deterministic Strategy). *A non-deterministic strategy for the agent is defined as a function* $\alpha : (2^{\mathcal{X}})^* \rightarrow 2^{2^{\mathcal{Y}}}$. *The set of deterministic strategies induced by a non-deterministic strategy* α *is the set*

$$[[\alpha]] = \{\sigma : (2^{\mathcal{X}})^* \rightarrow 2^{\mathcal{Y}} \mid \sigma(h) \in \alpha(h), \text{ for } h \in (2^{\mathcal{X}})^*\}.$$

Definition 4 (Maximally Permissive Strategy). *A non-deterministic strategy α is at least as permissive as α' if $[[\alpha']] \subseteq [[\alpha]]$. A non-deterministic strategy α is a maximally permissive strategy if $[[\alpha']] \subseteq [[\alpha]]$, for every non-deterministic strategy α'.*

Theorem 2 ([3]). *Let $\mathcal{G}$ be a safety game. We have that if $\mathcal{G}$ is realizable, then $\mathcal{G}$ has a maximal permissive strategy that is* memoryless, *i.e., $\alpha : S \to 2^{2^{\mathcal{Y}}}$.*

3   Compositional Approaches for Safety LTL Synthesis

3.1   From Safety LTL to DSA

Consider a Safety LTL formula φ, since every trace rejected by its corresponding DSA $\mathcal{D}_\varphi^s$ can be rejected in a finite number of steps, we can alternatively define the language accepted by $\mathcal{D}_\varphi^s$ by the finite prefixes that it rejects [20]. Therefore, the DSA construction can be achieved by first obtaining the DFA $\mathcal{D}_\varphi^f$ that accepts all the bad prefixes of φ, and then complementing it, which gives us the DSA of φ [33]. The construction shown in [33] is processed as follows: given a Safety LTL formula φ, first negate it to obtain a Co-Safety LTL formula $\neg\varphi$, then translate it into a first-order logic formula $fol(\neg\varphi)$. The DFA of $fol(\neg\varphi)$ is able to accept exactly the set of bad prefixes for φ, and can be constructed using MONA [18], a DFA construction tool from logic specifications.

Note that the key step here is to leverage the technique and tools developed for constructing $\mathcal{D}_\varphi^f$. To do so, we make use of LYDIA [9], which has shown better performance than MONA. In particular, this change does not require the explicit translation to first-order logic. Instead, we can directly consider the Co-Safety formula $\neg\varphi$ as an LTL_f formula, and give it to LYDIA as input. The returned automaton is the DFA that accepts all the good prefixes of $\neg\varphi$, e.g., the bad prefixes of φ.

Theorem 3. *Let ψ be a Co-Safety LTL formula in NNF, φ the same formula as ψ, but in LTL_f, and π a finite trace. Then π is good prefix of ψ iff $\pi \models \varphi$.*

Proof. We prove it by induction over the structure of φ.

– Base case, if $\psi = p$ is an atom, π is a good prefix for ψ iff $p \in \pi_0$. By definition of φ, we have that $\pi \models \varphi$. If $\psi = \neg p$, π is a good prefix of ψ iff $p \notin \pi_0$, then $\pi \nvDash \varphi$.
– If $\psi = \psi_1 \wedge \psi_2$, π is a good prefix for ψ implies π is a good prefix for both ψ_1 and ψ_2. By induction hypothesis, $\pi \models \varphi_1$ and $\pi \models \varphi_2$, where φ_1 and φ_2 are defined as ψ_1 and ψ_2, respectively, in LTL_f. Then, we have that $\pi \models \varphi_1 \wedge \varphi_2$.
– If $\psi = \psi_1 \vee \psi_2$, π is a good prefix for ψ implies π is a good prefix for either ψ_1 or ψ_2. Without loss of generality, suppose π is a good prefix for ψ_1. By induction hypothesis, $\pi \models \varphi_1$ where φ_1 is the LTL_f formula defined as ψ_1. Then, $\pi \models \varphi_1 \vee \varphi_2$, with φ_2 defined in LTL_f as ψ_2.
– If $\psi = \bigcirc\psi_1$, π is a good prefix for ψ iff suffix $\pi' = \pi_1\pi_2 \ldots, \pi_{|\pi|-1}$ of π is a good prefix for ψ_1. By induction hypothesis, $\pi', 1 \models \varphi_1$ where φ_1 is defined as ψ_1 in LTL_f. Then, we have that $\pi \models \bigcirc\varphi_1$.

- If $\psi = \psi_1 \, \mathcal{U} \, \psi_2$, π is a good prefix for ψ iff there exists $0 \leqslant i \leqslant |\pi| - 1$ such that suffix $\pi' = \pi_i \pi_{i+1}, \ldots, \pi_{|\pi-1|}$ of π is a good prefix for ψ_2, and for all $0 \leqslant j < i$, $\pi'' = \pi_j \pi_{j+1}, \ldots, \pi_{i-1}$ is a good prefix for ψ_1. By induction hypothesis, $\pi', i \models \varphi_2$ where φ_2 is defined as ψ_2 in LTL$_f$, and $\pi'', j \models \varphi_1$ with φ_1 defined as ψ_2 in LTL$_f$. Therefore, $\pi \models \varphi_1 \, \mathcal{U} \, \varphi_2$.
- The cases for $\mathcal{W}$, $\mathcal{M}$, and $\mathcal{R}$ are derived from the above.

3.2 Compositional Safety LTL Synthesis

The crux of our compositional approach is to avoid the DSA construction of the complete Safety LTL formula φ by performing the DSA construction for each conjunct φ_i, and, most importantly, solving the safety game over the DSA before composing it with the other DSAs. We first propose a compositional approach based on the computation of the agent winning states of safety games. In particular, inspired by the compositional automata construction technique presented in [2], we also employ here the explicit-DSA to symbolic-DSA switch heuristics to achieve promising practical benefits.

State-Based Compositional Approach. After checking realizability of each φ_i through the corresponding safety game, we prune the safety game wrt the winning states and then minimize the game; the algorithm then goes through a phase of combining two DSAs, minimizing the combined DSA, solving the safety game over the DSA, and pruning the game again, until a switch to a symbolic representation occurs. When we have switched to using the symbolic representation for DSAs, we will not perform minimization on the DSAs since it is time-consuming because of large DSA state space; instead, in each round we only combine the DSAs and solve the safety game over the corresponding DSA. Specifically, given a Safety LTL formula in the form of $\varphi = \bigwedge_{1 \leqslant i \leqslant n} \varphi_i$, and *switch-over threshold values* $t_1, t_2 > 0$ that represent the thresholds for the numbers of states in an individual DSA and in the product of two DSAs, respectively, to trigger the symbolic representation, the algorithm proceeds as follows.

1. **Decomposition.** Construct minimal DSA $\mathcal{D}_i$ for each sub-formula φ_i of φ in explicit-state representation as described in Sect. 3.1 and let $H_1 = \{\mathcal{D}_1, \ldots, \mathcal{D}_n\}$. Then, for all $i \in \{1, \ldots, n\}$,
   (a) compute the winning set W_i of the agent in the safety game $\mathcal{G}_i = \langle \mathcal{X}, \mathcal{Y}, \mathcal{D}_i \rangle$. Return φ is unrealizable if $\mathcal{G}_i$ is unrealizable.
   (b) Prune $\mathcal{D}_i$ such that only the states in W_i are retained. Formally, let $\mathcal{D}_i = (\Sigma, S, s_0, \delta)$. Then prune $\mathcal{D}_i$ with respect to W_i obtaining $\mathcal{D}_i^w = (\Sigma, W_i, s_0, \delta^w)$ where the transition function δ^w is defined as follows:
   $$\delta^w(s, \sigma) = \begin{cases} \delta(s, \sigma) & \text{if } \delta(s, \sigma) \in W_i, \\ \text{undefined} & \text{if } \delta(s, \sigma) \notin W_i. \end{cases}$$
   (c) Minimize $\mathcal{D}_i^w$. Note that, since DSAs are represented as DFAs, the pruning step is performed on DFAs, and therefore we can apply minimization techniques on DFAs to obtain the minimal DSA.
2. **Explicit-state composition.** For $j \in \{1, \ldots, n-1\}$, let $H_j = \{\mathcal{D}_1 \ldots \mathcal{D}_{n-j+1}\}$ be the set of DSAs in the j-th iteration. If H_j has only one DSA $\mathcal{D}_1$, then return

a winning strategy for the agent in $\mathcal{G} = \langle \mathcal{X}, \mathcal{Y}, \mathcal{D}_1 \rangle$. Otherwise, pick from H_j two DSAs, $\mathcal{D}_1$ and $\mathcal{D}_2$, chosen by the dynamic smallest-first heuristic [2] which always returns two DSAs in H_j with the smallest number of states. This allows to find an order that can optimize time and space in the composition phase. Indeed, if the algorithm would fail on the composition of the smallest two DFAs in that iteration, then it would probably fail on the composition of all other pairs of DFAs as well. Let $|\mathcal{D}|$ be the number of states in a DSA $\mathcal{D}$ represented in explicit-state form. If $|\mathcal{D}_1| > t_1$ or $|\mathcal{D}_2| > t_1$, or $(|\mathcal{D}_1| \cdot |\mathcal{D}_2|) > t_2$, then change state representation moving to Step 3 and let k be the iteration in which this occurs, i.e., take $k = j$. If not, continue with the explicit-state representation and perform the following steps.

(a) Construct $\mathcal{D}_{1,2} = \mathcal{D}_1 \cap \mathcal{D}_2$, and minimize $\mathcal{D}_{1,2}$ to generate $\mathcal{D}$.
(b) Compute the winning set W of the agent in safety game $\mathcal{G} = \langle \mathcal{X}, \mathcal{Y}, \mathcal{D} \rangle$. Return φ is unrealizable if $\mathcal{D}$ is unrealizable.
(c) Prune $\mathcal{D}$ such that only the states in W are retained (see Step 1(b)), and minimize it. Then, create $H_{j+1} = \{\mathcal{D}, \mathcal{D}_3 \ldots \mathcal{D}_{n-j+1}\}$.
(d) Go to Step 2.

3. **Change state representation.** Convert all DSAs in $H_k = \{\mathcal{D}_1, \ldots, \mathcal{D}_{n-k+1}\}$ from explicit-state to symbolic-state representation, and proceed to Step 4. Note that the state space of each DSA $\mathcal{D}_i$ is encoded symbolically using a different set of state variables $\mathcal{Z}_i$, where all $\mathcal{Z}_i$ are disjoint. Since no more minimization occurs after this point, the total set of state variables $\mathcal{Z} = \mathcal{Z}_1 \cup \ldots \cup \mathcal{Z}_{n-k+1}$ defines the state space of the final DSA.

4. **Symbolic-state composition.** For $j \in \{k, \ldots, n\}$, let $H_j = \{\mathcal{D}_1, \ldots, \mathcal{D}_{n-j+1}\}$ be the set of DSAs in the j-th iteration. If H_j has only one DSA, return a winning strategy for the agent, otherwise return φ is unrealizable. Otherwise, assume w.l.o.g. that $\mathcal{D}_1$ and $\mathcal{D}_2$ are the two DSAs chosen by the DSF heuristic and perform the following steps:

(a) Construct $\mathcal{D} = \mathcal{D}_1^w \cap \mathcal{D}_2^w$. Recall that, since $\mathcal{D}_1$ and $\mathcal{D}_2$ are in symbolic form, we do not perform DSA minimization of $\mathcal{D}_{1,2}$.
(b) Compute the winning set W of the agent in the safety game $\mathcal{G} = \langle \mathcal{X}, \mathcal{Y}, \mathcal{D} \rangle$. Return φ is unrealizable if any of the two $\mathcal{G}$ is unrealizable. Then, create $H_{j+1} = \{\mathcal{D}, \mathcal{D}_3 \ldots \mathcal{D}_{n-j+1}\}$.
(c) Go to Step 4.

To prove the correctness of the algorithm described above, i.e., to prove that the algorithm correctly evaluates realizability of the input safety formula φ and synthesizes a valid winning strategy (if realizable), we make use of the following result.

Lemma 1. *Let $\mathcal{D}$ be a DSA with winning set W for the agent player in the safety game played over $\mathcal{D}$. Let $\mathcal{D}^w$ be the pruning of $\mathcal{D}$ w.r.t. W, as described above. Then, every winning strategy in the safety game over $\mathcal{D}$ is a winning strategy in the safety game over $\mathcal{D}^w$, and vice-versa.*

Proof. We begin by showing that every winning strategy in the safety game $\mathcal{G} = \langle \mathcal{X}, \mathcal{Y}, \mathcal{D} \rangle$ is also a winning strategy in the safety game $\mathcal{G} = \langle \mathcal{X}, \mathcal{Y}, \mathcal{D}^w \rangle$.

Let $\sigma : (2^{\mathcal{X}})^* \to 2^{\mathcal{Y}}$ be a strategy. Let $\pi_\sigma = (X_0, \sigma(\epsilon)), (X_1, \sigma(X_0)), \ldots, (X_n, \sigma(X_0, X_1, \ldots X_{n-1}))$ be a play of finite-length induced by σ. Given a DSA

$\mathcal{D}' = (\mathcal{X} \cup \mathcal{Y}, S, s_0, \delta)$, let s_σ be the unique state in which the run of π_σ beginning in s_0 in DSA $\mathcal{D}'$ terminates. We will show that when σ is a winning strategy for the agent, then the terminal state s_f of the run of all finite plays π_σ is such that $s_\sigma \in W$.

By means of contradiction, suppose σ is a winning strategy such that there exists a finite play π_σ such that the terminal state of its run in DSA $\mathcal{D}$ is $s_\sigma \in S \backslash W$. Then, since DSAs are determined games and both players have memoryless winning strategies, the environment can begin executing a memoryless environment winning strategy from s_σ. Then, by definition of winning strategies of the environment, this ensures that every resulting play is winning for the environment. Thus, we have a contradiction.

Therefore, every agent winning strategy σ in the safety game over $\mathcal{D}$ can be executed in a game over $\mathcal{D}^w$ since $\mathcal{D}^w$ is defined over the winning set of $\mathcal{D}$. Finally, since $\delta^*(\pi_\sigma) \in W$ in DSA $\mathcal{D}$ for all π_σ, we get that $(\delta^w)^*(\pi_\sigma) \in W$ in DSA $\mathcal{D}^w$ for all π_σ, where δ^* and $(\delta^w)^*$ are the transitive closures of δ and δ^w. Thus, σ is also a winning strategy in safety game over $\mathcal{D}^w$ as it never encounters an undefined transition in $\mathcal{D}^w$.

Next, we show that a strategy that is not winning for the agent in a safety game over $\mathcal{D}$ is also not a winning strategy for the agent in the safety game over $\mathcal{D}^w$. The proof for this is the dual of the earlier case. For strategies that are not winning for the agent, the terminal state of the run of every finite-play in $\mathcal{D}$ lies in $S \setminus W$. Then, it is easy to see that these strategies will encounter an undefined transition in the game over $\mathcal{D}^w$. Meaning, that the strategy is not winning for the agent in the safety game over $\mathcal{D}^w$.

Theorem 4. *The state-based compositional approach is sound and complete for Safety LTL synthesis.*

Proof. Clearly, σ is a winning strategy for the agent for the input formula φ iff σ is a winning strategy in every DSA in H_1. Suppose $\mathcal{D}_1$ and $\mathcal{D}_2$ are chosen in the first iteration of the algorithm. Then, by Lemma 1, since winning strategies are preserved via pruning, we get that σ is a winning strategy in every DSA in $H_1 \setminus \{\mathcal{D}_1, \mathcal{D}_2\} \cup \{\mathcal{D}_1^w, \mathcal{D}_2^w\}$. Since σ is a winning strategy in both $\mathcal{D}_1^w$ and $\mathcal{D}_2^w$, σ is a winning strategy for $\mathcal{D}_1^w \cap \mathcal{D}_2^w$. Since the language of $\mathcal{D}_1^w \cap \mathcal{D}_2^w$ is equivalent to that of its minimal DSA $\mathcal{D}_{1,2}$, we get that σ is also a winning strategy in $\mathcal{D}_{1,2}$. Thus, σ is a winning strategy for the input formula iff σ is a winning strategy in every DSA in H_2. By repeated application of this argument, we show that σ is a winning strategy for the input formula iff it is a winning strategy over the single DSA in H_n.

It should be noted that when pruning each DSA, the state-based decomposition approach focuses only on winning states and therefore trims the DSAs by clustering all losing states into a single one and minimizes the resulting DSA. Nevertheless, certain transitions, though leading to winning states, do not contribute to the realizability of the conjunct since such transitions do not belong to the maximally permissive strategy of the safety game, e.g., a finite-state transducer that encompasses all the necessary information to ensure the satisfaction of the conjunct under all circumstances [3]. Furthermore, trimming also these transitions might result in an even smaller DSA. We now give a compositional approach based on the computation of the maximally permissive strategy of safety games over DSAs.

Strategy-Based Compositional Approach. Unlike the state-based approach, in each round, it trims from the DSAs not only all states but also *transitions* that do not belong to the maximally permissive strategy. The algorithm proceeds as follows.

1. **Decomposition.** Let $\mathcal{D}_1 \ldots \mathcal{D}_n$ be the minimal DSAs for each sub-formula φ_i of the input formula φ in the explicit-state representation as described in Sect. 3.1. Then, for all $i \in \{1, \ldots, n\}$, proceed as follows.
   (a) Compute the set of winning states W_i in the safety game $\mathcal{G}_i = \langle \mathcal{X}, \mathcal{Y}, \mathcal{D}_i \rangle$. Return φ unrealizable if $\mathcal{G}_i$ is unrealizable.
   (b) Compute the maximally permissive strategy α_i based on the set of winning states W_i. To do so, we define a strategy generator, which is a nondeterministic transducer $\mathcal{T} = (2^{\mathcal{X} \cup \mathcal{Y}}, W_i, s_0, \varrho, \tau)$, where
       - $W_i \subseteq S$ is the set of winning states;
       - $\tau : W_i \to 2^{(2^{\mathcal{Y}})}$ is the output function such that
       $$\tau(s) = \begin{cases} \{Y \mid \forall X. \delta(s, X \cup Y) \in W_i\} & \text{if } s \in W_i, \\ \emptyset & \text{otherwise.} \end{cases}$$
       - $\varrho : W_i \times 2^{\mathcal{X}} \to 2^{W_i}$ is the transition function such that $\varrho(s, X) = \{s' \mid s' = \delta(s, X \cup Y) \text{ and } Y \in \tau(s)\}$;

       This transducer represents the maximally permissive strategy $\alpha : (2^{\mathcal{X}})^* \to 2^{2^{\mathcal{Y}}}$ in the following way: $\alpha(\epsilon) = \tau(s_0)$, and $\alpha(\xi^k) = \tau(s_{k+1})$ for every $\xi^k \in (2^{\mathcal{X}})^+$, where s_{k+1} is the ending state of $\text{Run}(A, \pi^k) = s_0 s_1 s_2 \ldots s_k$, $\pi^k = (X_0 \cup Y_0)(X_1 \cup Y_1) \ldots (X_k \cup Y_k)$ and $Y_k \in \alpha(\xi^{k-1})$.
   (c) Prune $\mathcal{D}_i$ according to α_i. Intuitively, this pruning trims all states and transition that do not belong to α_i, unlike the state-based approach which only cuts states. Let $\mathcal{D} = (\Sigma, S, s_0, \delta)$ be a DSA. We prune $\mathcal{D}$ with respect to $\mathcal{T} = (\Sigma, W, s_0, \varrho, \tau)$ such that obtaining $\mathcal{D}^t = (\Sigma, W, s_0, \delta^t)$, where transition function δ^t is defined as follows:
       $$\delta^t(s, X \cup Y) = \begin{cases} \delta(s, X \cup Y) & \text{if } Y \in \tau(s), \\ \text{undefined} & \text{if } Y \notin \tau(s). \end{cases}$$
   (d) Minimize $\mathcal{D}_i^t$, and create $R = \{\mathcal{D}_1^t, \ldots, \mathcal{D}_i^t\}$.
2. **Explicit-state composition.** For $j \in \{1, \ldots, n-1\}$, let $R_j = \{\mathcal{D}_1 \ldots \mathcal{D}_{n-j+1}\}$ be the set of DSAs in the j-th iteration. If R_j has only one $\mathcal{D}_1$, then return a deterministic strategy for the agent. Otherwise, pick from R_j two DSAs, $\mathcal{D}_1$ and $\mathcal{D}_2$, chosen by the DSF heuristic. If $|\mathcal{D}_1| > t_1$ or $|\mathcal{D}_2| > t_1$, or $(|\mathcal{D}_1| \cdot |\mathcal{D}_2|) > t_2$, then change state representation moving to Step 3 and let k be the iteration in which this occurs, i.e., take $k = j$.
   If not, continue with explicit-state representation as follows.
   (a) Compute Step 2(a) and 2(b) as for the state-based approach, obtaining the DSA $\mathcal{D}$, which is the minimal DSA of $D_{1,2}^t = \mathcal{D}_1 \cap \mathcal{D}_2$, and the winning set W.
   (b) Compute maximally permissive strategy α based on W (see Step 1(b)).
   (c) Prune $\mathcal{D}$ in according to α (see Step 1(c)), obtaining D^t, and minimize it. Then, create $R_{j+1} = \{\mathcal{D}, \mathcal{D}_3 \ldots \mathcal{D}_{n-j+1}\}$.
   (d) Go to Step 2.
3. Step 3 and 4 are performed as Step 3 and 4 of the state-based approach.

Lemma 2. *Let $\mathcal{D}$, W and $\mathcal{D}^t$ be as above, then the agent has a winning strategy in the safety game $\mathcal{G} = \langle \mathcal{X}, \mathcal{Y}, \mathcal{D} \rangle$ iff the agent has a winning strategy in the safety game $\mathcal{G}^t = \langle \mathcal{X}, \mathcal{Y}, \mathcal{D}^t \rangle$.*

Proof. The proof follows Lemma 1.

Lemma 3. *The agent has a winning strategy in safety game $\mathcal{G} = \langle \mathcal{X}, \mathcal{Y}, \mathcal{D}_{i,j}^t \rangle$ iff $\varphi_i \wedge \varphi_j$ is realizable.*

Proof. We first obverse that $\varphi_i \wedge \varphi_j$ is realizable iff there exists an agent strategy σ that is winning in both safety games $\mathcal{G}_i = \langle \mathcal{X}, \mathcal{Y}, \mathcal{D}_i \rangle$ and $\mathcal{G}_j = \langle \mathcal{X}, \mathcal{Y}, \mathcal{D}_j \rangle$, where $\mathcal{D}_i$ and $\mathcal{D}_j$ are the DSAs for φ_i and φ_j, respectively. By Lemma 2, we know that the σ is also winning in both safety games over $\mathcal{D}_i^t$ and $\mathcal{D}_j^t$, and then it is also a winning strategy for $\mathcal{D}_{i,j}^t = \mathcal{D}_i^t \cap \mathcal{D}_j^t$, as required.

Theorem 5. *The Safety LTL synthesis problem $\mathcal{P} = \langle \mathcal{X}, \mathcal{Y}, \varphi \rangle$, where $\varphi = \bigwedge_{1 \leqslant i \leqslant n} \varphi_i$, is realizable iff the agent has a winning strategy in safety game $\mathcal{G} = \langle \mathcal{X}, \mathcal{Y}, \mathcal{D}^t \rangle$, where $\mathcal{D}^t$ is the last DSA obtained executing the strategy-based compositional approach.*

Proof. We can prove it by repeatedly applying Lemma 3, then we have that σ is an agent winning strategy for the input formula φ iff it is a winning strategy in the safety game over the single DSA $\mathcal{D}^t$.

4 Experimental Evaluation

4.1 Implementation

We implemented our two compositional synthesis approaches described in Sect. 3.2 in a prototype tool Gelato, on top of the Safety LTL synthesis tool SSyft [33]. We first use SPOT [10] to parse the input Safety LTL formula φ in the form of $\varphi_1 \wedge \cdots \wedge \varphi_k, k \geqslant 1$ and then call LYDIA [9] to obtain the DSAs for the smaller Safety LTL conjuncts $\varphi_i, 1 \leqslant i \leqslant k$. Note that all the explicit-state DSAs are, in fact, stored with their corresponding bad-prefixes DFAs. In this way, we can exploit the advanced compositional approach in LYDIA for constructing the DFAs of bad prefixes from small Safety LTL conjuncts. We then employ MONA for the minimization, state-pruning/strategy-pruning and product operations for explicit-state DSAs by operating on their bad-prefixes DFAs. Note that Gelato needs to take switch-over thresholds t_1, t_2 from explicit-states to symbolic-states representations and then performs synthesis on symbolic-state DSAs [34], where CUDD 3.0.0 [30] is used as the BDD library. The thresholds t_1 and t_2 are empirically set to 700 and 1500, respectively, in all experiments. We use native support of SSyft for solving safety game over symbolic DSAs and extracting the winning strategies if φ is realizable; we refer to [33] for more details.

4.2 Experimental Methodology

We compare our tool Gelato with two state of the art tools, namely SSyft, the synthesis tool dedicated for *Safety* LTL [33], and Strix (version 21.0.0) [22], the state-of-the-art synthesis tool for *general* LTL. In particular, we optimize SSyft by using LYDIA rather than MONA to construct the DSA, which highly speeds up the performance of SSyft used in [33]. Experiments were run on a computer cluster, where each instance took exclusive access to a computing node with Intel-Xeon processor running at 2.6 GHz, with 8 GB of memory and 30 min of time limit.

We consider large-scale Safety LTL synthesis instances in the form of $\varphi = \varphi_1 \wedge \varphi_2 \wedge \ldots \wedge \varphi_k$. We collected in total 2,500 Safety LTL synthesis instances, consisting of 1,250 instances from the *Conjunction* benchmark family and 1,250 instances from the *Random-Conjunction* benchmark family. Since Strix only supports the synthesis setting where the environment acts first, the instances taken by them had to be modified slightly to add a ◯ (Next) operator in front of all environment variables. The *Conjunction* benchmark family has 1,250 instances that are constructed from basic cases taken from Safety LTL synthesis datasets [33]. In particular, these basic cases are Safety LTL formulas splitting into 5 categories. Every category i ($1 \leqslant i \leqslant 5$) consists of a set of Safety LTL formulas with i nesting ◯ (Next) operators. Indeed, the more nesting ◯ operators are, the more difficult the basic case is. In order to evaluate the performance on scalability of handling conjunction formulas, for every category of Safety LTL formulas, we obtain 50 scalable conjunction instances by increasing the number of conjuncts from 1 to 5. The *Random-Conjunction* benchmark family also has 1,250 instances that are constructed in the similar way as the *Conjunction* instances. The key difference is that, all the variables in the randomly conjuncted formula are chosen randomly from a set of 20 candidate variables. Moreover, if a variable v is an environment-variable in the basic case, then the replacement variable v' of v is also an environment-variable in the randomly conjuncted formula. The same applies to the agent-variables.

We have evaluated the results from Gelato with those from Strix and SSyft, and we only find consistent results for the commonly solved cases.

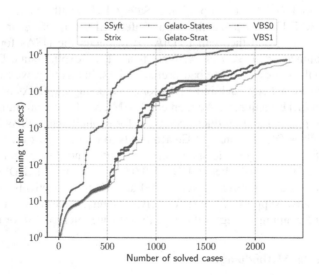

Fig. 1. Cactus plot indicating number of benchmarks solved by each tool over time.

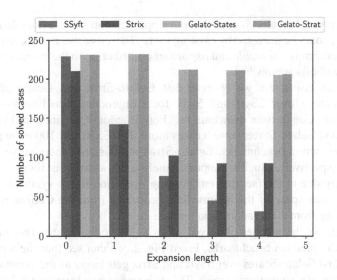

Fig. 2. Number of solved cases for different number of conjunctions in conjunction benchmarks

4.3   Results

We denote the winning states-based variant and the winning strategy-based variant of our algorithm in Sect. 3.2 by Gelato-States and Gelato-Strat, respectively. We compare both Gelato-States and Gelato-Strat against SSyft and Strix in terms of the number of solved cases and the running time. Additionally, we also consider two *virtual best solvers*, VBS0 (two existing tools, *without* Gelato) and VBS1 (*all* implementations).

The cactus plot in Fig. 1 reports how many benchmarks solved by each tool over time; we do not show the part where the running time is below 1 s for clarity. We can see that Gelato-Strat only has a slight advantage comparing to Gelato-States, with Gelato-Strat solving 2,325 cases and Gelato-States 2,324 cases, out of a total 2,500 cases. The performance of Gelato-Strat is similar to that of Gelato-States on most of the cases and is better on large instances. Regarding the number of solved cases, the performance of Gelato-Strat is significantly better than SSyft and Strix, since they only manage to solve 1,753 and 1,771 cases, respectively. In particular, Strix solved 554 cases less than Gelato-Strat did while taking more time to solve as many instances as both implementations in Gelato. This is reasonable since Strix considers the whole set of LTL while Gelato is carefully designed for big conjunctions of Safety LTL formulas. It is clear to see that our Gelato-Strat has the *best* performance regarding the number of solved cases within the same time limit. Between two virtual best solvers, VBS1 is significantly better than VBS0, with 2,369 cases solved by VBS1 and 1,979 cases by VBS0. It is worth mentioning that both our implementations Gelato-Strat and Gelato-States perform even better than VBS0.

The experimental results showed that our approach can solve a notable number of instances that cannot be managed by existing tools. Therefore, we believe that our compositional algorithm is a *valuable* and *important* contribution to the current portfolio of Safety LTL synthesis approaches.

On a closer inspection, we observe that Gelato-Strat and Gelato-States have a bigger advantage over SSyft and Strix for Conjunction benchmarks than they do for Random-Conjunction benchmarks. For Random-Conjunction benchmarks, Gelato-Strat and Gelato-States solve 3 cases more than SSyft and 100 more than Strix; while for Conjunction benchmarks, Gelato-Strat and Gelato-States solve 1,092 and 1,091 cases, respectively, which are approximately twice as many as those of SSyft and Strix. This may due to the fact that our pruning operation in the synthesis procedure reduces more state space of the intermediate programs from the Conjunction benchmarks than those from the Random-Conjunction cases.

Figure 2 shows the number of solved cases of all tools for different numbers of conjuncts in Conjunction benchmarks. From Fig. 2, we can see that the advantage of Gelato-Strat and Gelato-States over SSyft and Strix gets larger as the expansion length (i.e., the number of conjunctions) grows. This is because constructing DSAs by LYDIA for each small conjunct in Gelato does not get much harder as the length increases; it is more dependent on the size of the small conjunct formulas than the number of conjuncts. In contrast, the performance of SSyft, which relies on LYDIA to construct the DSA for the whole formula, decreases greatly when the expansion length grows. Moreover, we observe that the performance of Gelato does not vary too much when the expansion length grows. This confirms that our compositional synthesis approaches indeed can mitigate the difficulty encountered by other approaches that solve the game only after obtaining the game arena. We also observe similar performance trend of each tool when the expansion length grows for Random-Conjunction benchmarks, except that the advantage of our Gelato-Strat and Gelato-States over SSyft and Strix is not as significant as depicted in Fig. 2.

Finally, we compared the running time of Gelato-States and Gelato-Strat on all benchmarks. It is surprising to see that Gelato-States is competitive with Gelato-Strat in general, although, Gelato-Strat solves one more case than Gelato-States and performs better than Gelato-States in hard cases. Gelato-Strat in particular, was expected to benefit from the fact that the transducer of the maximally permissive strategy is supposed to more compact than the one of the winning states. Indeed, both transducers have the same number of states, thus leaving no state space to prune for Gelato-Strat. Nevertheless, the transducer of the maximally permissive strategy should contain fewer propositional evaluations on the transitions. However, this does not lead to a more compact transducer when the transducers are in an explicit-state symbolic-transition representation. On the one hand, the transition conditions are represented symbolically in BDDs, it is possible that removing evaluations that do not belong to the maximally permissive strategy generate larger BDDs. On the other hand, removing evaluations even bring an extra cost. Thereby, we can not expect significant advantage of applying the strategy-based compositional approach.

5   Conclusion

We presented a novel compositional synthesis technique *specialized* for Safety LTL formulas in the form of $\varphi = \varphi_1 \wedge \varphi_2 \wedge \cdots \wedge \varphi_2$. In contrast to extant compositional synthesis approaches that solve the game after obtaining the game arena, our algorithm synthesizes a program for each smaller conjunct $\varphi_i, 1 \leqslant i \leqslant n$ separately and then composes them one by one. A big advantage of our algorithm is that the intermediate programs will be made smaller with pruning techniques, mitigating the possibility of blow-up of program state space. Empirical evaluation shows that our proposed algorithm outperforms the state of the arts in terms of the number of solved cases and running time. We believe that our compositional approach is a valuable contribution to the portfolio of Safety LTL synthesis algorithms. As future work, we plan to study how to further improve the construction of DSAs for each conjunct, which is the current bottleneck of our approach. Alternatively, we can investigate how to decompose the specification better to obtain smaller conjunct formulas. It is also interesting to see how our approach performs on practical benchmarks. We leave this to future work as well.

Acknowledgement. This work is supported in part by the ERC Advanced Grant WhiteMech (No. 834228), the EU ICT-48 2020 project TAILOR (No. 952215), the PRIN project RIPER (No. 20203FFYLK), the National Natural Science Foundation of China (Grant Nos. 62102407 and 61836005), CAS grant QYZDB-SSW-SYS019, NSF grants IIS-1527668, CCF-1704883, IIS-1830549, CNS-2016656, DoD MURI grant N00014-20-1-2787, and an award from the Maryland Procurement Office.

References

1. Baier, C., Katoen, J.: Principles of Model Checking. MIT Press, Cambridge (2008)
2. Bansal, S., Li, Y., Tabajara, L.M., Vardi, M.Y.: Hybrid compositional reasoning for reactive synthesis from finite-horizon specifications. In: AAAI, pp. 9766–9774 (2020)
3. Bernet, J., Janin, D., Walukiewicz, I.: Permissive strategies: from parity games to safety games. RAIRO Theor. Inform. Appl. **36**(3), 261–275 (2002)
4. Bloem, R., Jobstmann, B., Piterman, N., Pnueli, A., Sa'ar, Y.: Synthesis of reactive (1) designs. J. Comput. Syst. Sci. **78**(3), 911–938 (2012)
5. Bohy, A., Bruyère, V., Filiot, E., Jin, N., Raskin, J.-F.: Acacia+, a tool for LTL synthesis. In: Madhusudan, P., Seshia, S.A. (eds.) CAV 2012. LNCS, vol. 7358, pp. 652–657. Springer, Heidelberg (2012). https://doi.org/10.1007/978-3-642-31424-7_45
6. Chang, E., Manna, Z., Pnueli, A.: Characterization of temporal property classes. In: Kuich, W. (ed.) ICALP 1992. LNCS, vol. 623, pp. 474–486. Springer, Heidelberg (1992). https://doi.org/10.1007/3-540-55719-9_97
7. Church, A.: Application of recursive arithmetic to the problem of circuit synthesis. J. Symb. Log. **28**(4), 289–290 (1963)
8. Cimatti, A., Geatti, L., Gigante, N., Montanari, A., Tonetta, S.: Expressiveness of extended bounded response LTL. In: GandALF 2021, pp. 152–165 (2021)
9. De Giacomo, G., Favorito, M.: Compositional approach to translate LTL_f/LDL_f into deterministic finite automata. In: ICAPS, pp. 122–130 (2021)

10. Duret-Lutz, A., Lewkowicz, A., Fauchille, A., Michaud, T., Renault, É., Xu, L.: Spot 2.0—a framework for LTL and ω-automata manipulation. In: Artho, C., Legay, A., Peled, D. (eds.) ATVA 2016. LNCS, vol. 9938, pp. 122–129. Springer, Cham (2016). https://doi.org/10.1007/978-3-319-46520-3_8

11. Ehlers, R., Raman, V.: Slugs: extensible GR(1) synthesis. In: Chaudhuri, S., Farzan, A. (eds.) CAV 2016. LNCS, vol. 9780, pp. 333–339. Springer, Cham (2016). https://doi.org/10.1007/978-3-319-41540-6_18

12. Esparza, J., Křetínský, J., Sickert, S.: From LTL to deterministic automata - a safraless compositional approach. Formal Methods Syst. Des. **49**(3), 219–271 (2016)

13. Faymonville, P., Finkbeiner, B., Tentrup, L.: BoSy: an experimentation framework for bounded synthesis. In: Majumdar, R., Kunčak, V. (eds.) CAV 2017. LNCS, vol. 10427, pp. 325–332. Springer, Cham (2017). https://doi.org/10.1007/978-3-319-63390-9_17

14. Filiot, E., Jin, N., Raskin, J.: Antichains and compositional algorithms for LTL synthesis. Formal Methods Syst. Des. **39**(3), 261–296 (2011). https://doi.org/10.1007/s10703-011-0115-3

15. Finkbeiner, B., Geier, G., Passing, N.: Specification decomposition for reactive synthesis. In: NFM, pp. 113–130 (2021)

16. Finkbeiner, B., Passing, N.: Dependency-based compositional synthesis. In: Hung, D.V., Sokolsky, O. (eds.) ATVA 2020. LNCS, vol. 12302, pp. 447–463. Springer, Cham (2020). https://doi.org/10.1007/978-3-030-59152-6_25

17. Giacomo, G.D., Vardi, M.Y.: Linear temporal logic and linear dynamic logic on finite traces. In: IJCAI, pp. 854–860 (2013)

18. Henriksen, J.G., et al.: Mona: monadic second-order logic in practice. In: Brinksma, E., Cleaveland, W.R., Larsen, K.G., Margaria, T., Steffen, B. (eds.) TACAS 1995. LNCS, vol. 1019, pp. 89–110. Springer, Heidelberg (1995). https://doi.org/10.1007/3-540-60630-0_5

19. Kupferman, O., Piterman, N., Vardi, M.Y.: Safraless compositional synthesis. In: Ball, T., Jones, R.B. (eds.) CAV 2006. LNCS, vol. 4144, pp. 31–44. Springer, Heidelberg (2006). https://doi.org/10.1007/11817963_6

20. Kupferman, O., Vardi, M.Y.: Model checking of safety properties. Formal Methods Syst. Des. **19**(3), 291–314 (2001). https://doi.org/10.1023/A:1011254632723

21. Kupferman, O., Vardi, M.Y.: Safraless decision procedures. In: FOCS, pp. 531–542 (2005)

22. Meyer, P.J., Sickert, S., Luttenberger, M.: Strix: explicit reactive synthesis strikes back! In: Chockler, H., Weissenbacher, G. (eds.) CAV 2018. LNCS, vol. 10981, pp. 578–586. Springer, Cham (2018). https://doi.org/10.1007/978-3-319-96145-3_31

23. Michaud, T., Colange, M.: Reactive synthesis from LTL specification with spot. In: SYNT@CAV (2018)

24. Plaku, E., Kavraki, L.E., Vardi, M.Y.: Falsification of LTL safety properties in hybrid systems. Int. J. Softw. Tools Technol. Transf. **15**(4), 305–320 (2013). https://doi.org/10.1007/s10009-012-0233-2

25. Pnueli, A.: The temporal logic of programs. In: FOCS, pp. 46–57 (1977)

26. Pnueli, A., Rosner, R.: On the synthesis of a reactive module. In: POPL, pp. 179–190 (1989)

27. Sickert, S., Esparza, J.: An efficient normalisation procedure for linear temporal logic and very weak alternating automata. In: LICS, pp. 831–844 (2020)

28. Sistla, A.P.: Safety, liveness and fairness in temporal logic. Formal Aspects Comput. **6**(5), 495–512 (1994). https://doi.org/10.1007/BF01211865

29. Sohail, S., Somenzi, F.: Safety first: a two-stage algorithm for the synthesis of reactive systems. Int. J. Softw. Tools Technol. Transf. **15**(5–6), 433–454 (2013). https://doi.org/10.1007/s10009-012-0224-3

30. Somenzi, F.: CUDD: CU decision diagram package 3.0.0. University of Colorado at Boulder

31. Tabajara, L.M., Vardi, M.Y.: Partitioning techniques in LTL$_f$ synthesis. In: IJCAI, pp. 5599–5606 (2019)

32. Vardi, M.Y.: From verification to synthesis. In: Shankar, N., Woodcock, J. (eds.) VSTTE 2008. LNCS, vol. 5295, p. 2. Springer, Heidelberg (2008). https://doi.org/10.1007/978-3-540-87873-5_2

33. Zhu, S., Tabajara, L.M., Li, J., Pu, G., Vardi, M.Y.: A symbolic approach to safety LTL synthesis. In: Strichman, O., Tzoref-Brill, R. (eds.) HVC 2017. LNCS, vol. 10629, pp. 147–162. Springer, Cham (2017). https://doi.org/10.1007/978-3-319-70389-3_10

34. Zhu, S., Tabajara, L.M., Li, J., Pu, G., Vardi, M.Y.: Symbolic LTL$_f$ synthesis. In: IJCAI, pp. 1362–1369 (2017)

35. Zhu, S., Tabajara, L.M., Pu, G., Vardi, M.Y.: On the power of automata minimization in temporal synthesis. In: GandALF, pp. 117–134 (2021)

Leroy and Blazy Were Right: Their Memory Model Soundness Proof is Automatable

Pedro Barroso[1,2][✉], Mário Pereira[1,2], and António Ravara[1,2]

[1] NOVA School of Science and Technology, Caparica, Portugal
p.barroso@campus.fct.unl.pt
[2] NOVA-LINCS, Caparica, Portugal

Abstract. Xavier Leroy and Sandrine Blazy in 2007 conducted a formal verification, using the Coq proof assistant, of a memory model for low-level imperative languages such as C. Considering their formalization was performed essentially in first-order logic, one question left open by the authors was whether their proofs could be automated using a verification framework for first-order logic. We took the challenge and automated their formalization using Why3, significantly reducing the proof effort. We systematically followed the Coq proofs and realized that in many cases at around one third of the way Why3 was able to discharge all VCs. Furthermore, the proofs still requiring interactions (e.g. induction, witnesses for existential proofs, assertions) were factorized isolating auxiliary results that we stated explicitly. In this way, we achieved an almost-automatic soundness and safety proof of the memory model. Nonetheless, our development allows an extraction of a correct-by-construction concrete memory model, going thus further than the preliminary Why version of Leroy and Blazy.

Keywords: C memory model · Formal proof · Theorem proving · Why3

1 Introduction

Formal semantics are concerned with the process of building a mathematical model to serve as a basis for understanding and reasoning about how programs behave. A mathematical model is important because the activity of trying to precisely define the behavior of program constructions can reveal all types of subtleties of which it is crucial to be aware [10]. Many programs that require formal verification are written in imperative languages that accommodate pointer-based data structures with in-place modifications. To reason about the contents of the memory or even the behavior of operations over it, one needs to develop an adequate memory model.

A. Lal and S. Tonetta (Eds.): VSTTE 2022, LNCS 13800, pp. 20–32, 2023.
https://doi.org/10.1007/978-3-031-25803-9_2

Leroy and Blazy in 2007 formalized and verified, using the Coq proof assistant, a memory model for C-like imperative languages [5]. Coq proofs tend to be a very time consuming task and in fact, Leroy and Blazy's proof was almost the length of the specification and theorems (970 and 1070 lines, respectively). Considering their formalization was performed essentially in first-order logic, one question the authors addressed was whether their proofs could be automated using a verification framework for first-order logic, e.g. Why3 [3]. The authors translated their memory model to Why (a former version of Why3), the authors claim that at the time some recursive definitions were hard to define in the Why syntax and therefore, they only translated the axiomatizations and derived properties of the memory model. Their preliminary study (Figure 1) showed that could be automated, but no further study or complete formalization of their memory model has been automated so far.

	Ergo	Simplify	Z3	At least one
Derived properties from sections 3 and 4	15/15	15/15	15/15	15/15
Generic memory embeddings (section 5.1)	7/12	1/12	6/12	9/12
Memory extensions (section 5.2)	0/7	1/7	5/7	5/7
Refinement of stored values (section 5.3)	2/8	3/8	6/8	6/8
Memory injections (section 5.4)	4/8	4/8	7/8	7/8
Total	28/50	24/50	39/50	42/50

Fig. 1. Leroy and Blazy's Why formalization

Nonetheless, the problem we address here is:

Is it possible (15 years later) to automate the complete abstract and concrete implementation of the authors memory model?

In this paper we translate Leroy and Blazy's memory model to Why3 and develop an almost-automatic soundness and safety proof. Moreover, our code, implementing a concrete memory model, is extractable. This requires some manual work, namely re-organizing modules, that we believe with some refactoring of the WhyML code could be avoided.

Concretely, our contributions are:

- two Why3 versions (one containing interactive proofs and one "fully" automatic) that reduce up to 90% the Coq proof effort;
- general techniques to achieve a more automatic proof;
- a proof effort comparison between ours and the original Coq ones;
- a correct-by-construction memory model extracted from our development.

The rest of the article is organized as follows. Section 2 describes memory models and briefly presents the one of Leroy and Blazy. Also, Sect. 2 shows how to prove the memory model sound and safe (which includes semantics preservation for three passes of the Compcert compiler), and the Coq proof statistics that Leroy and Blazy stated in their paper. Section 3 outlines our Why3 development and the techniques used to explicitly state interactive transformations. Section 4 compares both versions with the Coq version and presents our approach to extract correct-by-construction OCaml code, followed by conclusions in Sect. 6. Our Why3 development and OCaml extracted code is publicly available[1].

2   The Memory Model

Memory models provide the necessary abstraction between the behavior of a program and the behavior of the memory it reads and writes. When reasoning about compilers and low-level code we need to account for several factors such as memory management, concurrency behavior, casts, structured pointers, overlapping locations, etc. Therefore, it is not sufficient to interpret memory as an assignment of values to locations.

2.1   Concept

The generic idea behind a memory model is to explicitly describe and provide some guarantees on the behavior of certain operations that manipulate memory (e.g. read, write, allocation, free). This allows to make concrete assumptions about the "state of the memory" at any time of the execution of a program. One example is that reading after writing a value into a location should return the value that was previously stored. Figure 2 shows this simple scenario and the natural assertions one can make over the execution of the program.

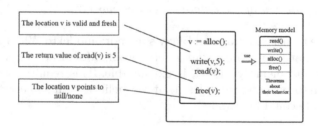

Fig. 2. Concrete assertion over a simple program

There are several ways to define a memory model: as a description of the set of valid traces of operations fulfilled by the execution of a program (e.g. IBM POWER multiprocessors [6]); as an abstract machine that receives and replies to messages (e.g. CompCertTSO [9]); and as a set of functions that can be invoked along with some guarantees on their results (e.g. Leroy and Blazy's memory model [5]). Note that in most cases a definition in one of these styles is provably equivalent to a definition in another style [7].

---

[1] https://gitlab.com/p.barroso/memory-model-c-why3/.

The memory model presented by Leroy and Blazy is used in the formal verification of the Compcert [4] compiler, which transforms the Clight subset of the C programming language down to PowerPC assembly code.

2.2   Leroy and Blazy's Memory Model

Leroy and Blazy start by giving an abstract, incomplete specification of a memory model to formalize the memory-related aspects of C and related languages. The abstract type val represents values, which includes the constant vundef to describe an undefined value. To describe references to memory blocks they use an abstract type block and to represent memory states an abstract type mem.

Memory Definitions. A memory *state* is a collection of separated blocks where each block behaves as an array of bytes, and is addressed using byte offsets $i \in \mathbb{Z}$. A memory *location* is a pair (b, i) of a block reference b and an offset i within this block. Lastly, the constant empty : mem represents the initial memory state.

Operations. They define four operations that manipulate memory states as total functions:

$$\text{alloc} : \text{mem} \times \mathbb{Z} \times \mathbb{Z} \to \text{option(block} \times \text{mem)}$$
$$\text{free} : \text{mem} \times \text{block} \to \text{option mem}$$
$$\text{load} : \text{memtype} \times \text{mem} \times \text{block} \times Z \to \text{option val}$$
$$\text{store} : \text{memtype} \times \text{mem} \times \text{block} \times Z \times \text{val} \to \text{option mem}$$

All these functions return option types to take into account potential failures. The function alloc(m,l,h) allocates a fresh memory block, where m is the initial memory state, $l \in \mathbb{Z}$ is the lower bound of the block (inclusive), and $h \in \mathbb{Z}$ the upper bound (exclusive) of the fresh block. Allocation can fail if not enough memory is available. Otherwise, Some (b,m) is returned, where b is the reference to the new block and m the updated memory state.

Contrarily, free(m,b) deallocates block b in memory m. In case of success, an updated memory state is returned.

The function store(τ,m,b,i,v) writes value v of type τ at offset i in block b of m. If successful, the updated memory state is returned.

Symmetrically, load(τ,m,b,i) reads a data type of τ from block b of memory state m at byte offset i. If successful, the value from block b is returned.

Axiomatization and Additional Properties. The authors axiomatize the expected behavior of the operations.[2] Recall that any implementation of the model must satisfy all these properties.

---

[2] The complete set of hypotheses can be consulted online.

Good and Not so Good Variables (Axioms S5 to S8). Define the correct behavior (operation succeeds) of a `load` after an `alloc`, `free` or `store` operation. Concretely, these hypotheses specify that: `alloc` and `free` preserve `load`s performed in any other disjoint block; reading from the same location with a compatible type τ' succeeds and returns the value `convert(v,`τ'`)`; and storing a value of type τ' in block `b` at offset `i` commutes with loading. Furthermore, Leroy and Blazy also specify when the `load` operation returns an undefined value.

Block Validity (Axioms S9 to S13). The correct behavior of a `load` after an `alloc`, `free` or `store` depends on separation properties between blocks. In order to capture such properties, Leroy and Blazy axiomatize the relation $m \models b$, which means that block `b` is valid in memory `m`. A block is valid if it was previously allocated and was not yet deallocated.

Bounds of Block (Axioms S14 to S17). The authors also axiomatize the function $\mathcal{B}(m, b)$ that associates low and high bounds to a block `b` in memory state `m`. The axiomatization specifies that a freshly allocated block has the bounds that were given as argument to the `alloc` function and the bounds of a block are preserved by an `alloc`, `store` or `free` operation over a different block.

Valid Access (Axiom S18 and Derived Properties D19 to D22). Combining the definitions of block validity and of bounds of a block, Leroy and Blazy define the "valid access" relation $m \models \tau @ b, i$, which means that in state `m`, the block `b` is a valid block and the range of byte offsets being accessed is included in the bounds of `b`. Intuitively, the `store` and `load` operations succeeds if and only if the corresponding memory reference is valid.

Freshness Property (Properties P30 to P34). In Leroy and Blazy's concrete memory model, `alloc` never reuses block identifiers. Therefore, they define the relation $m \# b$ stating that block `b` is fresh in memory `m`. This relation is mutually exclusive with block validity.

Alloc Determinism (Property P35). Lastly, Leroy and Blazy state that alloc is deterministic with respect to the domain of the current memory state, i.e. alloc chooses the same free block when applied twice to memory states that have the same domain, but may differ in block contents.

2.3   Compiler Passes and Their Soundness Proof

The axiomatization of the previous section specify precise handling of undefined values, behavior of operations over memory states and "good-variable" properties. This theory is used to prove the correctness of program transformations performed by three passes of the `Compcert` compiler. Our approach follows the same process presented by Leroy and Blazy and, therefore, we also prove the correctness of these transformations.

To prove soundness and safety of each transformation, one need to guarantee specific results between the memory operations performed by the original and transformed program. For that, invariants are defined to describe the memory states at every point of the execution of the original and transformed programs.

Leroy and Blazy use four relations between memory states: memory embeddings; memory extensions; refinement of stored values; and memory injections. For each of them, they define several properties the program needs to hold in order to prove soundness and safety. We decided to omit the exact definitions, as the list is exhaustive and falls out of the scope of this paper.[3]

2.4   Original Coq Proof

Coq uses *Gallina*, a functional programming language. The close connection between functional languages and mathematical definitions eases the implementation of mathematical theories. The Coq development of Leroy and Blazy is very close to the definitions presented in their paper. In fact, most of the definitions in their paper were transcribed directly from their Coq development, which has approximately 1070 lines of theorems and specifications, and 970 lines of proof scripts.

Coq does not grant much support for proof automation. Therefore, Leroy and Blazy manually conducted most of the proofs. Yet, their proofs exhaustively use the omega tactic, a procedure that automates reasoning about equations and inequalities over the type **nat** of natural numbers. They also occasionally use other tactics (e.g. **eauto**, **congruence**), which the authors say were useful.

3   Our Approach in Why3

The formalization of Leroy and Blazy was conducted mostly in first-order logic: the authors use functions as data, but only to implement finite maps, which allows a first-order axiomatization. Henceforth, the definitions in Why3 are very similar to the fragment from Gallina (Coq's language). In fact, our development is very similar to the specification and theorems of the Coq version.

Implementation. The Why version of Leroy and Blazy only contained the axiomatization of the abstract memory model. Our Why3 development have the axioms of the abstract memory model and additionally, the implementation of a concrete memory model, which allows an extraction of a correct-by-construction memory model. Our formalization have approximately 1040 lines of theorems and specifications, roughly the same amount of the Coq version.

Proofs. The automatic theorem provers discharges automatically 114 from a total of 125 verification conditions using the auto level 3 tactic, which attempts

---

[3] The authors did not presented a summarized list of properties for each of the four relations.

to apply recursively four transformations (split_all_full, introduce_premises, inline_goal and split_vc) and calls the provers with a larger time and memory limit (30 s and 4 Gb of memory). Using the key 3 of the keyboard (shortcut for the auto level 3 tactic) we automatically prove the equivalent of approximately 870 lines of proof scripts in Coq (89.6% of the total proof scripts lines). Appendix A on page 13 of [1] shows the corresponding proofs in Coq and Why3 of one lemma of the 114.

For the remaining 9 verification conditions (VCs), we follow closely the Coq proof script, applying transformations one by one and calling the solvers for each transformation. Three of the VCs require simple induction; four case analysis before applying the induction hypothesis; one additional properties in the context that we introduce with assertions and the last one a mix of induction, case analysis, assertions and additionally proves an existential statement (Table B1 on page 14 of [1] summarizes the results). Yet, in all nine, the amount of transformations to complete the proof were significantly less than the steps of the proof in Coq (circa 117 transformations versus a total of 220).

General Strategies to Achieve a More Automatic Proof. The primary cons of Why3 regarding proofs with manually conducted interactions are: it is hard to have a concise global view of all transformations applied, especially on larger proof trees; moreover after making change in the code, most of the times Why3 is not able to propagate the exact transformations through the correct proof nodes, which quite often leads to losses of the whole proof session [2].

To circumvent this, we present the following general techniques to explicitly state the interactions required for the remaining 9 proofs as WhyML code. This allows the reader to have the essence of the whole proof just by looking at the source code. Bellow, we explain and illustrate the approaches namely in the treatment of induction, assertions and existential properties. The remainder 9 proofs use these techniques. These techniques can be used as general recipes for provers.

Induction. Why3 provides a way to define lemma functions, which are special functions that serve not as actual code to execute but to prove the function's contract as a lemma. These are useful when proving properties by induction, as any recursive call to the functions means an application of the induction hypothesis. Lets consider the following lemma:

```
lemma set_cont_outside:
    forall n, f:(int → option (fset 'a, fset 'a)) , ofs i.
```

We prove the lemma by induction on n. Let us now convert our lemma to a recursive lemma function. Recursive lemma functions are declared with the keywords `let rec lemma` and its parameters are the universally quantified variables in the normal lemma:

```
let rec lemma set_cont_outside (n: int)
        (f: (int → option (memtype, value))) (ofs i: int)
```

Now we give a contract to the lemma, where each premise is now a precondition (declared with the `requires` keyword) and the conclusion a postcondition (declared with the `ensures` keyword). To guarantee the function terminates we state a variant, in this case n itself, which is the argument we are applying induction:

```
let rec lemma set_cont_outside (n: int)
        (f: (int → option (memtype, value))) (ofs i: int)
    requires { n ≥ 0 }
    requires { i < ofs  ∨  i ≥ ofs + n }
    ensures { set_cont f ofs n i = f i }
    variant { n }
```

Finally, we construct the correct recursive call by looking at the definitions of the functions within the postconditions. In this case we have the function `set_cont`, which definition is as follows:

```
let rec ghost function set_cont (f: int → content)
        (ofs: int) (n: int) : int → content
    requires { n ≥ 0 }
    variant { n }
= if n = 0 then f else set_cont (update ofs None f) (ofs + 1) (n-1)
```

The recursive call of the lemma uses the same argument modifications of the recursive call of `set_cont`:

```
let rec lemma set_cont_outside (n: int)
        (f: (int → option (memtype, value))) (ofs i: int) ...
= if n > 0 then set_cont_outside (n-1) (update ofs None f) (ofs + 1) i
```

Why3 is now able to automatically generate a valid induction hypothesis and prove the lemma. The technique can be used as a general recipe for provers.

Asserts. We introduce assertions in the body of `let lemmas`. For example in the lemma `store_mapped_emb`, we assert that b1 is a valid pointer in memory state m1 and b2 is a valid pointer in memory state m2:

```
let lemma store_mapped_emb
        (val_emb: (int → option (int, int))) → value → value → bool)
        (emb: int → option (int, int)) (m1 m2: mem_)
        (b1 ofs b2 delta: int) (v1 v2: value) (ty: memtype) (m1': mem_)
    requires { ... }
    ensures { ... }
= assert { valid_pointer_ ty m1 b1 ofs };
  assert { valid_pointer_ ty m2 b2 (ofs + delta) }
```

The assertions are introduced in the hypotheses of the lemma and Why3 generates two new VCs to prove both the assertions are valid.

Witnesses for Existential Statements. When one needs to prove an existentially quantified formula, sometimes the automatic theorem provers are not able to easily find the specific witness. Therefore, one needs to manually build it. Consider the following lemma:

```
lemma store_lessdef:
  forall m1 m2 ty b ofs v1 m1' v2. mem_lessdef m1 m2 →
      store_ ty m1 b ofs v1 = Some m1' → val_lessdef v1 v2 →
      exists m2'. store_ ty m2 b ofs v2 = Some m2' ∧ mem_lessdef m1' m2'
```

We convert the lemma to a let lemma and as the lemma now needs to return a value, we change the signature of the function to return the type of the witness:

```
let lemma store_lessdef (m1 m2: mem_) (ty: memtype) (b ofs: int)
    (v1: value) (m1': mem_) (v2: value) : (m2': mem_)
```

We also need to change the postcondition, which should now ensure the same properties over the result of the function. This is achieved by replacing the existential quantified variable with the output value m2':

```
ensures { store_ ty m2 b ofs v2 = Some m2' ∧ mem_lessdef m1' m2'}
```

Lastly, the function needs to return a proper witness that satisfied the post-conditions. In this case, we manually build a new memory state with updated fields:

```
let lemma store_lessdef (m1 m2: mem_) (ty: memtype) (b ofs: int)
    (v1: value) (m1': mem_) (v2: value) : (m2': mem_)
  ... = ...
  (mem_'mk (m2.nextblock) (m2.bounds_) (m2.freed)
    (update b (store_contents (m2.contents @ b) ty (ofs + 0) v2)
    (m2.contents)))
```

The proof is now automatic and again, the technique is general.

Outcome. Applying these three techniques to the remainder 9 lemmas, we reduce 100% the number of manually conducted transformations needed to complete the proofs. Table 1 compares the before and after applying these techniques.

Table 1. Number of transformations before and after

Lemma	Number of interactions (Why3)	
	Before	After
1. check_cont_charact	7	0
2. set_cont_outside	2	0
3. set_cont_inside	2	0
4. free_list_left_emb	6	0
5. free_list_not_valid_block	6	0
6. embedding_no_overlap_free_list	6	0
7. free_list_fresh_block	3	0
8. alloc_list_left_inject	75	0
9. alloc_list_alloc_inject	10	0

4   Proof Effort

Coq support for proof automation is limited, as one needs to explicitly apply a sequence of tactics and transformations to prove the desired goal. In contrast, one of the main focus of Why3 is automation, linking with SMT solvers to discharge proof obligations, what allows to develop proofs with less effort.

In this section we present metrics to compare our proofs with the Coq version. We used the original authors' proof as we are not aware of any improved version – nowadays Coq has much more support to automation and experts may reduce significantly the amount of transformations. Anyway, our goal is not a direct comparison between lines of proof scripts, but how much automation can be achieved, being this actually the original challenge left by Leroy and Blazy.

Why3 Fully Automatic Proof. All lemmas were automatically proved using the auto_level_3 tactic of Why3. The detailed proof results are available here. The Table 2 summarizes the structure of the proof.

Table 2. Number of lemmas per module

	Module							Total
	Gen_Mem_Facts	Ref_Gen_Mem_Facts	Concrete_Mem	Rel_Mem	Mem_Extends	Mem_Lessdef	Mem_Inject	
Number of lemmas	7	12	61	16	7	6	15	124

These results take into consideration the interactions stated explicitly in the code. Although the automatic theorem provers were able to prove all the lemmas automatically, we had to use the techniques in Sect. 3 to aid the verification process. One might think these techniques do exactly the same thing as the transformations in the Coq proof scripts. In some sense that is true, we closely followed the Coq proof script and applied transformations one by one. However, when explicitly stating the transformations, one gives auxiliary results (e.g. auxiliary lemmas, assertions, concrete definitions) not a sequence of transformations/tactics as in Coq. On one hand, in Why3 we have the certainty that all auxiliary results are required to complete the proof (without them it is not possible to prove the lemmas). On the other, in Coq, one does not have the certainty that all the tactics are essential to the proof (one just knows that specific sequence completes the proof). Nonetheless, even without explicitly stating the interactive proofs, the effort to prove the lemmas in Why3 was way less than in Coq. Let us compare the non-fully automatic Why3 proof with the Coq version.

Why3 Semi-automatic Proof. The implementation and proofs without explicit interaction in the code can be consulted here. Even without stating explicitly the interactions, the theorem provers were able to prove 115 VCs automatically, which translates into a gain of automation circa 93%. Table 3 summarizes the results.

Table 3. Number of lemmas proved automatically

Module								Total
	Gen_Mem_Facts	Ref_Gen_Mem_Facts	Concrete_Mem	Rel_Mem	Mem_Extends	Mem_Lessdef	Mem_Inject	
Number of lemmas	7	12	61	16	7	6	15	124
Automatically proved	7 (100%)	12 (100%)	58 (95%)	14 (87.5%)	7 (100%)	6 (100%)	11 (73.3%)	115 (92.7%)

These 115 VCs corresponds to a total of approximately 870 lines of the Coq proof script, which in turn consists of 89.6% of the total lines of the entire Coq proof script. Table B2 on page 14 of [1] compares the amount of transformations used in interactive proofs in Why3 and Coq. One can see that in Why3 we have a reduction of 46.8% of the transformations compared to the Coq version, which means significantly less proof effort.

5   Code Extraction

One extra contribution of our work is the extraction of a correct-by-construction OCaml implementation of the memory model.

The implementation of Leroy and Blazy uses several undefined functions (e.g. `enough_free_memory`, `alignof`). In order to extract OCaml code, we need to organize the code involving these functions and insert them into a parameterized module (functor). For example, considering the function `enough_free_memory`, we include its signature in the scope of the following `Make` functor:

```
scope Make
   scope X
       val function enough_free_memory (mem: mem_) (i: int) : bool
   end = struct ... end
```

With this manual transformation in the WhyML code (with the respect to the one we originally used for the proofs), the extraction becomes automatic in the sense that the obtained OCaml code compiles.

6   Conclusions

In this paper we present two versions in Why3 of the memory model of Leroy and Blazy, which is used in the Compcert compiler: from the proof point of view one is semi-automatic and the other results from an engineering effort to attain full automation (e.g. turning tactics into auxiliary results). Using the Why3 code extraction mechanism [8], from both versions we get correct-by-construction OCaml implementations of the memory model.

The first version is a direct translation from the Coq development to Why3. We immediately gain 93% of automation. The remaining 7% were proved following closely the Coq proof script. Nonetheless, in Why3 the amount of transformations required for the theorem provers to validate the proofs were significantly less (117 transformations versus a total of 220).

The second version is a fully automatic proof. We performed general techniques (explained in Sect. 3) to explicitly define the interactive proofs of the first version within the WhyML code. This improves readability, as one does not need to open the Why3 IDE to verify which transformations are used, it is possible to have the essence of the proof just by analyzing the code. Furthermore, as the proof is fully automatic, this approach also preserves the proof-sessions, allowing a simple replay to check the reproducibility of the results.

Lessons Learned. Nothing of the memory model was inexpressible in WhyML. This confirms the premise that automatic verification tools are well-good candidates to defiant proofs of complex programs without losing expressiveness.

Furthermore, most of the proofs required a handful of transformations and nevertheless 93% of the proof was performed by merely pressing a button (hence using automatic tactics, like `split`, etc.). It is possible to save time and effort to the proofs that are actually challenging.

It is undoubtedly that we are, at some point, limited to first order logic, however if one reaches the limits of these type of provers, one can still prove the remaining goals in Coq for example. In fact, Why3 provides a Coq tactic to call external theorem provers as oracles.

Nonetheless, to achieve an even higher level of automation we performed some refactoring to expose properties to the WhyML code: created auxiliary lemmas from patterns that constantly appear in the Coq proof script; defined inductive predicates to avoid proofs by induction; and transformed existential proofs to `lemma` functions which return the desired witness.

Acknowledgement. Work partially supported by the Portuguese Fundação para a Ciência e Tecnologia via NOVA LINCS (UIDB/04516/2020) and by the first author PhD grant (UI/BD/151265/2021).

References

1. Barroso, P., Pereira, M., Ravara, A.: Leroy and blazy were right: their memory model soundness proof is automatable (extended version) (2022). https://doi.org/10.48550/ARXIV.2212.02425, https://arxiv.org/abs/2212.02425
2. Bobot, F., Filliâtre, J.-C., Marché, C., Melquiond, G., Paskevich, A.: Preserving user proofs across specification changes. In: Cohen, E., Rybalchenko, A. (eds.) VSTTE 2013. LNCS, vol. 8164, pp. 191–201. Springer, Heidelberg (2014). https://doi.org/10.1007/978-3-642-54108-7_10
3. Filliâtre, J.-C., Paskevich, A.: Why3—where programs meet provers. In: Felleisen, M., Gardner, P. (eds.) ESOP 2013. LNCS, vol. 7792, pp. 125–128. Springer, Heidelberg (2013). https://doi.org/10.1007/978-3-642-37036-6_8
4. Leroy, X.: A formally verified compiler back-end. J. Autom. Reason. **43**(4), 363–446 (2009). https://doi.org/10.1007/s10817-009-9155-4
5. Leroy, X., Blazy, S.: Formal verification of a C-like memory model and its uses for verifying program transformations. J. Autom. Reason. **41**, 1–31 (2008). https://doi.org/10.1007/s10817-008-9099-0

6. Mador-Haim, S., et al.: An axiomatic memory model for POWER multiprocessors. In: Madhusudan, P., Seshia, S.A. (eds.) CAV 2012. LNCS, vol. 7358, pp. 495–512. Springer, Heidelberg (2012). https://doi.org/10.1007/978-3-642-31424-7_36
7. Mansky, W., Garbuzov, D., Zdancewic, S.: An axiomatic specification for sequential memory models. In: Kroening, D., Păsăreanu, C.S. (eds.) CAV 2015. LNCS, vol. 9207, pp. 413–428. Springer, Cham (2015). https://doi.org/10.1007/978-3-319-21668-3_24
8. Pereira, M.J.P.: Tools and techniques for the verification of modular stateful code. (Outils et techniques pour la vérification de programmes impératives modulaires). Ph.D. thesis, University of Paris-Saclay, France (2018). https://tel.archives-ouvertes.fr/tel-01980343
9. Ševčík, J., Vafeiadis, V., Zappa Nardelli, F., Jagannathan, S., Sewell, P.: CompCertTSO: a verified compiler for relaxed-memory concurrency. J. ACM **60**(3), 1–50 (2013). https://doi.org/10.1145/2487241.2487248
10. Winskel, G.: The Formal Semantics of Programming Languages: An Introduction. MIT Press, Cambridge (1993)

Shellac: A Compiler Synthesizer
for Concurrent Programs

Christopher K. Chen(✉)📧🆔, Margo I. Seltzer🆔, and Mark R. Greenstreet🆔

The University of British Columbia, Vancouver BC V6T 1Z4, Canada
cchen@nougat.org, {mseltzer,mrg}@cs.ubc.ca

Abstract. Formal specification languages such as TLA+ and UNITY are
used to design and verify concurrent programs. These languages are
intended for analysis rather than for execution. A compiler or a human
must implement the specified program in a lower-level executable language. We present Shellac, a *compiler synthesizer* that completes a sketch
of a syntax-directed compiler by using program synthesis to derive translation rules. This approach produces a correct-by-construction compiler
without burdening the compiler writer with manual specification and
verification. We evaluate Shellac by synthesizing a compiler from UNITY
to Arduino C++ and Verilog, then compiling Paxos consensus in UNITY
to implementations in Arduino C++ for microcontrollers and Verilog for
reconfigurable hardware.

Keywords: Automatic programming · Compilation · Concurrency ·
Formal models · Program synthesis

1 Introduction

Concurrent programs are notoriously difficult to write, debug, and verify. This is
especially the case with imperative programs that mix state mutation and control
flow, where the resulting state explosion makes formal analysis intractable.

Formal specification languages and program logics, e.g., TLA+ and UNITY,
enable the design and verification of concurrent programs at an abstract level
[7,10]. A specification written in such a language describes a state machine
by formally defining valid initial states and permitted state transitions. Such
specifications are *behavioural* as opposed to *logical*, e.g., a temporal logic formula.

A behavioural specification by itself is useful for analysis and as a design
tool, but in general, it is too abstract for direct execution. Often, a programmer
manually translates a specification to a lower-level implementation language.
This process is error-prone and verifying correctness, e.g., showing refinement,
requires substantial proof effort, e.g., seL4 [5]. Alternatively, a programmer could
write a compiler from a specification to an implementation language, e.g., CompCert, but still, the engineering and verification effort remains incredibly high

We acknowledge the support of the Natural Sciences and Engineering Research Council
of Canada (NSERC).

A. Lal and S. Tonetta (Eds.): VSTTE 2022, LNCS 13800, pp. 33–51, 2023.
https://doi.org/10.1007/978-3-031-25803-9_3

[8]. We are interested in *automatic* and *verified* techniques for generating programs that meet their specifications. In particular, we exploit *program synthesis* to reduce the proof burden of verifying an implementation against its behavioural specification.

Program synthesis is any procedure that generates a program that satisfies some constraint. If the constraint is a correctness condition with regard to a specification, then the synthesized implementation is correct by construction. This means that, assuming the correctness of the synthesis procedure, no further proof is required. We focus on counterexample-guided inductive program synthesis (CEGIS), where a search-verify-refine loop uses verification counterexamples to prune the search space [15]. Any decidable, search-based synthesis procedure places bounds, e.g., expression depth or number of instructions, over the infinite space of programs. This exponential search space explosion makes it difficult for CEGIS to find programs that satisfy nontrivial specifications.

We present a method to construct a compiler by generating verified translation rules via program synthesis. Our synthesized compiler accepts UNITY specifications and generates implementations in Arduino C++ and Verilog [1,4]. Instead of synthesizing concrete C++ or Verilog *programs* from a complete specification, we synthesize implementations of *elements* of UNITY's expression syntax. Each of these synthesized implementations takes the form of a rewrite rule from source to target. These synthesized rewrite rules are assembled into a recursive syntax-guided compiler pass. We show that for channel-based UNITY programs, syntax-guided translation preserves the specification's safety and liveness properties. Shellac, our compiler synthesizer, is written in Rosette [16]. The programs that Shellac synthesizes have all the benefits of traditional compilation: they are deterministic and handle arbitrary source programs that satisfy a channel-based schema. We provide:

1. A rewrite rule synthesizer that includes language embeddings in Rosette and a procedure for generating rewrite rules between languages.
2. A proof that the compiler preserves safety and liveness properties for channel-based UNITY programs.
3. An evaluation of rewrite rule synthesis performance and the compilation of Paxos consensus from UNITY to Arduino C++ and Verilog.

2   Preliminaries

Shellac starts with a partial compiler, or a sketch, whose organization is illustrated in Fig. 1. We begin with an discussion of our state and process model. Next, we describe an abstract channel model for asynchronous communication and a dataflow merge specification used as a running example. Given that context, we introduce the UNITY specification, boolean-bitvector parallel, boolean-bitvector scalar, boolean-bitvector sequential, Arduino C++, and Verilog languages.

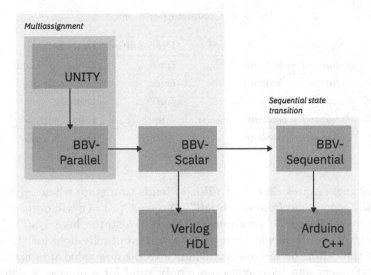

Fig. 1. Source (salmon), intermediate (indigo), and target (tangerine) languages with compiler passes. Boxes highlight semantic similarities.

2.1 State, Assignment, and Processes

The source and target languages modelled here are all imperative: we effect computation by mutating state. Each program is defined over a set of variables, and a state is a mapping from those variables to values. Programs operate by inspecting the current state of their variables and, if permitted, assigning new values to a subset of them, effecting a state transition. Variables are either *internal* or *shared*. Shared variables are reserved for channel communications, described below. The languages presented differ in their assignment/state transition semantics. In particular, UNITY, boolean-bitvector parallel/scalar, and Verilog state transitions are parallel and atomic, while boolean-bitvector sequential and Arduino C++ state transitions occur sequentially with each assignment statement.

Our coarse-grained concurrency model is based upon communicating processes. Each such process, P, must be coherent: if P writes to some variable, v, no other process writes to v; if process P reads v and some other process, C, writes to v, then C must be a channel as described below. Processes execute one assignment at a time. Concurrency is a property of a system of processes, not of a process itself.

2.2 Channels

Interprocess communication is via point-to-point channels. At the specification level, a channel, c is an abstract data type. Channel operations are listed in Table 1.

Table 1. Channel operations

Function	Signature	Precondition	Description
empty?(c)	*channel → boolean*	*true*	Empty predicate
full?(c)	*channel → boolean*	*true*	Full predicate
drain(c)	*channel → channel*	*full?(c)*	Drains *c*
fill(c, v)	*channel × boolean → channel*	*empty?(c)*	Fills *c* with *v*
read(c)	*channel → boolean*	*full?(c)*	Extracts value from *c*

The channel ensures that $c' := fill(c, v)$ leads to a state where $\neg empty?(c')$ holds for the sender and from which $full?(c') \wedge read?(c') = v$ will eventually hold for the receiver. Likewise, $c' := drain(c, v)$ leads to a state where $\neg full?(c')$ holds for the receiver and from which $empty?(c')$ will eventually hold for the sender. The use of the $'$ after the variable name indicates the new value after assignment. The *empty?* query and *fill* operation are only valid for a process designated as the sender. Likewise, *full?*, *read*, and *drain* are only valid for the receiver.

2.3   Dataflow Merge Element

We use a merge operator as a running example; it takes two input channels, *inA* and *inB*, and transmits anything received on those channels to the output channel, *out*. In the case where both input channels are full and *out* is empty, the specified behaviour is nondeterministic, and either assignment can occur.

2.4   UNITY

UNITY is a language for specifying parallel and distributed programs [10]. We provide an informal overview of assignment syntax and semantics here – and provide a formalization of expressions and state transitions later. We do not cover Chandy and Misra's UNITY program logic. A specification defines variables, initial state, and next-state assignments. A UNITY program may reach a fixed point, but it does not halt in the traditional sense. We discuss datatypes, followed by parallel assignment, then nondeterministic choice. Our examples include merge and channel processes.

Datatypes. Our model of UNITY includes primitive datatypes, send/receive buffers, and channels. Send/receive buffers are fixed length lists with a cursor for serializing data to be sent over a channel. Presently, Shellac supports booleans and natural numbers for primitive datatypes, send/receive buffers that are lists of booleans, and channels for boolean data.

Simultaneous Assignment. A simultaneous assignment statement has a list of variables on the left side and an expression list on the right side. The expression list is either *simple* or *conditional*. A simple list contains expressions corresponding to the assignment's variables: e.g., $a, b := 42, a + 3$ assigns the value 42 to a and the sum of 3 and the *original* value of a to b. Parallel assignments are *independent* and *simultaneous*: the expressions are evaluated to values *before* any assignments are made, and all assignments occur in one atomic action. A conditional list pairs simple expression lists with boolean guard expressions: e.g., for the dataflow merge assignment from *inA* to *out*:

$$inA, out := \left\{ drain(inA), fill(out, read(inA)) \text{ if } full?(inA) \wedge empty?(out) \right.$$

In the above case, there is only one guarded assignment, but in general, a conditional list may contain an arbitrary number of expression list and guard pairs. Guards are not required to be exhaustive. If no guard is true, the state is left unchanged. If two guards are true, their corresponding expression lists must evaluate to the same values. Parallel assignment is deterministic.

Nondeterministic Choice. Note that our description of dataflow merge does not specify what to do if both input channels were full, when both assignments are permitted. We express this nondeterminism in UNITY by composing simultaneous assignments with the *box* operator $\square$:

$$inA, out \quad := \left\{ drain(inA), fill(out, read(inA)) \text{ if } full?(inA) \wedge empty?(out) \right.$$

$$\square$$

$$inB, out \quad := \left\{ drain(inB), fill(out, read(inB)) \text{ if } full?(inB) \wedge empty?(out) \right.$$

Nondeterministic choice is subject to a *fair selection* or *absolute fairness* constraint: every assignment is executed infinitely often. Note that this property implies weak fairness, but not strong fairness.

Channel Asynchrony. As described previously, channels are asynchronous processes accessed via shared variables, with channel processes responsible for propagating state between senders and receivers. Because state propagates asynchronously, parallel atomic channel actions by one process may appear to an observer in any sequence or simultaneously.

2.5 Boolean-Bitvector Parallel

The boolean-bitvector parallel intermediate language is a lowering of UNITY to tuples booleans and fixed-length bitvectors. Booleans are encoded as boolean singletons and bounded naturals are encoded as bitvector singletons. Send/receive buffers are encoded as the bitvector pairs $\langle cursor, data \rangle$. Channel values are already encoded in UNITY as boolean triples $\langle req, ack, data \rangle$, resembling signals on a serial communication line. A boolean-bitvector channel is empty if $req = ack$, full if $req \neq ack$. Senders cannot modify ack, and receivers cannot modify req or $data$.

Assignment semantics are identical to UNITY, where individual assignments are deterministic, parallel, and atomic. Nondeterministic choice over assignments is also subject to a fair selection constraint. We describe the behaviour of dataflow merge for inA in boolean-bitvector parallel:

$$inA.ack, out.req, out.data \quad := \begin{cases} \langle inA.req, \neg out.req, inA.data \rangle \\ \quad \text{if } inA.req \neq inA.ack \wedge out.req = out.ack \end{cases}$$

2.6   Boolean-Bitvector Scalar

The boolean-bitvector scalar intermediate language is a scalar version of boolean-bitvector parallel, with tuple values split into scalars. Assignment semantics are unchanged.

2.7   Boolean-Bitvector Sequential

The boolean-bitvector sequential intermediate language is a sequential version of boolean-bitvector scalar. Parallel atomic assignments are replaced by sequences of scalar assignments, with fair selection over sequences. We describe the behaviour of merge for inA in boolean-bitvector sequential:

$$\text{if } inA.req \neq inA.ack \wedge out.req = out.ack$$
$$\begin{cases} out.data & := inA.data; \\ out.req & := \neg out.req; \\ inA.ack & := inA.req; \end{cases}$$

A boolean-bitvector sequential program executes variable assignments one at a time and in order. This exposes intermediate states not accounted for in the specification, opening the possibility to a violation of a specification property. We describe in Sect. 3.4 ordering constraints that rewrite rules must encode such that sequential implementations preserve the behaviours of the original specification.

2.8   Target Platforms

To demonstrate Shellac, we use Arduino mkr Vidor 4000 prototyping boards with ARM microcontrollers and Intel FPGAs. This allows us to demonstrate compilation to both hardware and software. With several boards and some wire, we demonstrate a small-scale distributed system.

Arduino. The Arduino language is an API in C++ derived from the Wiring language [1,3]. The API provides functions for reading and writing from hardware input/output pins.

Shellac generates a compiler with a backend from boolean-bitvector sequential to Arduino C++. The Arduino project toolchain compiles C++ into ARM machine code and programs the microcontroller.

Verilog. Verilog is a simulation and design language for digital circuits [4]. The non-simulation subset of the language that can be realized in digital circuits is referred to as *synthesizable* Verilog.

Shellac generates a compiler with a backend from boolean-bitvector scalar to synthesizable Verilog. An Intel toolchain compiles Verilog into a *bitstream* for configuring the FPGA, turning it into a custom digital device.

3   Formalization and Mechanization

The UNITY specification language is structured around an explicit separation between functional expression evaluation and atomic state transition. This separation allows us to formulate correctness by focusing on each concern independently. Two compilation passes engage in a semantic transformation that requires a formalization of correctness:

1. UNITY assignment to boolean-bitvector parallel assignment, where we show that specification expression semantics are preserved
2. Boolean-bitvector scalar to sequential assignment, where we show that target state transitions are a refinement of the specification

We describe these formal relations, their mechanization in Rosette, and how Shellac generates verification conditions for synthesizing rewrite rules.

3.1   The Implements Relation Between Expressions

Our language embeddings give a functional interpretation of expression semantics. The expressions of a language L are defined over:

- A set of values $vals(L)$
- A set of variables $vars(L)$
- A set of operators $ops(L)$
- An inductively defined set of expressions $exprs(L)$
  - If $t \in vals(L)$, then $t \in exprs(L)$
  - If $t \in vars(L)$, then $t \in exprs(L)$
  - If n-ary $op \in ops(L)$ and $a_0, \ldots a_n \in exprs(L)$, then $op(a_0, \ldots a_n) \in exprs(L)$
- A set of states, $states(L)$, each a mapping function $vars(L) \rightarrow vals(L)$
- A partial function $eval_L : exprs(L) \times states(L) \rightarrow vals(L)$

We describe relations between a source language S and a target language T. Because S and T may be at different levels of abstraction, we describe a scheme where values in $vals(S)$ can be encoded using n-tuples of values in $vals(T)^n$. That is, for any source variable, there exist a tuple of target variables, and the value of those target variables is related to the value of the source variable. We define a variable mapping function $varmap_{ST}$ from S variables to T variable tuples:

$$vartuples(T) = \bigcup_{n=1}^{\infty} vars(T)^n$$

$$varmap_{ST} \subset vars(S) \times vartuples(T)$$

Similarly, we define a value mapping function $valmap$ from T value tuples to S values:

$$valtuples(T) = \bigcup_{n=1}^{\infty} vals(T)^n$$

$$valmap_{TS} \subset valtuples(T) \times vals(S)$$

We treat $valmap_{TS}$ as a partial function and $varmap_{ST}$ as a total function. The direction of each relation is motivated by the desire to translate target type environments from source to target and to lift values from target to source.

Given value and variable mappings between source and target languages, we can now describe a relation between source and target states, where a state is a mapping from variables to values. We say that st_t in $states(T)$ encodes st_s in $states(S)$, or $st_t \precsim st_s$ iff st_t reflects st_s under variable and value mapping:

$\forall st_t \in states(T), st_s \in states(S).$

$st_t \precsim st_s \iff$

$\quad \exists valmap_{TS}, varmap_{ST}.$

$\quad \forall \langle var_s, val_s \rangle \in st_s.$

$\quad val_s = valmap_{TS}(st_t(varmap_{ST}(var_s)_0) \ldots, st_t(varmap_{ST}(var_s)_n))$

where subscripts $0, n$ refer to elements of the target variable tuple.

The evaluation function maps expressions and states to values. Now that we have a relation between source and target states, we can describe what it means for a tuple of target expressions to implement a source expression. We define a set of expression tuples over the expressions of T:

$$exprtuples(T) = \bigcup_{n=1}^{\infty} exprs(T)^n$$

We say that $exprt$ in $exprtuples(T)$ implements $expr_s$ in $exprs(S)$, or $exprt \lhd expr_s$ iff $exprt$ in st_t and $expr_s$ in st_s evaluate to the same value under value mapping when st_t encodes st_s:

$\forall exprt \in exprtuples(T), expr_s \in exprs(S).$

$exprt \lhd expr_s \iff$

   $\exists valmap.$

   $\forall st_t \in states(T), st_s \in states(S).$

   $st_t \precsim st_s \implies$

      $valmap_{TS}(eval_T(exprt_0, st_t) \ldots, eval_T(exprt_n, st_t)) = eval_S(expr_s, st_s)$

where subscripts $0, n$ refer to elements of the target expression tuple.

3.2   Mechanizing the Implements Relation

Shellac is implemented in the Rosette solver-aided language. UNITY, Arduino C++, and Verilog are modelled by deep embeddings: primitive values and abstract syntax are encoded as data structures and the semantics are defined by an evaluation function over those data structures. Boolean-bitvector interme-diate languages are modelled by shallow embeddings: they use Rosette's native boolean and bitvector primitives and functions.

Value and Variable Mapping. The user provides a *typemap* function from UNITY types to tuples of boolean-bitvector types. Simple datatypes such as booleans and the natural numbers map respectively to singleton tuples of boolean and bitvector. More complex types such as channels and booleans map respec-tively to a triple of booleans and a pair of bitvectors. In addition, the user provides *valmap* functions for each UNITY type that translate corresponding boolean-bitvector tuples to UNITY values, e.g., booleans, natural numbers, chan-nels, and buffers. Combined with a UNITY specification's variable declarations, *typemap* is used to generate the appropriate variable mapping function.

Generating the Verification Condition. Shellac synthesizes tuples of boolean-bitvector expressions for each UNITY operator. These synthesized expressions satisfy the implements relation described above. We express this con-straint as a *verification condition* generated via symbolic execution in Rosette. The verification condition is parameterized over *typed holes*: variables that rep-resent boolean-bitvector expressions. The types of these holes are determined by applying the type mapping over the domain and codomain of the UNITY operator. For example, *fill : channel × boolean → channel* type maps to the corresponding boolean-bitvector signature:

$$\langle boolean, boolean, boolean \rangle \times \langle boolean \rangle \rightarrow$$
$$\langle boolean, boolean, boolean \rangle$$

From here we can see the shape of the rewrite: from a triple and singleton of booleans in the domain to a triple of booleans in the codomain. We establish related UNITY and boolean-bitvector inputs by creating a symbolic representa-tion of the boolean-bitvector domain then lift it with value mapping functions.

For example, we first allocate fresh variables for the boolean-bitvector channel: $c_{req}, c_{ack}, c_{data}$ and boolean: val. Next, we lift the boolean-bitvector inputs to UNITY inputs by value mapping:

$$valmap_{channel}(c_{req}, c_{ack}, c_{data}) : channel$$
$$valmap_{boolean}(val) : boolean$$

We can now use the lifted values in our UNITY model. This allows us to express pre- and post-conditions. The fill operator is only defined over empty channels, so our precondition P is generated by applying the predicate *empty?* from the UNITY model to the lifted channel:

$$P = empty?(valmap_{channel}(c_{req}, c_{ack}, c_{data}))$$

Similarly, we generate our postcondition Q by applying *fill* from the UNITY model to the lifted channel and value:

$$Q = fill(valmap_{channel}(c_{req}, c_{ack}, c_{data}), valmap_{boolean}(val))$$

Now that we have pre- and post-conditions in terms of lifted boolean-bitvector values in UNITY, we turn our attention to the boolean-bitvector codomain. We generate additional fresh boolean variables for the channel in the codomain, using $\square$ to denote a typed hole: $\square_{req}, \square_{ack}, \square_{data}$.

We can also express boolean-bitvector invariants. In the case of fill, a channel sender can modify only the request and data lines, so the acknowledge line should remain unchanged: $I = \square_{ack} = c_{ack}$.

We now state the verification condition: for all inputs, if the precondition P holds, the invariant I holds and the lifted codomain channel equals the postcondition Q:

$$\forall c_{req}, c_{ack}, c_{data}, val \in \mathbb{B}.$$
$$P \implies I \wedge valmap_{channel}(\square_{req}, \square_{ack}, \square_{data}) = Q$$

3.3   Searching the Space of Expressions

The verification condition presented above is in terms of holes that represent arbitrary expressions. Synthesis as done in Rosette is done over a symbolic syntax graph that represents all productions over an inductive syntax, bounded, in this case, by expression depth. Shellac drives synthesis by substituting a symbolic syntax graph for each typed hole in a verification condition and using Rosette's CEGIS procedure to drive a SMT solver until either a satisfying model is found or the solver returns unsat. If the solver returns a satisfying model, we have a solution, and after applying the model to the symbolic syntax graph, we are left with a boolean-bitvector abstract syntax tree that satisfies the verification condition. If the solver returns unsat, Shellac expands the bound on the symbolic syntax graph and retries synthesis, or if a depth limit is reached, returns a failure.

Symbolic Syntax Graphs. A symbolic syntax graph is a boolean encoding of a set of abstract syntax trees. Shellac symbolic syntax graphs are s-expressions containing Rosette choose expressions. For example, (choose 1 2 3) evaluates in Rosette into a boolean expression encoding the choice:

```
> (define choices (choose* 1 2 3))
> choices
(ite xi?$1 1 (ite xi?$2 2 3))
```

In this simple example Rosette allocates fresh boolean variables xi?$1 and xi?$2 whose truth values govern the value of the expression. For example, this choose expression can be included in an assertion that can be sent to an SMT solver:

```
> (solve (assert (= 1 choices)))
(model
 [xi?$1 #t]
 [xi?$2 #f])
```

Verification Condition Partitioning. The number of boolean variables induced by the Rosette runtime when generating a symbolic syntax graph grows exponentially with expression depth. In the case where a verification condition for synthesis contains multiple typed holes, each one replaced with a symbolic syntax graph, the number of variables can grow to the point where SMT solver performance begins to suffer. We observe that when the verification condition is a conjunction, if typed holes occur in distinct sets of subterms, we can partition the verification condition into subproblems, simplifying the task. We show the effectiveness of this optimization in Sect. 4.

3.4 Ordering to Satisfy Refinement

In the case of channel fill, the order of assignments on a sequential execution matters a great deal. The final phase of rewrite rule synthesis finds an ordering of assignments such that the externally visible states induced by the assignments satisfy refinement, i.e., intermediate states map to P or Q, and the transition is monotonic. The notion of refinement used here is of Lynch and Vaandrager on simulation relations between automata [9].

The final rewrite rule for the fill operation is encoded in a translation-rule form:

```
(translation-rule
    ;; Precondition (channel empty)
    (<=> req ack)
    ;; Domain
    (list (list req ack data) (list value))
    ;; Codomain (synthesized expressions)
    (list (! req) ack value) ;; Codomain
    ;; Ordering constraints (indices into codomain)
    (list (ordering 2 0) (ordering 1 0)))
```

A translation-rule form contains symbolic constants, e.g., `req`, `ack`, `data`, and `value`; these are substituted with compiled subexpressions by the recursive syntax-directed pass. The ordering constraints specify *happens-before or simultaneously with* relationships between indices in the tuple of synthesized expressions for sequential assignment. For example, (`ordering 2 0`) specifies that the `value` assignment must come before or synchronously with the (`! req`) assignment. The (`ordering 1 0`) is a trivial constraint: the `ack` assignment is a no-op.

3.5 Correctness of the Synthesized Programs

The asynchronously composed simultaneous assignments are partitioned by the user into *processes*. Processes can be channels or compute-processes. Channels provide point-to-point communication between two (not-necessarily distinct) processes. A property is stable in a process if no actions by *other* processes can falsify it. The channel protocol ensures that a channel being full is a stable property of the process that reads the channel; furthermore, the value of such a channel is stable when the channel is full. Likewise, a channel being empty is a stable property of the process that writes the channel.

The rules for translating channels to boolean-bitvector (parallel or sequential) are provided by the Shellac developer – they are effectively an API. These rewrite rules ensure that a receive channel is only read or drained from states in which a channel is full, and likewise for send channels. When synthesizing sequential code, all read operations on a channel in a simultaneous assignment must be performed before any drain operation; likewise, the data value of a send channel must be updated before the status is set to full. Finally, guards on receive channels must be monotonic in the channel being full, and guards on send channels must be monotonic in the channel being empty. We can now sketch the correctness and liveness properties for programs synthesized by Shellac.

Correctness of Synthesized Sequential Implementations. For each simultaneous assignment of the compute process, Shellac synthesizes code that evaluates the guard(s), then evaluates the right-hand side(s), and finally updates the left-hand side(s) of the assignment. When execution reaches a point where the guard(s) have been shown to be satisfied, the abstraction function can map the implementation state, and all subsequent states until the code block is finished, to the state corresponding to a completed simultaneous assignment. The careful reader might note that a single simultaneous assignment could fill and/or drain several channels, that the sequential implementation will perform these operations in some order, and this could enable external processes to fill or drain channels written or read by this process before the sequential implementation of the simultaneous assignment is complete. This is indeed the case. Such operations are non-interfering due to the stable properties noted above, and thus they do not affect the outcome of the simultaneous assignment. The "explanation" in the abstraction of implementation state to specification state is that the simultaneous assignment completed (as soon as it was started), and these operations by other processes happened later.

Correctness of Parallel Implementations. Each simultaneous assignment is performed on a single clock "tick" and the state update matches the specification.

Liveness. UNITY requires fair selection but does not provide stronger fairness guarantees. Both the sequential and parallel implementations produced by Shellac perform round-robin execution of the simultaneous assignments in each process. This ensures fair selection.

4 Evaluation

We evaluate Shellac by measuring the performance of the rewrite rule synthesizer and of the synthesized compiler itself. Is rewrite rule synthesis feasible, and does the search conclude with a reasonable timeframe? Is the synthesized compiler capable of processing a nontrivial specification, the single-proposer version of the Paxos consensus algorithm [6]?

4.1 Experimental Setup

We ran Shellac on an Intel Xeon W-2275 3.30 GHz CPU with 128 GiB of memory. Shellac ran on Rosette 4.1 on Racket 8.6, with Z3 4.8.8. We ran the output of the synthesized compiler on Arduino MKR Vidor 4000 development boards, each of which contains an ARM Cortex-M0 microprocessor and an Intel Cyclone FPGA [2].

4.2 Rewrite Rule Synthesis

We study the synthesis time for various UNITY operations, presented in Table 2. The number of boolean variables tracks the exponential growth in the number of boolean-bitvector expressions encoded in each symbolic syntax graph. Operators are categorized by their general types: boolean, natural numbers, channels, and arbitrary-length boolean list buffers. Rewrite rules for boolean, natural number, and channel operators synthesize quickly due to the narrow semantic gap between source and target. UNITY list-of-booleans buffers are encoded as bitvectors in boolean-bitvector, so buffer operations become bitwise expressions. In the case of `recv-buf-put`, a satisfying boolean-bitvector was only found after expanding the depth bound on the symbolic syntax graph to 4. In addition to the exponential growth in the search space as expression depth increases, it is known that CEGIS is less efficient at finding useful counterexamples for bitvector program synthesis [13].

Verification Condition Partitioning. Table 3 shows the effect of verification condition partitioning for applicable operator synthesis runs. For smaller symbolic syntax graphs, the overhead of processing and managing multiple SMT solver runs leads to a slowdown, but as the search space grows, i.e., `recv-buf-put`, the significant reduction in each partition's search space leads to a significant performance increase, 4.33× faster.

Table 2. UNITY operator to boolean-bitvector expression rule synthesis. Variables and time are grouped by search round: the number referring to the depth of that round's symbolic syntax graph. Variables refer to boolean variable count. Time refers to Rosette runtime and SMT solver time combined. A blank cell indicates success in the previous round.

Operator	Variables at search round				Time (ms) at search round				Time (ms)
	1	2	3	4	1	2	3	4	
not	4	22			35	90			125
and	6	28			37	131			168
or	6	28			44	143			187
<=>	6	28			43	150			193
empty?	8	34			42	115			157
full?	8	34			49	160			209
read	8				24				24
drain	18				33				33
fill	22	110			54	270			324
recv-buf-full?	2	22			43	159			202
send-buf-empty?	2	22			42	161			203
empty-recv-buf	7				27				27
empty-send-buf	9				26				26
nat->send-buf	10				45				45
recv-buf->nat	8				128				128
recv-buf-put	16	50	118	254	153	447	2038	68076	70714
send-buf-get	2	22	86	274	67	297	26269	73608	100241
send-buf-next	13	43			72	326			398
+	8	23			68	191			259
=?	2	22			42	1058			1100
<?	2	22			51	314			365

4.3 Paxos Consensus

We implemented Lamport's *single-decree synod* consensus algorithm [6] in UNITY. Paxos solves the problem of achieving *distributed consensus*: getting a collection of distributed processes to agree on a value. The processes execute in a *shared nothing* environment, which means that they interact with each other only through message passing.

The basic Paxos protocol defines three classes of participants: proposers, acceptors, and learners. Proposers and acceptors are active participants and learners are passive. Proposers initiate a protocol round by sending *prepare* messages to a majority of the acceptors. The acceptors reply with *promise* messages, promising to accept a proposed value. Once a proposer receives promise replies from the majority of the acceptors, it sends *accept* messages to acceptors to commit a value. Acceptors reply to the accept message with an *accepted* message, indicating that the value is committed and the round is complete. After a value is accepted by an acceptor, additional *accepted* messages are sent from acceptors to learners: this propagates the consensus value.

Table 3. The effect of verification condition partitioning on expression rule synthesis for applicable operators. Results are shown for each partition. Cumulative times are compared against Table 2 to determine speedup. A blank cell indicates success in the previous round.

Operator	Variables at search round				Time (ms) at search round				Time (ms)	Speedup
	1	2	3	4	1	2	3	4		
read	0				21				43	0.56×
	8				22					
drain	13				30				52	0.63×
	8				22					
fill	16	75			51	199			299	1.08×
	10				49					
empty-recv-buf	4				20				50	0.54×
	4				30					
empty-send-buf	4				23				53	0.49×
	4				30					
nat->send-buf	6				37				110	0.41×
	6				73					
recv-buf-put	10	27			41	199			16329	4.33×
	10	27	61	129	151	321	2217	13400		
send-buf-next	8	23			36	153			257	1.55×
	8				68					

The safety guarantee of the Paxos algorithm ensures that once a value has been chosen, that value will remain stable. The algorithm guarantees this by associating each protocol round with a *ballot number*. Proposer's *prepare* messages are required to have a ballot number greater than that of any existing prepare request. Acceptors are required to inform proposers in promise messages if they have already accepted a value and the associated ballot number. When an acceptor sends a *promise* reply, it promises to ignore any requests with lesser ballot numbers. Proposers are required to propose the previously accepted value with the greatest ballot number, ensuring the stability of the previously accepted value.

Table 4. Paxos compilation time for boolean-bitvector (BBV) parallel and sequential passes in milliseconds

Role	UNITY to BBV parallel	to BBV scalar	to BBV sequential
Proposer	2560	40	768
Acceptor	1045	11	252

4.4   Specification of Paxos

Specifications for the proposer and acceptor in UNITY use a pair of channels between each proposer and acceptor. Each pair of channels require six I/O pins. With a 22 pin budget, this limits specifications to three channel pairs using 18 pins. The specification defines a topology with one proposer and three acceptors. The acceptor and proposer specifications contain 14 and 34 clauses respectively.

Topologies containing up to three proposers and three acceptors are possible. A 3×3 topology requires a modified acceptor specification to include the additional proposers. No changes to the proposer specification are required, because proposers communicate only with acceptors.

Compilation of Proposer and Acceptor. Compilation times for proposer and acceptor specifications are shown in Table 4. Translating from UNITY to boolean-bitvector parallel takes a few seconds. This is due to verification that any preconditions generated during compilation are implied by the guards. In comparison, translating from boolean-bitvector parallel to sequential only requires solving for ordering constraints and completes very quickly.

5   Related Work

We are not aware of other work in the synthesis of rewrite rules for compiling concurrent specifications. However, we consider related work in inductive program synthesis, compiler synthesis, and asynchronous circuit design.

The space of expressions is encoded as a symbolic syntax graph structure, where the choice of possible children for a node is taken from the grammar of the language. Many of the expressions we are interested in synthesizing involve bitwise manipulations and comparisons. This is the case when encoding buffers as bitvectors. Solar-Lezama et al. provide the first example of *sketch-based* program synthesis, referring to their technique as compilation by constraint-solving [14]. This work also provided the first example of the insight behind the CEGIS technique. Sketch-based programming requires the user to provide a *partial program* with *holes* that the program synthesizer fills to satisfy a constraint.

There have been previous efforts in exploiting program synthesis to guarantee compiler correctness. Van Geffen et al. use sketch-based program synthesis to build a just-in-time compiler from the eBPF virtual instruction set to RISC-V [18].

The search space of assembly routines for an instruction set like RISC-V is huge, so they partition the search space an ordered set of *compiler metasketches*. Our work differs in the relative abstraction difference between source and target languages. Both eBPF and RISC-V are load-store register machines, while our focus on UNITY is to enable the compilation of concurrent or distributed programs.

Our focus on channel-based UNITY specifications was inspired by self-timed digital circuit design. Udding described three classes of circuit specifications invariant to signal delay: for synchronization, data communication, and arbitration [17]. Our channel model is defined to satisfy the properties of Udding's *arbitration* class of specifications. Our notion of channel state and a specification of a channel as a participant in data propagation is descended from Roncken's link-and-joint model, where channels are equivalent to links [11,12]. Roncken gives us a model to bifurcate our specifications between processes with parallel atomic assignment and concurrent communications.

6   Future Work

Shellac has shown that given a domain-specific language, a compiler with a high-level of assurance can be built using program synthesis. Developing and synthesizing compilers for domain-specific languages for operating systems concerns such as memory management, interrupt handling, and processor context management, etc. would improve safety in those critical areas.

Synthesizing compilers to intermediate languages such as LLVM, MLIR, or Webassembly would enable reuse of already existing toolchains for analysis or further compilation.

The current syntax-guided compilers generated by Shellac preserve liveness by following a round-robin scheduling that guarantees fair selection. Static or dynamic analysis should enable more efficient schedulings.

7   Conclusion

Concurrent, imperative programs that mix state mutation and control flow admit a state explosion that makes debugging notoriously difficult and formal analysis intractable. The advent of formal specification languages allow for a concurrent program or system of concurrent programs to be described as a state machine. Such a specification enables automated reasoning. Unfortunately, formal specifications are usually too abstract for direct execution. Instead of manually translating a specification to a low-level implementation, which can introduce errors, we describe a method for exploiting program synthesis to generate compiler rewrite rules. We show that such a compiler can process UNITY specifications with channel-based communication and output both hardware and software implementations that preserve safety and liveness properties. Source code is available at https://github.com/chchen/shellac-can.

References

1. Arduino: Arduino language reference (2020). https://www.arduino.cc/reference/en/. Accessed 02 Sept 2020
2. Arduino: Arduino MKR vidor 4000 (2020). https://store.arduino.cc/usa/mkr-vidor-4000. Accessed 06 Jan 2021
3. Barragán, H.: Wiring: prototyping physical interaction design. Master's thesis, Interaction Design Institute Ivrea (2004). https://people.interactionivrea.org/h.barragan/thesis/thesis_low_res.pdf
4. IEEE Standards Association, et al.: IEEE standard for verilog hardware description language. Design Automation Standards Committee, IEEE Std 1364TM-2005 2 (2005)
5. Klein, G., et al.: SeL4: formal verification of an OS kernel. In: Proceedings of the ACM SIGOPS 22nd Symposium on Operating Systems Principles, SOSP 2009, pp. 207–220. Association for Computing Machinery, New York (2009). https://doi.org/10.1145/1629575.1629596
6. Lamport, L.: The part-time parliament. ACM Trans. Comput. Syst. 16(2), 133–169 (1998)
7. Lamport, L.: Specifying concurrent systems with TLA+. Calculational Syst. Design 183–247 (1999). https://www.microsoft.com/en-us/research/publication/specifying-concurrent-systems-tla/
8. Leroy, X.: Formal certification of a compiler back-end or: programming a compiler with a proof assistant. In: Conference Record of the 33rd ACM SIGPLAN-SIGACT Symposium on Principles of Programming Languages, POPL 2006, pp. 42–54. Association for Computing Machinery, New York (2006). https://doi.org/10.1145/1111037.1111042
9. Lynch, N., Vaandrager, F.: Forward and backward simulations. Inf. Comput. 121(2), 214–233 (1995)
10. Mani Chandy, K., Misra, J.: Parallel Program Design: A Foundation. Addison-Wesley, Reading (1988)
11. Roncken, M., Gilla, S.M., Park, H., Jamadagni, N., Cowan, C., Sutherland, I.: Naturalized communication and testing. In: 2015 21st IEEE International Symposium on Asynchronous Circuits and Systems, pp. 77–84 (2015). https://doi.org/10.1109/ASYNC.2015.20
12. Roncken, M., et al.: How to think about self-timed systems. In: 2017 51st Asilomar Conference on Signals, Systems, and Computers, pp. 1597–1604 (2017). https://doi.org/10.1109/ACSSC.2017.8335628
13. Solar-Lezama, A., Rabbah, R., Bodík, R., Ebcioundefinedlu, K.: Programming by sketching for bit-streaming programs. In: Proceedings of the 2005 ACM SIGPLAN Conference on Programming Language Design and Implementation, PLDI 2005, pp. 281–294. Association for Computing Machinery, New York (2005). https://doi.org/10.1145/1065010.1065045
14. Solar-Lezama, A., Tancau, L., Bodik, R., Seshia, S., Saraswat, V.: Combinatorial sketching for finite programs. SIGARCH Comput. Archit. News 34(5), 404–415 (2006). https://doi.org/10.1145/1168919.1168907
15. Solar-Lezama, A., Tancau, L., Bodík, R., Seshia, S.A., Saraswat, V.A.: Combinatorial sketching for finite programs. In: Proceedings of the 12th International Conference on Architectural Support for Programming Languages and Operating Systems, ASPLOS 2006, San Jose, CA, USA, 21–25 October 2006, pp. 404–415 (2006). https://doi.org/10.1145/1168857.1168907

16. Torlak, E., Bodik, R.: A lightweight symbolic virtual machine for solver-aided host languages. SIGPLAN Not. **49**(6), 530–541 (2014)
17. Udding, J.T.: A formal model for defining and classifying delay-insensitive circuits and systems. Distrib. Comput. **1**(4), 197–204 (1986)
18. Van Geffen, J., Nelson, L., Dillig, I., Wang, X., Torlak, E.: Synthesizing JIT compilers for in-kernel DSLs. In: Lahiri, S.K., Wang, C. (eds.) CAV 2020. LNCS, vol. 12225, pp. 564–586. Springer, Cham (2020). https://doi.org/10.1007/978-3-030-53291-8_29

A Sequentialization Procedure for Fault-Tolerant Protocols

Cezara Drăgoi[2,3] and Patricio Inzaghi Pronesti[1,2](✉) (iD)

[1] Département d'informatique de l'ENS, École normale supérieure, CNRS,
PSL Research University, 75005 Paris, France
`pinzaghi@ens.fr`
[2] Inria, Paris, France
[3] Informal Systems, Toronto, Canada

Abstract. We introduce a sequentialization procedure for fault-tolerant protocols that takes as input a Distal program and produces a sequentialized counterpart as output. The sequentialization procedure captures a representative subset of the behaviors of the input system and is easier to model check; for a broad class of protocols, it captures a representative for every behavior. Our notion of sequentialization-equivalence extends the well-studied notion of communication closure in distributed protocols, which relates asynchronous and synchronous executions. We implemented our sequentialization and applied it to verify several consensus protocols, including ZooKeeper Atomic Broadcast, and Raft, using the P framework. We considered P models that include critical safety bugs present in implementations and known by the community. The P model checker found these bugs only when using the sequential model but not in the original asynchronous counterparts.

1 Introduction

Correctly designing and implementing fault-tolerant distributed systems is hard. Many bugs appear both at the protocol and at implementation level and the design of effective tools to find bugs early is an important challenge in formal methods. One successful direction of research is the development of high-level Domain Specific Languages designed for facilitating verification or testing of distributed systems, together with efficient verification and testing tools. Notable examples are Ivy [1] Promela/Spin [2], Coyote [3] and P [4]. The bane of all these tools is state-space explosion: as the complexity of the protocols grow, systematic exploration can only cover a minuscule portion of the state space.

We show how systematic testing of fault-tolerant distributed protocols can be improved by using the *sequentialization* approach, which produces a sequential version that captures an interesting subset of all behaviors. The sequential version has fewer behaviors, allowing systematic testing tools to scale better, but

Supported by: French National Research Agency ANR project SAFTA (12744-ANR-17-CE25-0008-01).

any bug in the sequentialization is also a bug in the original protocol. For shared memory systems, sequentialization techniques have proved effective in increasing the number of bugs found in concurrent programs [5,6]. However, existing sequentialization techniques for message passing protocols are either manual [7], or consider only non-faulty protocols [8], or prove equivalence between given asynchronous and sequential protocols, given both protocols as well as complicated inductive invariants [9]. In contrast, we propose a new automated sequentialization technique for fault-tolerant protocols that uses minimal annotations.

Our sequentialization uses the notion of communication-closure [10], which identifies the conditions under which a set of asynchronous executions is equivalent to one *round-based* execution. In round-based executions, processes proceed in lock-step: all processes *send* messages, *receive* (possibly a subset of) the sent messages, and *update* their state based on the received messages. There are no delayed messages: a message that is not received after it was sent (a.k.a. *rendez-vous*) is lost forever. Round-based executions have no interleaving across rounds and faults are localized within the round boundaries. Compared with asynchronous protocols, they have exponentially fewer behaviors.

We define a sequentialization procedure for protocols written in Distal [11], a DSL for fault-tolerant systems aligned with the syntax of text-book protocols but also with the syntax of P [4], a modeling language used for writing and testing state machine models in industry (roughly, P embeds Distal constructs). First, we compute a round-based representation of Distal protocols, building on the procedure in [12] that takes an asynchronous program (from an appropriate class) and computes an equivalent round-based representation. We extend their procedure to handle common features required by asynchronous programs such as high-level primitives for message passing. Second, we propose a sequentialization of the round-based representation that is complete for arbitrary networks, like the ones required by Paxos [13] or Raft [14], but also for stronger network assumptions, as required by Ben-Or or 2PC [15].

To sum up, we take a Distal program as input and produce as output a new Distal program that is the sequentialization of the input. Since the sequentialization has fewer behaviors, testing tools have an easier time finding bugs.

We implement and evaluate our algorithm using the P framework [4]. We applied the sequentialization on P models for Paxos, Raft, Ben-Or, View-Stamped, UniformVoting, and 2PC. Running P's testing tool on their sequential versions uncovered subtle bugs that were not always found in the original asynchronous P model (due to state explosion). Most notable bugs found exclusively in the sequentialization were in Paxos and Raft. We modeled a version of Paxos that captures the bug scenario in ZAB [16,17]. The bug is a violation of agreement, where replicas disagree on the order of the commands executed by the replicated state machine and is used as a running example. We modeled the protocol that handles the cluster's configuration in Raft [14,18]. The bug is a safety violation, where processes disagree on the replicas that run the state machine. To catch it, the sequentialization of Raft takes into account process creation.

Related Work. Communication closure has been used in verification [12,19] and testing [17]. In [12,19] the authors define a transformation of an asynchronous protocol into a synchronous one, that is further verified using Hoare-style of reasoning ([19] uses communication closure implicitly). Both works consider a highly-constrained input language, chosen to suit the requirements of the transformation procedure. For example, they do not consider high level message passing primitives. In contrast, we consider Distal protocols as input. Distal is an established language in the theoretical community and in industry (in the form of P). Therefore, our method makes transformations based on synchronizations accessible to a wider audience. Moreover, we define a sequentialization procedure that uncovers bugs which are not found by state-of-the art testing tools for asynchronous protocols. There are many verification and testing tools for sequential programs and shared memory systems [20,21], that could be applied on the sequentialization computed by our method, contrary to the output of [12,19], where tools for distributed synchronous protocols are not available.

The communication closure hypothesis has been empirically used in testing large scale systems models [17,22,23]. In [17] the authors start from an instrumented large scale system and explore a subset of its executions checking for violations. The current submission starts from a model of the program and proposes a more systematic and efficient exploration of the executions.

2   Overview

We illustrate our sequentialization procedure using the replicated state machine protocol in Fig. 1, inspired from Paxos [13]. Processes receive different commands, and the goal of the protocol is to make processes agree on a total order over a set of received commands, even when messages are lost or delayed. Each process maintains the log of commands it agreed on, e.g. *abcd*, which is visible to an external observer (line 30). The outputted log of any two processes must respect the prefix order over sequences. A violation of the prefix order, e.g., one process outputs *a* and another one outputs *b*, means that the two processes disagree on the first command to be executed by the machine. However, it is correct to have one process output *a* and another one output *ab*, it happens when the process outputting *a* is late and didn't learn yet the second command to be executed.

The protocol in Fig. 1 has a bug in line 9 which generates an execution violating the prefix order property. This bug is fixed by moving this statement to line 23. We choose this example because (1) testing it using P [4] did not find the bug, and (2) it is a simplified version of the bug[1] in the implementation of ZAB [16]. Using P on the sequentialization found the bug.

The protocol is written in Distal [11], an event-driven programming model with upon statements defining how the protocol reacts to receiving a message.

---

[1] https://issues.apache.org/jira/browse/ZOOKEEPER-2832.

```
1:  init                                         21:       ballot = m.ballot; ▶ Propose
2:    ballot = 0; log = ε;                       22:       log = m.log;
3:    if primary(ballot+1) then                  23:       //Bugfix: last = ballot;
4:      ballot = ballot+1;                        24:       m = Promise(ballot,log); ▶ Promise
5:      m = PrepareMsg(ballot);▶ Prepare         25:       send m to ALL;
6:      send m to ALL;                            26:   upon Promise with m.ballot ≥ ballot ∧
7:  while true do                                      m.log = log times n/2 do
8:    upon Prepare with m.ballot > ballot do     27:       ballot = m.ballot; ▶ Promise
9:      last = ballot;                           28:       log = m.log;
10:     ballot = m.ballot;                        29:       promised = true;
11:     promised = false;                         30:       output(log);
12:     primary = m.sender;                       31:       if primary(ballot+1) then
13:     m = Ack(ballot, last, log); ▶ Ack         32:         ballot = ballot+1; ▶ Prepare
14:     send m to primary;                        33:         m = Prepare(ballot);
15:   upon Ack with m.ballot = ballot times n/2   34:         send m to ALL;
      do                                          35:   upon timeout() with true do
16:     log = longest_log(ballot); ▶ Ack          36:     if primary(ballot+1) then
17:     log.add(newCommand());                    37:       ballot = ballot+1;
18:     m = Propose(ballot, log); ▶ Propose       38:       m = Prepare(ballot); ▶ Prepare
19:     send m to ALL;                            39:       send m to ALL;
20:   upon Propose with m.ballot ≥ ballot ∧
      ¬promised do
```

Fig. 1. Simple Paxos protocol in Distal containing a bug (marked in red) where the `last` variable is updated too early. The ▶ marker denotes a new round in the code. (Color figure online)

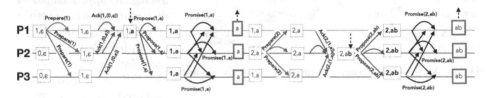

Fig. 2. An execution over two ballots where all messages are delivered.

The code given in Fig. 1 is executed by all processes[2] using the standard inter-leaving of steps executed by different processes. To communicate, processes use point-to-point or broadcast. Messages may be dropped of delayed.

Processes go through a sequence of ballots, and in each ballot they try to add a new command to their log. If enough messages are delivered, then the log is extended, otherwise they move on to the next ballot and retry, maybe with a different command. This is a leader-based protocol, where the function *primary*(*b*) takes as input a ballot number *b* and returns the identity of the leader of the ballot, using for example a round-robin scheme. The leader is in charge of (1) starting a new ballot, (2) collecting logs of a quorum of processes, and selecting the longest most recent log out of the received ones, and (3) extending this log with a new command and proposing it to all processes in the network. All processes that receive the new log from the leader broadcast it. Finally, a process

---

[2] This does not mean all processes go through the same sequence of states, because (1) local state updates based on the received messages and (2) processes might receive a different set of messages.

outputs a log when it learns that $n/2$ of its peers received the same log from the leader. Figure 2 shows an execution of the protocol, where all messages are delivered and all processes store a in their logs in the first ballot, and extend the log with b in the second ballot. Figures 4 and 3 show other executions where the messages send by P3 are delayed or dropped. A naive and inefficient sequentialization scheme produces a sequential behavior for each interleaving. For example it generates two different sequentializations, one where first P1 sends a `Prepare` message and then P2, and the other way around. Moreover, from one interleaving multiple sequential executions are possible depending on which messages are delayed, lost, or delivered. For example, there will be three sequential executions one when P3 receives the `Prepare` message, one when it is lost, and one when it is delayed.

We propose a more efficient sequentialization procedure, which produces one non-deterministic sequential protocol that is equivalent to an asynchronous one. This equivalence relation is that processes go through the same sequence of states modulo *stuttering* (i.e., consecutive repetition of equivalent states).

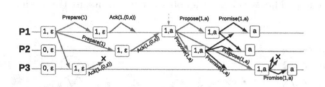

Fig. 3. An execution where all messages sent by P3 are lost.

The sequentialization exploits *the round structure* of the protocol following the approach based on communication-closure [12,17]. The asynchronous semantics allows an arbitrary interleaving of steps of different processes, executed over a non-deterministic network that can delay, drop, or reorder messages. However, this semantics includes a set of synchronous executions, where all messages are delivered in-time, e.g., Fig. 2. Observing this happy path, we see that the protocol is structured in four rounds, executed in the same sequence in each ballot. Each round only sends/receive one type of message. Processes update their state using only messages of this type.

In the first round the leader sends a `Prepare` message containing the number of the leading ballot. The processes that receive its message update their ballot, if the leader leads a higher or equal ballot. In the next round, processes reply to the leader with an `Ack` message that contains the leader's ballot, the current log stored by the process, and the value of the last ballot the process participated in. If the leader receives more than $n/2$ `Ack` messages it selects the longest log out of the one coming from processes that participated in the most recent ballot.

In the next round the leader extends this log and broadcasts a `Propose` message with the current ballot and the new log. In the final round all processes that receive the new proposed log, broadcast this log and the current ballot number in a `Promise` message. A process that receives more than $n/2$ `Promise` messages with the same log and the current ballot outputs that log.

Faulty executions respect the round structure as well: locally, processes respect the ballot order and the round order within a ballot. Figure 3 shows an execution of the first ballot where sent messages by P3 are lost. To transform it into a synchronous execution we use the fact that any send, receive, or update of some round r, it's a *left mover* [24] w.r.t. actions of other processes from rounds higher than r and a right mover w.r.t. actions from earlier rounds.

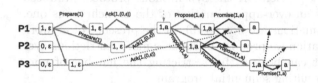

Fig. 4. Messages sent by P3 are delayed. Dotted lines represent stale messages that are not used by the receiver.

The execution in Fig. 4 respects the round structure, even if the messages sent by P3 are delivered after P1, and P2 moved past the round the messages coming from P3 were sent for. In [10,12] it's proved that a message received with a delay causes a violation of the round structure only if (1) the process is in a higher round and (2) the process use the message's payload to update its local state. In the considered execution, P1 and P2 are in the second ballot where the messages from P3 arrive, and they ignore all messages coming from the first ballot, like the ones sent by P3, therefore their reception does not cause a change of state in P1 and P2.

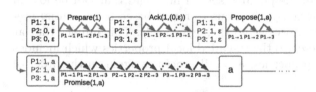

Fig. 5. Sequential execution equivalent to Fig. 3. Boxes represent the global state, arrows are messages (dashed are lost messages) and the color its round.

All executions of the protocol in Fig. 1 are equivalent to potentially faulty round-based executions, like those in Fig. 2, where messages can be lost but not delayed. Round-based executions impose a total order over actions performed by processes across rounds. The sequentialization maintains this order, and adds a total order over actions performed by processes within one round. Note that within one round there are only message chains of length at most one, and each process sends at most one message. Therefore the order in which processes send messages does not matter, all are equivalent and the sequentialization picks one. For each receive, it adds a non-deterministic choice modeling a message dropped by the network. Let us consider round-based executions where no messages are lost in Fig. 2. In this case, an equivalent sequential execution replaces any send and its matching receive by one assignment, and order them according to a chosen order over processes. In the presence of faults, the equivalent sequential execution consists only of those assignments corresponding to not dropped messages (Fig. 5).

In [12] and [19] the authors exploit the round structure for verification. They compute the synchronous version of the protocol (over a more restricted input). The resulting synchronous protocol is equivalent with the original asynchronous one in the absence of network assumptions, i.e., any message can be lost or delayed. When the protocol is correct under a network that meets a certain amount of reliability, e.g., Ben-Or, the synchronous protocol produced by these previous methods is an over-approximation of the asynchronous one. Since for testing over-approximations are not useful, in the presence of network assumptions, the sequentialization we propose introduces more restrictions over the number of messages that can be lost, by restricting the number of non-deterministic choices in the resulting sequential program.

In summary, we propose a method to obtain a non-deterministic sequential protocol, that is equivalent with an asynchronous one, where the equivalence relation is that processes go through the same sequence of states modulo stuttering. The sequentialization is precise for fault models commonly used in distributed protocols. As an intermediate step of the sequentialization we compute the round-based version of a Distal asynchronous protocol, where all executions are structured in rounds, and messages sent in a round are either received in the same round or lost, a.k.a., communication-closed protocols. For this step we extend the work in [12] to a more general input language and the procedure we propose uses lighter annotations where the user needs to specify the rounds only in the message types. The sequential protocol is non-deterministic because for each round it will consider all the possible sets of messages that can be lost in that round. The reduction from asynchronous to round-based to sequential preserves the sequence of states processes go through locally. This implies that at the global system level it preserves the so-called local properties which includes consensus. We tested safety properties, e.g., all processes agree on the order of commands.

3   Asynchronous Protocols

In this section we present Distal [11], a DSL for fault-tolerant systems, and P [4] a modeling language for event-driven systems equipped with a bug-finding tool.

3.1   Distal: Syntax and Semantics

We consider asynchronous protocols written in Distal [11]. The system is composed of N processes, where N is a parameter. Each process is associated with a unique identifier, which serves as an address for sending and receiving messages. All processes execute the same protocol $\mathcal{P}$ written using the syntax in Fig. 6. Protocols are composed by an *init* statement and a main loop, composed by a sequence of *upon* statements. An upon statement is followed by a predicate *guard* and a body with instructions to be executed. Processes can access a read-only mailbox variable mbox, which contains the received messages. Distal follows the event-driven paradigm where the state of a process tries to be updated upon the reception of a message. Processes exchange messages using instructions send and send to all that take m a message of type T as input and a PID. All variables are local to a process, there are no global or shared variables. The guard of each upon is a formula over the local state and mbox. Guards apply to different message types and check the values of the received message, e.g., upon Prepare with m.ballot > ballot in Fig. 1 line 8, or cardinally conditions upon Ack with m.ballot=ballot times n/2 which says more than $n/2$ Ack messages have been received with the same ballot value as the process' ballot (Fig. 1 line 15).

$$
\begin{array}{lll}
\text{type } \mathbb{M} ::= & \text{struct } \{ \text{ field } \textbf{Identifier}; \} & \\
e ::= & \text{const } | \text{ x } | f(\vec{x}) & \textbf{Expressions} \\
\text{Action} ::= & \text{x} = \text{e} & \textbf{Statements} \\
& | \text{ if e then Action else Action} & \\
& | \text{ send}(\text{p, m}) | \text{ send}(\text{m}) \text{ to ALL } | \text{ send to p} & \\
& | \text{ Action ; Action} & \\
U ::= & \text{upon } \mathbb{M} \text{ with Guard do Action} | U ; U & \textbf{Upon block} \\
\mathcal{P} ::= & \text{init : Action; loop : U} & \textbf{Program}
\end{array}
$$

Fig. 6. Syntax of Distal protocols, p is a PID, $x \in$ *Identifier*, m is a message of some message type in $\mathbb{M}$.

The semantics of a protocol $\mathcal{P}$ is the asynchronous parallel composition of the actions performed by all processes. Formally, the state S of a protocol is a tuple $\langle s, msg \rangle$ where $s \in [P \mapsto \textit{Vars} \cup \textit{Loc} \rightarrow \mathcal{D}]$ is a valuation of the local variables of each process, including the program location in the local state and $msg : P \rightarrow \textit{Msg}$ is the global set of messages in transit. Given a process $p \in P$, s_p is the local state of p, which is a valuation of p's local variables, and msg_p is the set of messages in transit towards p. When a replica starts, it executes the *init* code block and then runs the main loop forever. Executing an action makes a process change its state. Every process has a message pool that other processes write messages to. The semantics of $send(p, m)$ adds the message m to p's message pool.

```
1   state Propose {                    8    on Propose do (m: Propose) {
2     entry {                          9      if(m.phase == phase){
3       if(primary(phase, ps) == this){ 10       log = m.payload; goto Promise;
4         BroadCast(Propose, (phase, log)); 11     }
5       }                             12    }
6     }                               13  } // END state Propose
7
```

Fig. 7. A snippet of Paxos in P.

In every iteration of the loop a process checks for new messages, moving a subset of its message pool to its local mbox. Messages dropped by the network never appear in mbox. Several upons could be enabled in the same iteration, but to keep local determinism only the first one will be executed, i.e., the listing order breaks the ties[3]. The network assumptions are defined at execution time in Distal. We consider both protocols: the ones that make no assumptions for safety, where messages can be reordered, delayed or dropped; or those whose network assumptions for safety are given as first-order formulas over the messages received by processes (examples are given in Sect. 4.1).

P and Distal. P programs are composed of a state machine with several states, where each state has an *entry* function and handlers for different event types which are essentially messages. Figure 7 shows a snippet of the running example in P. There is a one-to-one correspondence between the upon statements and P message handlers. The latter does not include a guard, it triggers on reception. We incorporate the guard as an if statement (line 9).

Distal has the high level concept of times that is not present in P, we emulate it using a counter variable. In general, P models consist of a single state that handle all system messages, making the translation even more direct. Distal does not provide any implementation nor tools for doing random testing. On the other hand, P provides a well maintained state-of-the-art random testing framework that is used extensively.

4   Round-Based Protocols

In this section we introduce round-based protocols, we define a set of sufficient conditions for an asynchronous protocol to have an equivalent round-based version, and we sketch a rewriting that computes this round-based version.

4.1   Round-Based Syntax and Semantics

The syntax of round-based protocols consists of an initialization function init and a phase consisting of a non-empty finite sequence of rounds $r_1, ..., r_k$.

All processes execute the initialization function followed by the given sequence of rounds in lock-step, in a loop. The round number is an abstract notion of time: all processes are in the same round. In each round processes send messages in one synchronized step, using SEND. Each process receives in one atomic step a non-deterministically chosen subset of the messages that were sent to it. We denote by $mailbox : P \rightarrow 2^{Msg}$ the set of received messages in the current round per process. Messages sent in a round, are either received in the same round or lost. All processes update the local state synchronously, using UPDATE.

There are protocols, like Paxos or ViewStamped, that do not make any assumptions on the set of delivered messages to guarantee safety, e.g. agreement,

---

[3] Distal does not emphasize the loop and allows multiple upon statements to be executed in a sequence. The latter is captured by multiple loop iterations where no new messages are delivered in between.

all processes agree on an order of commands[4]. Other protocols are designed for stronger networks. Two representative network assumptions come with Ben-Or [25] and UniformVoting [26]. Ben-Or requires that in each round each process receives at least $n - f$ messages, where f is the number for faulty processes, i.e., $\forall r \in rounds : \forall p \in P : |mbox(p, r)| > n - f$. UniformVoting requires that in every round, there is one process called *kernel*, such that the message exchanges between any process p and the kernel are received. The kernel may change between rounds: $\forall r \in rounds : \exists k \in P : \forall p \in P : k \in mbox(p, r) \wedge p \in mbox(k, r)$, where $k \in mbox(p, r)$ is interpreted as follows: if there is a message sent by process k to p then it is received.

4.2   Round-Based Asynchronous Protocols

In this section we define a set of conditions which ensure that an asynchronous protocol is *round-based*, i.e., it has an equivalent round-based semantics. Two executions are equivalent if each process goes through the same sequence of local states, modulo stuttering, in both executions. We introduce synchronization tags, a lightweight annotation for checking the existence of a round structure.

Definition 1. *A synchronization tag in $\mathcal{P}$ is a tuple $\langle (phase, round), tagm \rangle$ where phase and round come from ordered domains and round takes a bounded number of values tagm : $\mathcal{M} \rightarrow [\{(phase, round)\} \rightarrow \mathcal{M} \cup Fields(\mathcal{M})]$ for each message type $\mathbb{M} \in \mathcal{M}$ maps phase and round over the fields of $\mathbb{M}$, or the type itself. For each message $m : \mathbb{M}$ we denote tagm by m.phase and m.round.*

A protocol is round-based if there is a synchronization tag and two variables *phase* and *round*, such that, (1) the values of $(phase, round)$ monotonically increase (w.r.t. the lexicographic order) in any execution of the protocol, (2) for every message sent m, either using $send(p, m)$ or $broadcast(m)$, m is timestamped with $m.phase = phase$ and $m.round = round$, (3) each guard uses messages timestamped with values greater or equal than the current value *phase* and *round* (4) actions only use (i.e., read) the messages from the mbox that are timestamped with current value of *phase* and *round* (5) between a send/broadcast and a receive either there are only receive statements or the values of *phase* and *round* have been updated. If there is any update between two receive steps then it must update also *phase* and *round*.

We require the user to annotate only the message type with a synchronization tag, and we add two fresh auxiliary variables *phase* and *round* to each protocol. Initially *phase* and *round* have minimal default values. We add assignments to these variables (1) before each send s.t. the second condition is satisfied, i.e., *phase* and *round* are equal to the tag of the sent message, and before each action such that the fourth condition is satisfied, i.e., *phase* and *round* are assigned to the maximal tag of the messages in the guard preceding the action.

---

[4] Consensus solutions always work under network assumption, at least for ensuring liveness, but checking liveness is beyond the scope of the paper.

The synchronization tag of Paxos in Fig. 1 is conformed by the variable `ballot` for the phase, where phase is an integer. The protocol has no variable that tracks the round, it's highlighted using the symbol ▶. The round domain takes `Prepare` $\preceq$ `Ack` $\preceq$ `Propose` $\preceq$ `Promise` as values. For all messages *round* is mapped onto the message type, and *phase* is mapped on the `ballot` field.

The synchronization tag of the P model in Fig. 7 consists of the field `phase` of each event, for the phase, and the event type for the round. Because the P version of the protocol has a state machine structure that groups handlers/upon statements into states, the round is the state the process is in, so both the phase and the round are present in the P model. The transformation to Distal replaces the states with a local variable that will track the round/state the process is in. The sequentialization method includes an additional testing tool that checks if the synchronization tag satisfy the five properties.

4.3   Computing a Protocol's Phase Structure

Given a Distal program, we want to compute its round-based counterpart. For this, we need to understand in which order the upons can be executed, under which conditions, and be able to delimit the boundaries between phases in the code. The statements between any two phase variable assignments is what we call the protocol's phase structure. We find it by unfolding the iterations of a Distal program, preserving the order in which the upons happen and their context. Figure 8 shows the syntax of an unfolded program $\mathcal{P}_{phase}$ and Fig. 9 describes the UNFOLD procedure. The output program satisfies Proposition 1.

$$
\begin{array}{lll}
\text{type M} & ::= \text{struct \{ field \textbf{Identifier}; \}} & \\
e & ::= \text{const} \mid \text{x} \mid f(\vec{x}) & \text{Expressions} \\
S & ::= x = e \mid \text{if e then S else S} \mid \text{S ; S} & \text{Statements} \\
\text{SEND} & ::= \text{send(p,m)} \mid \text{send(m) to ALL} \mid \text{noop} & \text{Send actions} \\
C & ::= \text{if e then ; SEND ; S ; U} \mid \text{C ; C} & \text{Conditionals} \\
U & ::= \text{mbox = havoc() ; C} \mid \text{continue} & \text{Statements} \\
\mathcal{P}_{phase} & ::= \text{init} : \mathcal{P}.\text{init() ; S ; loop} : U & \text{Program}
\end{array}
$$

Fig. 8. Syntax for the phase structure, p is a PID, $x \in$ *Identifier*, and m is a message type in M.

UNFOLD starts by creating a program with an initializing function and a `while(true)` statement with an empty body. It follows by *unfolding* the main loop, this is: 1) inserting a `mbox = havoc();` statement; 2) for each `upon guard do action` in $\mathcal{P}$ it creates an `if(guard) {action}` statement inside the while body (line 8). In the following iterations we repeat the unfolding for every `if` statement created in the previous one, given by the function *leafs*. This procedure is repeated K times, where K is the number of rounds in a phase.

Proposition 1. *For each execution $\tilde{\pi} \in \mathcal{P}_{phase}$ there is a $\pi \in \mathcal{P}$ s.t. π and $\tilde{\pi}$ are equivalent ($\pi \approx \tilde{\pi}$), i.e., their sequence of states is the same modulo stuttering.*

Proof. $\mathcal{P}_{phase}$ doesn't introduce or restrict behaviors of $\mathcal{P}$. Let $\overline{\pi} = [\langle \overline{s_0}, \emptyset \rangle]$ be an execution that starts with $\overline{s_0} = \mathcal{P}_{phase}.init()$ and an empty mailbox. UNFOLD defines $\mathcal{P}_{phase}.init() = \mathcal{P}.init()$ (line 2), so in $\mathcal{P}$ exists $\pi = [\langle s_0, \emptyset \rangle]$ such that $s_0 = \overline{s_0}$. $\langle \overline{s_1}, msg_1 \rangle$ is the result of executing $\mathcal{P}_{phase}$'s first iteration (*height* = 1) from state $\overline{s_0}$ where $havoc()$ returns msg_1. The unfolded conditionals respect the original order in $\mathcal{P}$. Given the same state and mailbox, the selected upon is uniquely determined. $\mathcal{P}_{phase}$ and $\mathcal{P}$ are in the same state with the same mailbox so they execute the same upon, i.e., $\overline{\pi} = \pi = [\langle \overline{s_0}, \emptyset \rangle, \langle \overline{s_1}, msg_1 \rangle]$. The same argument can be followed at most K times, when the unfolding stops with a phase variable increment. For the following $K + 1...$ transitions, we show that the code to execute is congruent to the first K iterations of UNFOLD. The phase variable is interpreted as a symbolic variable. When a new phase starts, the set of enabled upons is the same as the one considered from the initial state, but with a greater phase value.

4.4 Delimiting Rounds' Boundaries

Round boundaries are defined by round variable assignments. Processes can have different behaviors in the same round, depending on their local state and the messages received, although they execute the same code and go through the same sequence of rounds. Figure 10 shows the code of the Ack round extracted from our example's unfolded program $\mathcal{P}_{phase}$.

```
1:  procedure UNFOLD(P)
2:      P ← init : P.init(); loop : noop;
3:      for height ∈ 1 to K do
4:          for body in leafs(P_phase) do
5:              body.append(mbox_height = havoc())
6:              for upon in upons(P) do
7:                  ifStm ← if (upon.guard){upon.action}
8:                  body.append(ifStm)
9:      P ← deadCodeElimination(P)
10:     return P
```

Fig. 9. Procedure that translates an asynchronous program $\mathcal{P}$ into an unfolded program $\overline{\mathcal{P}}$

We start by iterating line by line starting from the *init* function of $\mathcal{P}_{phase}$ and traverse the main loop until we reach the first assignment of the round variable to Ack (line 13 in Fig. 1). Then, we start collecting a sequence of instructions until the next assignment of the round variable (line 18).

All the code before the first assignment is ignored. We introduce ghost flag variables, e.g., f, to preserve the conjunction of all the guards leading to the collected code, conserving the execution context. In this case, we cannot send an Ack message without having received a valid Prepare message.

Finally, the code of every round is split into a SEND block, consisting of the (unique) send statement guarded by the conditionals preceding them and an UPDATE block that contains the rest of the code except the mailbox's havoc. This completes the code of $\mathcal{P}_{round}$.

```
1  if(mbox(Prepare,m.ballot > ballot)){
2      f = true;
3      m = new Ack(ballot, last, log);
4      send(m, primary);
5      if(f && mbox(Ack,m.ballot == ballot,n/2)){
6          log = longest_log(ballot);
7          log.add(newCommand());
8      }
9  }
```

Fig. 10. Unfolded round Ack from motivating example.

This procedure is based on [12], but the input received in that work is significantly different. In [12] the reception loops are found explicitly in the code, these are replaced with calls to a havoc function that non-deterministicaly fills the mailbox. Their work also assumes that every iteration of the main loop moves to a (greater) new phase and it does not check that this holds. Algorithm 9 guarantees this property and the Proposition 2 too.

Proposition 2. *Let $[\![\mathcal{P}]\!]$ be the set of executions of $\mathcal{P}$. Given a protocol that makes no network assumptions, $[\![\mathcal{P}]\!] \approx [\![\mathcal{P}_{round}]\!]$, otherwise $[\![\mathcal{P}]\!] \subseteq [\![\mathcal{P}_{round}]\!]$.*

5 Sequentialization of Round-Based Protocols

In this section we define a transformation of a round-based protocol into a sequential one, that preserves safety properties.

5.1 Equivalence with No Network Assumptions

Reductions that over approximate the set of executions are not suitable for testing. If an equivalence exists, given a round-based protocol $\mathcal{P}_{round}$ we build a sequential protocol $\mathcal{P}_{seq}$ using Algorithm 1, such that, given an initial (global) state c_0, all the (global) states reachable from c_0 in $\mathcal{P}_{round}$ are also reachable executing $\mathcal{P}_{seq}$ from c_0. Equivalently, we say that Proposition 3 holds.

Proposition 3. *Given a round-based protocol that makes no network assumptions, $[\![\mathcal{P}_{round}]\!] \approx [\![\mathcal{P}_{seq}]\!]$.*

Proof. Let $\rho = \|_{i=1}^{n} send_*(i,1) \| ... \| send_*(i,n); \|_{i=1}^{n} update(i);$ be the execution of a $\mathcal{P}_{round}$ round where $\|$ denotes the non-determinism of actions.

The round-based semantics ensure that between any two processes p and q there is at most one message sent from p to q and vice versa. Consequently, the order in which send and receive actions are executed does not matter. We obtain $\rho' = send_*(1,1); ...; send_*(n,n); \|_{i=1}^{n} update(i);$ such that $\rho' \approx \rho$.

Two update functions of the same round, on different processes are independent, we can remove other source of non-determinism fixing an arbitrary order $\rho'' = send_*(1,1); send_*(1,n); ...; send_*(n,n); update(1); ...; update(n);$ and this results in $\rho'' \approx \rho$. This reasoning is valid for any arbitrary round.

Algorithm 1 does as follows. The state of $\mathcal{P}_{seq}$ is defined from the global state of $\mathcal{P}_{round}$. The sequential program manipulates the following variables: an integer variable n, corresponding to the number of processes executing the round-based protocol, for each variable v of type T in $\mathcal{P}_{round}$, it has s_v an array of type $ID \rightarrow T$, where each index i gives the value of the variable for process p_i. For example, in $\mathcal{P}_{round}$, mbox is a local variable that stores the messages received in a round. It changes its type in each round because each of them sends different types of messages. The sequentialization $\mathcal{P}_{seq}$ manipulates several arrays, each storing elements of some message type, and $\text{mbox}_r[p_i]$ is the value of mbox in round r on process p_i. The transition relation of $\mathcal{P}_{seq}$ defines a total order over all actions performed by all processes, i.e., an order across all **send** and **update**.

Round-based protocols impose a total order over actions performed by processes across rounds. The sequentialization maintains this order, and it is mainly concerned with the code of one round. The sources of non-determinism at the round level are: (1) the order in which processes send messages (2) the order in which processes execute update (3) the order in which messages are received and (4) which messages are received.

Algorithm 1. Sequentialization

```
1:  while true do ▶ Protocol
2:     for R = 1 to K do
3:        for s = 1 to n do ▶ Send
4:           for r = 1 to n do
5:              mailbox_R(p_r) += (*)p_s.send(p_r)
6:           for i = 0 to n do ▶ Update
7:              p_i.update(mailbox_R(p_i))
8:              mailbox_R(p_i) = ∅
```

The round-based semantics ensure that between any two processes p and q there is at most one message sent from p to q and vice versa. Consequently, the order in which send and receive actions are sequentialized does not matter.

The update function takes the set of received messages as input, and performs a local computation. Two update functions of the same round, on different processes are independent.

Therefore, we fix one order across processes, denoted $p_1, p_2, \ldots p_n$ where the index gives the order relation. The calls to send and update are sequentialized according to this order, where all sends go before all updates, lines 3 and lines 6 in Algorithm 1.

For each message sent the sequential program makes a non-deterministic choice whether to deliver it or not. Each **send-receive** pair is replaced with an assignment, that non-deterministically adds or not the sent message to the receiver's mailbox.

Algorithm 1 uses "*" to represent a non-deterministic choice in line 5, i.e., if the message sent by process p_s to process p_r is received by p_r.

A protocol consisting of K rounds is sequentialized in a while loop that executes the sequentialization of one round after another, in the order in which they are defined in the round-based protocol.

```
1:  procedure DELIVERFN(round)          1:  procedure KERNEL(round)
2:    for r = 1 to n do                 2:    kernel = pick(1, P)
3:      senders = pick(n − f, P)        3:    for s = 1 to n do
4:      for s = 1 to n do               4:      for r = 1 to n do
5:        if p_s ∈ senders then         5:        if p_s ∈ kernel then
6:          mbox_round(p_r) += p_s.send[p_r]    6:          mbox_round(p_r) += p_s.send[p_r]
7:        else                          7:        else
8:          mbox_round(p_r) += (*)p_s.send[p_r]  8:          mbox_round(p_r) += (*)p_s.send[p_r]
```

Fig. 11. Sequentialization for stronger network assumptions. The *Send* block is replaced accordingly with DELIVERFN or KERNEL procedures.

5.2   Protocols with Network Assumptions

If the protocol makes assumptions about the set of messages delivered then, by Proposition 4, we know that the sequentialization given in Algorithm 1 produces an over-approximation of the round-based executions. We strengthen Algorithm 1 for the most common fault models to preserve the equivalence between the synchronous protocol and the sequential one. For protocols that do not tolerate faults, e.g., 2PC, each sent message is received. The sequentialization is deterministic.

Ben-Or is not correct unless each process receives at least $n - f$ messages in each round, where f is the number of tolerated faults. In this case the equivalent sequentialization, (DELIVERFN in Fig. 11), picks randomly which $n - f$ messages to deliver to each process. When the network requires the existence of a non-empty kernel, a set of processes that everyone can communicate reliably with, e.g., UniformVoting, the sequentialization (KERNEL in Fig. 11) guesses the processes in the kernel in beginning of each round and always delivers messages between them.

Proposition 4. *Given a round-based protocol that assumes a Deliver n-f or a Kernel network, $[\![\mathcal{P}_{round}]\!] \approx [\![\mathcal{P}_{seq}]\!]$.*

6   Experimental Evaluation

We evaluated the proposed sequentialization on several consensus and replicated state machine protocols and looked for safety violations. For the evaluation we use P [4]. We consider implementation-inspired asynchronous models, and their sequential versions obtained with the algorithms in Sect. 4.3, 5.

First we check that the asynchronous models are round-based. Even though the evaluated protocols are known to be round-based, we test the conditions in Sect. 4.2 for a given synchronization tag using P's monitoring framework. Every send, receive or mailbox read makes a call to an **announce** primitive, where the monitor observes the state of the calling machine and asserts these conditions.

All modeled implementations[5] contain a safety bug. We compared every asynchronous model with its sequential counterpart using P model checker, measuring

---

[5] https://github.com/vstte22seqprocedure/artifacts.

the time needed for finding these bugs. We found that the most subtle bugs are not found in the asynchronous models, but they are in the sequential version. The experimentation setup consists of manually constructed models in P of the protocol in both asynchronous and sequential versions, a test driver that instantiates the experiment defining the size of the network and other environment variables, and a specification machine that monitors safety violations during the execution. The checking tool systematically explores behaviors of the system model, trying different interleavings of the processes' actions. Each experiment shows the average time (in seconds) to find the bug in 100 executions of 10,000 different schedulers with a timeout of 1 h.

Bugs are caused by messages being dropped/delayed and processes waiting for messages up to a timeout. To model faults, we implemented a `Timer` machine that each process instantiates. The timer machine non-deterministically informs the process that the time waiting for a message expired, making the process move to the next round of the protocol. We use a wrapper around `send`, every time a message is sent, a non-deterministic boolean function chooses to actually send it or to drop it. Next, we describe the bug in each benchmark.

Paxos. This is the example from Sect. 2. Both the asynchronous version and the sequential one contain a bug found in ZAB[6]. The bug occurs when a process sets the variable `last = ballot` at the very beginning of a new phase, when a `Prepare` message is received. This leads to a non-confirmed log being considered as the latest log in the cluster, and leads to a violation of agreement: one replica knows a to be the first command while another one thinks that b is the first. The assignment of `last` should be moved to the `Propose` state upon receiving a message from the primary, confirming that a quorum of processes already have the latest log. The bug requires ten rounds and four phases.

Raft (membership changes). Raft is another consensus algorithm for managing a replicated log. This protocol allows changes into the cluster's configuration, adding or removing nodes to the system. The version presented in [18] contains a bug that produces a safety violation[7]. This happens when there is a membership change during two consecutive terms and the two leaders have different knowledge of the system's configuration. This causes log entries to be considered as committed using disjoint sets of processes and corrupting the global state. Contrary to *Paxos*, the size of the network is not fixed. At each phase the set of processes might change. To capture this in the sequential model, we introduced a *global* configuration variable that includes all the processes of the system, including the new ones trying to join the cluster. Every process has a "local" knowledge about the current state of the cluster stored in a mapping from processes to set of processes. As we mentioned before, this incomplete knowledge about the system size leads to the mentioned bug.

Ben-Or/Uniform Voting. Ben-Or [25] and Uniform Voting [26] are not leader-based decentralized consensus algorithms. Ben-Or solves binary input consensus,

---

[6] https://issues.apache.org/jira/browse/ZOOKEEPER-2832.
[7] https://groups.google.com/g/raft-dev/c/t4xj6dJTP6E/m/d2D9LrWRza8J?pli=1.

while Uniform Voting considers arbitrary input values, and is a deterministic version of Ben-Or. Once a process decides a value, it keeps deciding the same value forever, the original estimate of each process must be overwritten by the decided value. The bug we introduced omits this, producing executions where all processes decide one value but, later on due to some messages being lost, a process decides a different value. The result for Ben-Or* in Table 1 read as follows: the time comes from using Algorithm 11 as described, but when an under approximation is used, using only two quorums for all the execution the number goes down to 9,12. Ben-Or is designed to work under a particular network assumption, where $n - f$ messages are delivered in each round, otherwise safety is not guaranteed. In the second Ben-Or experiment, we have weakened the network assumptions, and allowed the processes to move on to the next round/phase even if fewer than $n - f$ messages are received. As expected, this leads to a violation of agreement. However this violation is found only using the sequential model.

Table 1. Seconds to find a bug in Asynchronous and Sequential protocols under different network environments. † denotes a timeout (1 h). R means messages can be reordered, D means messages can be arbitrarily delayed, T means processes can timeout and move to the next round/phase, MD means messages drops.

Network assumption	Protocol	Network	Async	Sequential
Required	Paxos	R D T	†	0,53
	Paxos	R,D,T,MD	†	0,53
	Ben-Or*	R,D	15,04	30,97/9,12
	Raft	R,D,T,MD	†	158,44
Weaker	ViewChange	R,D,T,MD	22,02	0,21
	Ben-Or	R,D,T	†	0,19
	UniformVoting	R,D,T,MD	18,22	33,74

Similarly, Uniform Voting requires a non-empty set of processes, called the kernel, to communicate reliably with the entire network, otherwise safety is violated. The kernel is needed because Uniform Voting does not rely on a quorum, the vote and decision is based on a minimum argument. We weaken this network assumption and found a violation of agreement. Typically there is no proof showing that these assumptions cannot be weakened, and there is no understanding what happens if they are weakened. Protocol designers would like to play with the network assumptions and see how the protocol behaves.

Viewstamped Replication (view change). In this experiment we consider the leader election protocol used in Viewstamped Replication [27]. We introduced an artificial bug to the protocol where the function that returns the PID of the current leader to be elected is buggy, instead of returning the same PID for a given phase to all processes, it chooses one non-deterministically. Also, the original protocol gathers quorums of messages to guarantee safety, here we introduce another simple bug where the number of collected messages is less than $n/2$.

Table 1 shows our results. The upper half lists the experiments when the network assumptions of each protocol are respected, the lower one depicts the scenario when these networks are weakened.

7   Conclusions

We propose a technique that reduces testing event-driven asynchronous protocols to testing sequential ones. The sequentialization uses the round structure of protocols, which reduces the number of interleavings the sequentialized version needs to explore. The modularity of the method allows to add more sequentializations for network assumptions not considered in this work and therefore run the tool for new protocols. If no sequentialization produces an equivalent set of executions, the method remains interesting for testing because it can be used with a stronger network assumption that under approximates it.

References

1. Padon, O., McMillan, K.L., Panda, A., Sagiv, M., Shoham, S.: Ivy: safety verification by interactive generalization. In: Proceedings of the 37th ACM SIGPLAN Conference on Programming Language Design and Implementation, pp. 614–630 (2016). https://doi.org/10.1145/2908080.2908118
2. Holzmann, G.J.: The model checker SPIN. IEEE Trans. Softw. Eng. **23**(5), 279–295 (1997)
3. Deligiannis, P., et al.: Uncovering bugs in distributed storage systems during testing (not in production!). In: Proceedings of the 14th Usenix Conference on File and Storage Technologies, pp. 249–262. FAST 2016. USENIX Association (2016)
4. Desai, A., Gupta, V., Jackson, E., Qadeer, S., Rajamani, S., Zufferey, D.: P: safe asynchronous event-driven programming. In: Proceedings of the 34th ACM SIGPLAN Conference on Programming Language Design and Implementation, ser. PLDI 2013, pp. 321–332. Association for Computing Machinery, New York (2013). https://doi.org/10.1145/2491956.2462184
5. Bouajjani, A., Emmi, M., Parlato, G.: On sequentializing concurrent programs. In: Yahav, E. (ed.) SAS 2011. LNCS, vol. 6887, pp. 129–145. Springer, Heidelberg (2011). https://doi.org/10.1007/978-3-642-23702-7_13
6. Qadeer, S., Wu, D.: KISS: keep it simple and sequential. ACM SIGPLAN Not. **39**(6), 14–24 (2004)
7. Bertran, M., Babot, F., Climent, A.: Formal sequentialization of distributed systems via program rewriting. Electr. Notes Theor. Comput. Sci. **188**, 53–75 (2007)
8. Bakst, A., Gleissenthall, K.V., Kıcı, R.G., Jhala, R.: Verifying distributed programs via canonical sequentialization. Proc. ACM Program. Lang. **1**(OOPSLA), 1–27 (2017). https://doi.org/10.1145/3133934
9. Kragl, B., Enea, C., Henzinger, T.A., Mutluergil, S.O., Qadeer, S.: Inductive sequentialization of asynchronous programs. In: Proceedings of the 41st ACM SIGPLAN Conference on Programming Language Design and Implementation, pp. 227–242 (2020). https://doi.org/10.1145/3385412.3385980

10. Elrad, T., Francez, N.: Decomposition of distributed programs into communication-closed layers. Sci. Comput. Program. **2**(3), 155–173 (1982)
11. Biely, M., Delgado, P., Milosevic, Z., Schiper, A.: Distal: a framework for implementing fault-tolerant distributed algorithms. In: 2013 43rd Annual IEEE/IFIP International Conference on Dependable Systems and Networks (DSN), pp. 1–8. IEEE (2013)
12. Damian, A., Drăgoi, C., Militaru, A., Widder, J.: Communication-closed asynchronous protocols. In: Dillig, I., Tasiran, S. (eds.) CAV 2019. LNCS, vol. 11562, pp. 344–363. Springer, Cham (2019). https://doi.org/10.1007/978-3-030-25543-5_20
13. Lamport, L.: Paxos made simple. ACM SIGACT News (Distributed Computing Column) **32**, 4 (Whole Number 121, December 2001) (2001). https://www.microsoft.com/en-us/research/publication/paxos-made-simple/
14. Ongaro, D., Ousterhout, J.: In search of an understandable consensus algorithm. In: 2014 USENIX Annual Technical Conference (Usenix ATC 2014), pp. 305–319 (2014)
15. Mohan, C., Lindsay, B.: Efficient commit protocols for the tree of processes model of distributed transactions. ACM SIGOPS Oper. Syst. Rev. **19**(2), 40–52 (1985). https://doi.org/10.1145/850770.850772
16. Junqueira, F.P., Reed, B.C., Serafini, M.: Zab: high-performance broadcast for primary-backup systems. In: 2011 IEEE/IFIP 41st International Conference on Dependable Systems & Networks (DSN), pp. 245–256. IEEE (2011). http://ieeexplore.ieee.org/document/5958223/
17. Drăgoi, C., Enea, C., Ozkan, B.K., Majumdar, R., Niksic, F.: Testing consensus implementations using communication closure. Proc. ACM Program. Lang. **4**, 1–29 (2020). https://doi.org/10.1145/3428278
18. Ongaro, D.: Consensus: bridging theory and practice. Stanford University, CA, USA (2014). aAI28121474 ISBN-13: 9798662514218
19. Gleissenthall, K.V., Kıcı, R.G., Bakst, A., Stefan, D., Jhala, R.: Pretend synchrony: synchronous verification of asynchronous distributed programs. Proc. ACM Program. Lang. **3**(POPL), 1–30 (2019)
20. Demsky, B., Lam, P.: SATCheck: SAT-directed stateless model checking for SC and TSO. ACM SIGPLAN Not. **50**(10), 20–36 (2015). https://doi.org/10.1145/2858965.2814297
21. Kokologiannakis, M., Marmanis, I., Gladstein, V., Vafeiadis, V.: Truly stateless, optimal dynamic partial order reduction. Proc. ACM Program. Lang. **6**(POPL), 1–28 (2022). https://doi.org/10.1145/3498711
22. Gario, M., Cimatti, A., Mattarei, C., Tonetta, S., Rozier, K.Y.: Model checking at scale: automated air traffic control design space exploration. In: Chaudhuri, S., Farzan, A. (eds.) CAV 2016. LNCS, vol. 9780, pp. 3–22. Springer, Cham (2016). https://doi.org/10.1007/978-3-319-41540-6_1
23. Bornholt, J., et al.: Using lightweight formal methods to validate a key-value storage node in Amazon S3. In: Proceedings of the ACM SIGOPS 28th Symposium on Operating Systems Principles, pp. 836–850 (2021). https://doi.org/10.1145/3477132.3483540
24. Lipton, R.J.: Reduction: a method of proving properties of parallel programs. Commun. ACM **18**(12), 717–721 (1975)

25. Ben-Or, M.: Another advantage of free choice (extended abstract) completely asynchronous agreement protocols. In: Proceedings of the Second Annual ACM Symposium on Principles of Distributed Computing, pp. 27–30 (1983). https://doi.org/10.1145/800221.806707
26. Charron-Bost, B., Schiper, A.: The heard-of model: computing in distributed systems with benign faults. Distrib. Comput. **22**, 49–71 (2009). https://doi.org/10.1007/s00446-009-0084-6
27. Liskov, B., Cowling, J.: Viewstamped replication revisited. MIT, Tech. Rep. (2012). MIT-CSAIL-TR-2012-021, Jul 2012

Towards Practical Partial Order Reduction for High-Level Formalisms

Philipp Körner$^{(\boxtimes)}$⬡ and Michael Leuschel⬡

Heinrich Heine University, Universitätsstraße 1, 40225 Düsseldorf, Germany
{p.koerner,leuschel}@hhu.de

Abstract. Partial order reduction (POR) has considerable potential to
reduce the state space during model checking by exploiting independence
between transitions. This potential remains, however, largely unfulfilled
for high-level formalisms such as B or TLA$^+$. In this article, we report
on our experiments regarding POR: We empirically assess that our current implementation of POR in PROB does not have any impact for a
vast majority of B machines. We then analyse why POR fails to achieve
reductions and identify minimal examples without reduction that make
use of high-level constructs in B, and provide several new ideas to make
POR pay off for more complex formal models. A proof-of-concept implementation then yields two orders of magnitude reduction in the state
space for a particularly challenging case study, a railway interlocking
model that escaped our POR techniques thus far.

Keywords: B-method · Partial order reduction · Model checking ·
Analysis

1 Introduction

Partial order reduction (POR) [18,32,38] is a technique to tackle the state space
explosion problem in model checking [12]: Instead of executing all interleavings
of independent behaviour, only one is explored in the best case. In *low-level
formalisms*, such as Petri nets or Promela, and in process algebras like CSP or
mCRL2, POR is known to reduce the state space by several orders of magni-
tudes [7,17,19,25].

In contrast, the application of POR to *high-level formalisms* like TLA$^+$ [26] or
B [1,2] has been disappointing thus far. Attempts at using POR for TLA$^+$ using
TLC [39] were not successful and abandoned[1]. POR has also been implemented
for B using the ample set approach within PROB [13–15]. While considerable
reduction can be obtained for some specifications, the technique does not seem
beneficial for real-life examples. Another attempt of using POR for B was made
using LTSMIN together with PROB [6,25]. It uses PROB to solve predicates

---

[1] Private communication from Stephan Merz to Michael Leuschel at Schloß Dagstuhl;
see also the presentation by Kuppe [24].

A. Lal and S. Tonetta (Eds.): VSTTE 2022, LNCS 13800, pp. 72–91, 2023.
https://doi.org/10.1007/978-3-031-25803-9_5

```
1  MACHINE NoReduction
2  VARIABLES xx, locked
3  INVARIANT xx ∈ POW(1..2) ∧ locked ∈ 𝔹
4  INITIALISATION xx := ∅ ‖ locked := ⊥
5  OPERATIONS
6  add(yy) = SELECT locked = ⊥ ∧ yy ∈ 1..2 ∧ yy ∉ xx
7            THEN xx := xx ∪ {yy} END;
8  lock    = SELECT locked = ⊥ THEN locked := ⊤ END;
9  unlock  = SELECT locked = ⊤ THEN locked := ⊥ END
10 END
```

Listing 1. Adding a Value Into a Set—No Reduction

and calculate the next states while POR is provided by LTSMIN. LTSMIN's approach to POR is based on the stubborn set theory [38] and works well for *low-level* formalisms. Compared to PROB's approach in [13–15], the approach of LTSMIN is more fine-grained (wrt. guards), yet rarely achieves (mostly slightly) better reduction for B models[2]. Overall, POR rarely seems worth the effort for practical B models.

This article re-visits the implementation of POR in PROB: first, we evaluate its effectiveness in Sect. 3. The main insight we gained is that static analysis of a model (before model checking) often does not determine a precise enough independence relation. The techniques described in the rest of the paper focus on POR for deadlock checking (as effectiveness is already low and LTL model checking requires even more constraints): Many B models contain operations drawing a parameter from a known finite set; such operations are treated as a unit and, thus, independence between certain instances cannot be captured. We propose to *unroll* such operations by replacing them with a new operation for each parameter (Sect. 4). Additionally, operations that access a shared set variable usually only interact with a small subset of its elements. We discuss benefits and drawbacks of a constraint-based analysis as well as encoding sets to SAT variables before applying a syntactical analysis (Sect. 5).

As an example, the model in Listing 1 can (automatically) be re-written to an equivalent model depicted in Listing 2 by *unrolling* the add operation and encoding the set xx as booleans. The former model yields no state space reduction using PROB's POR, whereas the latter one does. Though some specifications may require additional re-writes or more involved analysis techniques, the combination of these two techniques allows state space reduction by POR on large, real-world models. In Sect. 6, we share key insights based on a grand challenge we set ourselves, a large model with many real-world features whose state space should be significantly reduced using POR, yet escaped our approach so far. With the techniques above, the expected reduction occurs.

---

[2] Already the results in Sect. 4.3 and Table 3 of [23] for POR were unsatisfying. Other techniques of LTSMIN were very effective, however.

```
 1  MACHINE HasReduction
 2  VARIABLES xx_1, xx_2, locked
 3  INVARIANT xx_1 ∈ 𝔹 ∧ xx_2 ∈ 𝔹 ∧ locked ∈ 𝔹
 4  INITIALISATION xx_1 := ⊥ ‖ xx_2 := ⊥ ‖ locked := ⊥
 5  OPERATIONS
 6  add_1  = SELECT locked = ⊥ ∧ xx_1 = ⊥ THEN xx_1 := ⊤ END;
 7  add_2  = SELECT locked = ⊥ ∧ xx_2 = ⊥ THEN xx_2 := ⊤ END;
 8  lock   = SELECT locked = ⊥ THEN locked := ⊤ END;
 9  unlock = SELECT locked = ⊤ THEN locked := ⊥ END
10  END
```

Listing 2. Unrolled and SAT Encoded Version of Listing 1—POR is Successful

2   Background

The B-Method. [1] and its successor Event-B [2] are methodologies that rely on a correct-by-construction approach, i.e., an abstract specification is proven correct and is iteratively refined as more details are added. Proofs accompany all refinement steps, linking each iteration to the ones before.

Both B and Event-B have seen particular use in the railway industry [9]. While the former focuses on software development, the latter is designed for modelling systems. Event-B is most commonly used via the Rodin toolset [3], and exported proof information can be used for model checking [5]. B and Event-B are very expressive, encompassing first-order logic with (higher-order) sets, sequences, functions, relations and records. Both formalisms are state-based with (possibly non-deterministic) initial assignments of constants and state variables, and guarded transitions (named operations in B and events in Event-B)[3] yielding successor states. A state of a B model is composed of values for all the constants and variables of the model.

While we study both B and Event-B models, we will use the term operation to denote both B operations and Event-B events. Small examples of a B specification are given in the motivating example in Listings 1 and 2. B machines might include additional clauses such as the CONSTANTS clause (that declares identifiers of constants similar to the VARIABLES clause), the PROPERTIES clause (constraining the constants) or the SET clause (that contains, e.g., enumerated sets). While the following concepts of operation and operation instance are related, it is important to distinguish between them:

Notation. *An* operation *is the name of a guarded substitution (aka statement) that may be parameterised. E.g.,* add *or* lock *in Listing 1 are operations. The guarded substitution is also called the* body *of the operation.*
An operation along with values for all its parameters is called an operation instance. *E.g.,* add(1) *is an operation instance. Another one is* add(2).

An operation instance is thus a transition label.

---

[3] Or actions in TLA+.

PROB. [28,29] is an animator, model checker and constraint solver for the B language. It is written in SICStus Prolog [10] and its constraint-solving backend makes use of coroutines and the CLP(FD) library [11]. Alternative backends are available via translations to SAT and SMT: the work of Plagge and Leuschel [34] uses the Kodkod [37] library to translate B to SAT, while the works of Krings, Schmidt and Leuschel [20,35] translate B to SMT for using Z3 [30] as a solver.

Partial Order Reduction. (POR) [4,32,33] is a model checking technique that only explores a subset of the state space. POR is considered to be appealing because, for n independent operation instances, one has to explore (in the best case) only a single ordering rather than $n!$ many. Thus, exponential reductions are possible in concurrent systems that synchronise on few events. While the underlying idea seems simple, the conditions to ensure correctness are intricate[4].

POR exploits *independent* operation instances: Two operation instances are independent, if they can be performed in any order without changing the resulting state. This is visualised in Fig. 1: If α and β are independent and simultaneously enabled in the original state space, this implies that β can be executed after α and vice-versa, and the resulting states are identical. In short, this is the case if the operation instances commute and do not disable each other.

Below, we will give a more formal definition. Note, as is usual when presenting POR, we assume that operation instances are deterministic, i.e., given an operation instance α and a state s there is at most one successor state s' such that $s \xrightarrow{\alpha} s'$.[5]

Notation (Enabling Predicate). *For an operation e, we define en_e to be its enabling predicate (its guard) that is evaluated over a state s.*

Definition 1 (Independence). *Two operation instances α and β are independent, if the following constraint holds. Otherwise, they are dependent.*

$$\forall s, s_1, s_2 : en_\alpha(s) \wedge en_\beta(s) \wedge s \xrightarrow{\alpha} s_1 \wedge s \xrightarrow{\beta} s_2 \implies \exists s' : en_\beta(s_1) \wedge en_\alpha(s_2) \wedge s_1 \xrightarrow{\beta} s' \wedge s_2 \xrightarrow{\alpha} s'$$

The operation instance `lock` depends on `add(1)` (and vice versa, as the independence relation is symmetric), because performing `lock` may (and will) disable `add(1)`. The operation instance `add(1)` is independent of `add(2)`.

Usually, one approximates the independence relation during static analysis before model checking based on operations. Two operations are independent if all respective operation instances are independent. As an example, the operations `add` and `unlock` are independent of each other because they write different variables (and the read in the guard of `add` of `unlock` is not conflicting)[6].

---

[4] For example, an error in a twenty-year-old algorithm was recently discovered [36].

[5] For Event-B it is straightforward to lift all non-determinism into parameters. In Classical B this is more difficult; but the formalisation of independence with non-determinism would make the presentation overly complex and detract from the main points of the article.

[6] More precisely, all operation instances of `add` are independent of `unlock` because they can never be enabled at the same time.

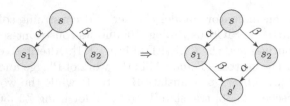

Fig. 1. Visualisation of the operation independence definition

The Ample Set Approach. As the POR implementation in PROB relies on the ample set approach[7], we introduce it more formally. For this article, it is not necessary to understand *why* POR works in detail, but only *what information* is required.

By $op(\alpha)$ we denote the operation associated with an operation instance α. We also define the enabled operations in a state s by $enabled(s) = \{op(\alpha) \mid \exists s' : s \xrightarrow{\alpha} s'\}$.

An ample set is a subset of enabled operations in a state (referred to as s in the following formulas) that are considered by model checking. In other words, all operation instances for operations not contained in the ample set are ignored. For example, in Fig. 1, we could choose $ample(s) = \{op(\alpha)\}$ and thus ignore β in s. To reach a sound reduction of the state space, one requires the following conditions to hold (taken from [15]):

(A 1) **Emptiness Condition:** $ample(s) = \varnothing \Leftrightarrow enabled(s) = \varnothing$
(A 2) **Dependence Condition:** Along every finite path in the original state space starting at s, an operation dependent on $ample(s)$ cannot appear before some operation $e \in ample(s)$ is executed.

The conditions (A 1) and (A 2) suffice for deadlock checking; LTL model checking (which is used for invariant checking) has additional conditions (stutter and cycle), yet those are out of scope for this paper. In PROB's implementation, two local criteria are used instead of (A 2). They have been proven correct in [14,15]:

(A 2.1) **Direct Dependence Condition:** Any (ignored) operation $e \in enabled(s) \setminus ample(s)$ is independent of all operations in $ample(s)$.
(A 2.2) **Enabling Dependence Condition:** Any (disabled) operation $e \in Events \setminus enabled(s)$ that depends on some operation $f \in ample(s)$ and is possibly co-enabled with f may not become enabled by execution of operations $e' \notin ample(s)$.

Two operations are considered to be possibly co-enabled if there exists a state s in which both guards are satisfied. Note that such a state may not be reachable.

Thus, in practice, the independence relation, an enabling relation and a "may be co-enabled" relation between operations are approximated during a static analysis phase (which we will refer to as *POR analysis*).

---

[7] The implementation in LTSMIN uses stubborn sets. There is not much difference concerning our argument as the analysis must extract mostly the same information.

3   Experiments and Results

In order to evaluate the impact of PROB's partial order reduction, we use a collection of B and Event-B specifications [22] and compare the state space sizes with and without applying POR. We consider 1894 B machines with at least two operations in order to have an opportunity for independent events to occur. The set of machines and produced results can be found on GitHub[8].

All machines were model checked for 30 min (per configuration) with 2 GB of RAM on a single CPU core of an Intel E5-2697v2 (Ivy Bridge EP) running at 2.70 GHz. A nightly version of PROB 1.11.0 was used (commit 1b6f14bbd533c2459b1ce675eb57ab24fee89caa).

For **deadlock checking**, we excluded 519 machines that time out with and without POR; 17 machines that time out only with POR; and 25 machines (4% of machines with timeout) only timed out using the vanilla baseline implementation. We assume some reduction occurred for these 25 machines. 3 machines are included due to some other error. Thus, 1330 machines are subject to this analysis. 1121 are deadlock-free, and 209 contain a deadlock.

The original and reduced state space sizes are given in Fig. 2a and Fig. 2b. Data points on the diagonal correspond to cases where no reduction occurs, while data points below the diagonal correspond to a reduction due to POR. In the right figure (Fig. 2b) data points can also be found above the diagonal, meaning that model checking with POR did find the deadlock later than without POR.

Of the 1121 deadlock-free machines, only 191 (17%) showed some reduction with POR. On average the reduced state space has 54% of the original size (i.e., a reduction of 46%) for these 191 machines. The median is 56% of the original size. Similar, of 209 machines containing deadlocks, we can observe 36 (17.2%) with a reduced state space and 9 with a larger one (as discussed earlier).

Thus, even when adding the 25 machines with timeout when not using POR above, we have less than 20% of models where POR reduces the state space.

For **invariant checking**, we can analyse 1385 machines after excluding 452 where both model checking algorithms time out, 2 machines that only time out with POR and 55 machines that only time out without POR. Again, we assume some reduction for the latter cases (around 11% of all machines featuring any timeout). Further, we exclude 55 additional machines due to other errors. This leaves 1331 machines to analyse here, of which 1169 machines preserve the invariant.

The (reduced) state space sizes are visualised in Fig. 3a. Of these, we can observe a state space reduction in 37 machines (3.2%). On average, the reduced state space has 76% of the original size (i.e., a reduction of 24%) for these 37 machines. The median is 86% of the original size. Unexpectedly, a single outlier lies above the diagonal, i.e., yields a larger state space with POR. This is a machine that acts as a test for PROB's randomisation library, and hence the state space can change with each run. Even when assuming that all 55 machines with timeout produce a reduction, we have a reduction in less than 10% of cases.

---

[8] https://github.com/hhu-stups/specifications/tree/por-experiments.

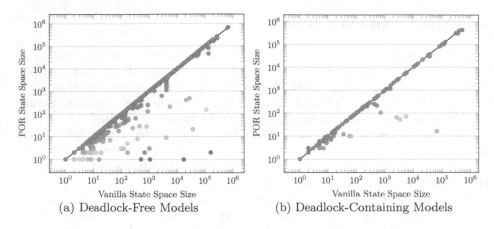

(a) Deadlock-Free Models   (b) Deadlock-Containing Models

Fig. 2. (Reduced) state space sizes for deadlock checking

Of 162 machines with invariant violations (Fig. 3b), we observe 30 machines (18.5%) with a reduced state space and 18 with a larger one.

Threats to Validity. Many machines time out and are excluded, though they might exhibit better reduction in reality. However, from our sample, we can also observe the trend that smaller machines exhibit state space reductions more often (cf. Figs. 2a and 3a). Indeed, our findings in Sect. 4 and Sect. 5 suggest that constructs to structure larger machines *hinder* POR.

Further, the set of machines may not be representative, as it includes many examples from literature, small machines used for teaching, different versions or instantiations of the same machine, etc., and not larger, confidential machines from industry. From our experience, POR does not work well for these machines. The bias may even be *towards* machines well-suited for POR, as several models meant for testing the POR implementation are included.

4   Idiom 1: Parameterised Operations

PROB's partial order reduction and the POR analysis identifies operations by their name. However, there may be several operation instances, i.e., combinations of a name and concrete parameter values. A trivial example is part of Listing 1.

From a high-level point of view, this machine has three operations where only add and lock can be enabled simultaneously but are dependent. Thus, the state space cannot be reduced. Yet, the operation instances add(1) and add(2) satisfy exactly our definition of independence (Fig. 1), as add(1) and add(2) commute (see Fig. 4)!

In this example, the independence of some operation instances within the same operation is not exploited. In many cases, certain operation instances of *one* operation are independent of certain operation instances of *another* operation. An example is described based on our grand challenge in Sect. 6.2.

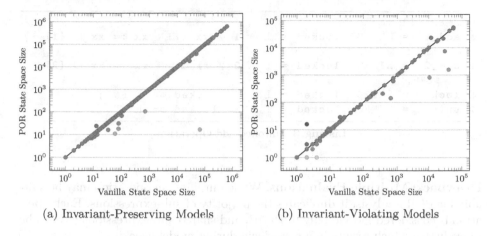

(a) Invariant-Preserving Models   (b) Invariant-Violating Models

Fig. 3. (Reduced) state space sizes for invariant checking

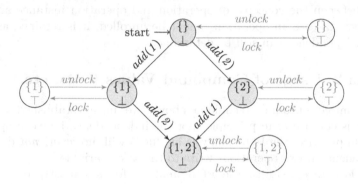

Fig. 4. State space of the machine in Listing 1. Each state consists of the set **xx** (at the top) and the boolean **locked** (at the bottom). The commutativity of the *add* operation instances is highlighted.

4.1   Solution: Unrolling of Operations

The example above has one important property: for the considered operation **add**, we can statically determine a finite set of possible values for the parameters (i.e., either $yy = 1$ or $yy = 2$). In this case we can replace the *operation* with all its *operation instances*, by hardwiring the parameter values. For the example above, this gives rise to two operations add_1 and add_2 in Listing 3.

Advantage: Necessary Preprocessing. This technique is the bare minimum to locate independence between operations that share at least one variable. Thus, it is the foundation for the techniques below.

Drawback: Infinite Sets. This unrolling technique is not always applicable given that parameter choices for all states have to be considered. Indeed, the calculation of all possible parameter values may be expensive and yield a large or infinite number of values (due to an overapproximation by the static analysis).

```
1  OPERATIONS
2  add_1  = SELECT locked = ⊥ ∧ 1 ∉ xx THEN xx := xx ∪ {1}
       END;
3  add_2  = SELECT locked = ⊥ ∧ 2 ∉ xx THEN xx := xx ∪ {2}
       END;
4  lock   = SELECT locked = ⊥ THEN locked := ⊤ END;
5  unlock = SELECT locked = ⊤ THEN locked := ⊥ END
```

Listing 3. Unrolled add Operation

Drawback: Multiple Evaluations. While unrolling an operation may be suitable for POR analysis, it duplicates the majority of sub-expressions. Each operation is considered individually in PROB, and shared sub-expressions have to be re-evaluated which results in a slow-down during model checking.

Below, we assume that all operation instances are unrolled. Thus, there is no difference between the concepts of operation and operation instance and their independence. In case an operation cannot be unrolled, it is retained as-is and syntactic independence can still be determined.

5 Idiom 2: Usage of Compound Values (Sets, etc.)

With the simple unrolling technique above, we have established that the POR analysis could now in principle spot the independence between operation instances. In practice, the POR analysis in PROB will, however, *not* determine the independence if two operations write to the same variable.

For performance reasons, the POR analysis focuses mostly on syntactic aspects in order to yield a fast approximation[9]. It considers the (action) **read** and **write** sets of two operations (AR_1, AR_2, R_1, R_2, W_1 and W_2). A variable is contained in the action read set AR of an operation, iff the substitution reads it; in the read set R iff the guard or the substitution reads it; and in the write set W iff the variable is written to. The POR analysis then follows the flowchart depicted in Fig. 5, where only the disabling analysis uses semantic aspects.

If we re-consider the operations in Listing 3, we can observe that both add_1 and add_2 write to the same variable xx. Obviously, the intersection of the two write sets $W_1 \cap W_2$ is not empty and a syntactic POR analysis yields that the two operations are (race) dependent. Yet, set union is associative and commutative and the operations *should* be classified as independent because $(xx \cup \{1\}) \cup \{2\} = (xx \cup \{2\}) \cup \{1\}$.

5.1 Solution 1: Constraint-Based POR Analysis

Since the original syntactic approach depicted in Fig. 5 does not suffice, we added a new constraint-based semantic approach. Instead of syntactically classifying a

---

[9] Which is precise enough for some formalisms (at least using LTSMIN's POR), but not for others [25].

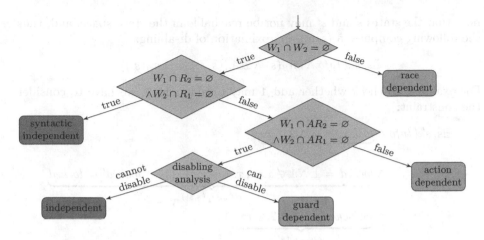

Fig. 5. Syntactically determining the independence relation of two operations

pair of operations as race or action dependent (see Fig. 5), we use a constraint solver (PROB, Kodkod or Z3) during the POR analysis. Below, we present how we determine operations to be independent by considering non-disabling and commutativity constraints separately (see Definition 1). Further, in order to be able to check 2 on the fly, we also use constraints to determine which other operations may (not) be enabled by a specific operation. Finally, again for 2, one also has to determine which operations may be co-enabled. For the overall approach, we use the notion of before-after predicates and enabling predicates:

Notation (Before-After Predicate). *For an operation instance e, we define $BA_e(s, s')$ to be the before-after predicate. It is a conjunction of the guard of operation $op(e)$ and the predicate whose solutions s' form the successor states of s using e.*

As an example, the before-after predicate for the operation `add_1` is[10]:

$$BA_{add_1}(s, s') \equiv \underbrace{locked = \bot \wedge 1 \notin xx}_{en_{add_1}(s)} \wedge \underbrace{xx' = xx \cup \{1\} \wedge locked' = locked}_{\text{substitution of } add_1}$$

Before-after predicates do not exist for all operations, e.g., those containing a WHILE-loop.

Non-disabling Constraint. Independent operations must not disable each other and commute. The constraint below checks whether operation α can disable the operation β. The conjunct *Info* might contain additional information, such as the values of constants, proven theorems or (parts of) the state invariant. Also

---

[10] We will directly refer to the state variables by their name; e.g., xx is part of state s, and xx' is a variable of s'.

note that the states s and s' may not be reachable in the state space, and, thus the following computes a (safe) approximation of disabling:

$$\exists s, s'.(\mathit{Info} \wedge en_\beta(s) \wedge BA_\alpha(s, s') \wedge \neg en_\beta(s'))$$

For example, to check whether add_1 may disable add_2, we have to consider the constraint:

$$\exists s, s'.(\mathit{Info} \wedge \underbrace{locked = \bot \wedge 2 \in xx}_{en_{add_2}(s)}$$

$$\wedge \underbrace{locked = \bot \wedge 1 \notin xx \wedge xx' = xx \cup \{1\} \wedge locked' = locked}_{BA_{add_1}(s,s')}$$

$$\wedge \underbrace{\neg(locked' = \bot \wedge 2 \in xx')}_{\neg en_{add_2}(s')})$$

As this constraint is a contradiction, we can conclude that add_1 cannot disable add_2 (and, analogously, vice versa). This does not suffice for independence, and we have to continue to check the commutativity of the operations (see below). However, lock can (and will) disable add_1 and the operations cannot be independent. The same holds for lock and add_2.

Commuting Constraint. The next constraint below encodes counter examples to commutativity in Definition 1. egain, if a solution is found, a timeout occurs or unknown is returned by the solver, we conclude that the operations might be non-commuting and thus dependent:

$$\exists s, s_1, s_2, s_3, s_4.(\mathit{Info} \wedge BA_\alpha(s, s_1) \wedge BA_\beta(s, s_2) \wedge BA_\alpha(s_2, s_3) \wedge BA_\beta(s_1, s_4) \wedge s_3 \neq s_4)$$

E.g., to find that add_1 and add_2 commute, the following constraint is used:

$$\exists s, s_1, s_2, s_3, s_4.(\underbrace{locked = \bot \wedge 1 \notin xx \wedge xx_1 = xx \cup \{1\} \wedge locked_1 = locked}_{BA_{add_1}(s,s_1)}$$

$$\wedge \underbrace{locked = \bot \wedge 2 \notin xx \wedge xx_2 = xx \cup \{2\} \wedge locked_2 = locked}_{BA_{add_2}(s,s_2)}$$

$$\wedge \underbrace{locked_2 = \bot \wedge 1 \notin xx_2 \wedge xx_3 = xx_2 \cup \{1\} \wedge locked_3 = locked_2}_{BA_{add_1}(s_2,s_3)}$$

$$\wedge \underbrace{locked_1 = \bot \wedge 2 \notin xx_1 \wedge xx_4 = xx_1 \cup \{2\} \wedge locked_4 = locked_1}_{BA_{add_2}(s_1,s_4)}$$

$$\wedge \underbrace{\neg(xx_3 = xx_4 \wedge locked_3 = locked_4)}_{s_3 \neq s_4})$$

Due to the associativity and commutativity of the set union, the two operations will commute. Further, as they do not disable each other, the constraint can be found to be unsatisfiable. Hence, we know for certain that for all states Definition 1 holds and the operations are independent of each other.

Non-Enabling Constraint. For condition (A 2.2), we also have to know which operations can *enable* each other. In order to determine whether operation α can enable β, we need a constraint similar to the non-disabling constraint:

$$\exists s, s'.(\textit{Info} \wedge \neg en_\beta(s) \wedge BA_\alpha(s, s') \wedge en_\beta(s'))$$

As an example, add_1 cannot enable add_2 and vice versa. However, both these operations can be enabled by unlock.

Co-Enabledness Constraint. Again, for condition (A 2.2), we need to know which operations are potentially co-enabled. The constraint below is true if the operations α and β are co-enabled in some state:

$$\exists s.(\textit{Info} \wedge en_\alpha(s) \wedge en_\beta(s))$$

For example, add_1 and add_2 are both enabled in the initial state. However, lock and unlock are never co-enabled as their guards form a contradiction.

Advantage: Precision. Overall, such a constraint-based analysis is very precise and, in an optimal world, would obtain all necessary information for POR.

Drawback: Required Information. In practice, (proven) invariants often are important to determine independence (i.e., they should be part of the *Info* predicate above). E.g., if $x > 0 \Rightarrow x = y$ is known, we can infer that the guards $x > 0$ and $y \leq 0$ are mutually exclusive. However, adding conjuncts to the *Info* predicate can also make a constraint solver time out. We were not able to find a heuristic that selects additional information for the solver and consistently succeeds for more complex models.

Drawback: Analysis Overhead. For many constraints the solvers time out, which vastly increases the POR analysis time. We found that for many models, such an analysis surpasses the actual model checking time for the full state space. The issue is further discussed regarding the interlocking example in Sect. 6.2.

Drawback: Instability of Solver Integrations. PROB's own constraint solver does not perform well in finding unsatisfiability of the commuting constraints. Other integrated solvers on the other hand, i.e., Kodkod and Z3 fit extraordinarily well. However, for some constraints Kodkod and Z3 will occupy all available memory (including swap space), leading to crashes during POR analysis.

5.2 Solution 2: SAT Encoding of Finite Sets

While the constraint-based approach above works well for smaller models, the blow up of analysis time renders it less favourable for larger ones. Thus, we have implemented a prototype[11] that aims to expose syntactic independence by automatically re-writing finite set variables (as well as finite relations) into a series of boolean variables. This is technique often refered to as "bit blasting", or "data refinement" in the context of modelling and refinement. It also is used in Kodkod's translation to SAT, and similar re-writes are required when encoding

---

[11] Available at: https://github.com/JanRossbach/fset.

such a model in lower-level formalisms, such as Promela. In Listing 2, an example encoding is given for the machine in Listing 3.

One can see that the (original) set variable xx can contain at most two values that can be determined statically (i.e., 1 and 2). Then, the original set xx is replaced by a group of boolean variables, here xx_1 (that equals TRUE iff $1 \in xx$) and xx_2 (that equals TRUE iff $2 \in xx$). Finally, a membership check is a comparison with TRUE (or FALSE for non-membership, e.g., in the guard of add_1), and the set union with a singleton set just sets the according boolean to true (e.g., in the body of add_1). Most operators concerning sets, functions and relations can be re-written (though some translations are rather involved [37], and are omitted here).

Advantage: Faster Analysis. The POR analysis yields a pretty precise result even if the original, fast syntactical analysis in Fig. 5 is re-used. For example, add_1 reads and writes only xx_1 and does not require xx_2, and vice versa for add_2, resulting in independent operations on a syntactical level. Further, as the behaviour of the machine is not altered, one could also verify that this is a valid refinement in order to ensure correctness.

Drawback: Performance. There are several aspects of performance overheads to consider here: first, the translation itself requires some time, especially if all operations are unrolled and if complicated invariants are used. For larger models, our prototype of the translation may take several minutes. Second, the translated model does not perform as well during model checking with PROB, and may be several times slower. Thus, a sensible option would be to use the translated model for POR analysis only and map the results to the original model.

Drawback: Translatable Subset. Unfortunately, not all operators in the B language have a straightforward mapping to a SAT encoding. As a fallback, one may re-calculate the original set by combining all boolean values it is spliced into. Yet, in these instances, one loses all syntactic independence again.

6 Case Study and Challenge: Railway Interlocking System

In his book on Event-B [2], Abrial presents a model[12] of a railway interlocking system. The role of an interlocking is to safely operate signals and points within an area of the train network. This means that the interlocking controller has to ensure that trains do not collide and that points are not moved while a train is driving over them.

In this section, we investigate the impact of the POR analysis techniques we presented above with this interlocking system by Abrial [2, Chapter 17] (cf. Listing 4). Although it is an academic model intended for teaching, we chose it because *(i)* it shares several features with real-world models, *(ii)* while SAT-based approaches are able to verify small to medium-sized interlockings [8,31], the verification of larger interlockings is still an active research area and challenge, *(iii)* applying PROB's *POR yields no state space reduction*, *(iv)* it requires

---

[12] https://github.com/pkoerner/train-por/blob/main/Train_1_beebook_TLC.mch.

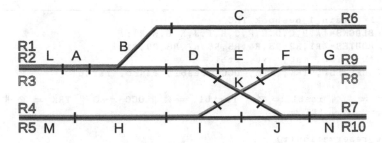

Fig. 6. Example interlocking track layout based on page 524 of [2] with 5 signals, 5 points, one crossing and 14 tracks segments

vast resources for model checking—its state space for the simple topology from Fig. 6 consists of 61 648 077 states and invariant checking with PROB would take about six days (based on estimates [21]—without distributed model checking, the process ran out of memory and crashed), *(v)* one can identify that partial-order reduction is in principle possible because the `route_freeing` operation is independent of all other operations. One can hand-code this insight into the model [27] by forcing this operation (`route_freeing`) to be taken as soon as it is enabled[13], thereby reducing the state space to 672 174 states. Our challenge for the last years has been to identify why our current approach fails and to obtain this two-order of magnitude reduction by (an improved) POR.

6.1   Interlocking Model Overview

The rail network is divided into individual *blocks*; the blocks in Fig. 6 are named A–N. The interlocking allows trains to follow a fixed number of statically determined *routes* through the network. Figure 6 contains 10 routes, named R1–R10. For example, route R1 goes through blocks L, A, B, C, while route R2 goes through L, A, B, D, E, F, G and route R6 is the reversed route of R1, going through C, B, A, L (analogously for R7–R10).

The model also contains the following constants and variables: `fst` and `lst` are functions that map a route to its first and last block, respectively. `nxt` is a function that—given a route—returns a function mapping a block to its successor. `rtbl` is a relation storing the routes for each block. `resbl` (reserved blocks) `resrt` (reserved routes) and `rsrtbl` (blocks reserved for routes) store information about reservations. `OCC` keeps track of blocks that are occupied. `frm` stores which routes are formed on the physical track (`TRK`). `LBT` maps a route to the last block of the train.

Operations are usually called within a certain order: first, a route has to be reserved (`route_reservation`) and the points need to be positioned to match the route (`point_positionning`). Then, these points are locked as the route is formed (`route_formation`). On formed routes, trains may enter and leave blocks

---

[13] https://github.com/pkoerner/train-por/blob/main/Train_1_beebook_tlc_POR.mch.

```
1   MACHINE Train_1_beebook_TLC
2   SETS  BLOCKS={A,B,C,D,E,F,G,H,I,J,K,L,M,N};
3         ROUTES={R1,R2,R3,R4,R5,R6,R7,R8,R9,R10}
4   CONSTANTS fst, lst, nxt, rtbl
5   VARIABLES LBT, TRK, frm, OCC, resbl, resrt, rsrtbl
6   INITIALISATION
7   resrt := ∅ || resbl := ∅ || rsrtbl := ∅ || OCC := ∅ || TRK := ∅ ||
8   frm   := ∅ || LBT := ∅
9   OPERATIONS
10  route_reservation(r) =
11    SELECT r ∉ resrt ∧ (rtbl⁻¹)[{r}] ∩ resbl = ∅
12    THEN resrt := resrt ∪ {r} ||
13         rsrtbl := rsrtbl ∪ (rtbl ▷ {r}) ||
14         resbl := resbl ∪ (rtbl⁻¹)[{r}] END;
15  route_freeing(r)
16    SELECT r ∈ resrt \ ran(rsrtbl)
17    THEN resrt := resrt \ {r} || frm := frm \ {r} END;
18  FRONT_MOVE_1(r) =
19    SELECT r ∈ frm ∧ fst(r) ∈ resbl \ OCC ∧ rsrtbl(fst(r)) = r
20    THEN OCC := OCC ∪ {fst(r)} || LBT := LBT ∪ {fst(r)} END;
21  FRONT_MOVE_2(b) =
22    SELECT b ∈ OCC ∧ b ∈ dom(TRK) ∧ TRK(b) ∉ OCC
23    THEN OCC := OCC ∪ {TRK(b)} END;
24  BACK_MOVE_1(B) =
25    SELECT b ∈ LBT ∧ b ∉ dom(TRK)
26    THEN OCC := OCC \ {b} || rsrtbl := {b} ◁ rsrtbl ||
27         resbl := resbl \ {b} || LBT := LBT \ {b} END;
28  BACK_MOVE_2(b) =
29    SELECT b ∈ LBT ∧ b ∈ dom(TRK) ∧ TRK(b) ∈ OCC
30    THEN OCC := OCC \ {b} || rsrtbl := {b} ◁ rsrtbl ||
31         resbl := resbl \ {b} || LBT := LBT \ {b} ∪ {TRK(b)} END;
32  point_positionning(r) =
33    SELECT r ∈ resrt \ frm
34    THEN TRK := ((dom(nxt(r)) ◁ TRK)
35               ▷ ran(nxt(r))) ∪ nxt(r) END;
36  route_formation(r) =
37    SELECT r ∈ resrt \ frm ∧
38         (rsrtbl⁻¹)[{r}] ◁ nxt(r) = (rsrtbl⁻¹)[{r}] ◁ TRK
39    THEN frm := frm ∪ {r} END
40  END
```

Listing 4. Grand Challenge: Abrial's Interlocking System (Excerpt)

in the corresponding order (via the operations FRONT_MOVE_1, FRONT_MOVE_2, BACK_MOVE_1 and BACK_MOVE_2). Once a train finishes its route, the route is freed again (route_freeing).

Since only some routes share blocks, several routes can be reserved, formed and several trains may be on the tracks at the same time. For example, route R1 does not share any block with route R4 or R5. On the other hand, route R3 and R4 both include the blocks F and G.

6.2 Insights

Operation Unrolling. As previously mentioned, this is the key technique for the POR analysis that avoids re-writing the POR implementation itself. In our case study, one can unroll all operations, as parameters are either one of the ten routes or fourteen blocks. Then, the unrolled model has 92 operations. If the operations were not unrolled, one could not exploit that some pairs of routes do not overlap (and the corresponding operation instances are, thus, *independent*). One consequence is that the POR analysis cannot infer the independence of, e.g., the route reservation of the disjoint routes R1 and R5. Another consequence is that, e.g., `route_reservation` and `route_formation` are overapproximated as dependent, even though *some* pairs of routes do not overlap (and the corresponding operation instances are, thus, *independent*).

Constrained-Based Analysis. The constraint-based approach is able to yield a precise independence analysis. This, however, comes with a cost: if operations *are* dependent on each other, solvers usually time out rather than returning a counterexample or unknown. As many operations do not commute (or may enable or disable each other), this drastically increases POR analysis time. As 4186 (unordered) pairs of operations exist, a full analysis that checks the non-disabling, commutativity (for independence) as well as non-enabling and co-enabledness constraints (for (A 2.2)) takes several hours even on modern hardware due to the amount of timeouts. Finally, even though the obtained information was pretty precise, we did not achieve any reduction with this approach. The POR analysis was not able to determine that a crucial pair of operations cannot be co-enabled (cf. (A 2.2)), and was not precise enough concerning the enabling relation. In particular, for the same parameter route R, the operation instance `route_freeing(R)` may disable both `point_positionning(R)` and `route_formation(R)` and, thus, is not independent of them. However, the operations are never enabled at the same time. If this co-enabledness was disproven, the reduction would occur as expected.

SAT Encoding. Finally, the SAT encoding of the original model[14] *in combination with* the constraint-based analysis yielded the most precise POR analysis results. In consequence, the technique also allowed the POR algorithm to achieve the same reduction as the hand-written version. Analysis and model checking takes about 30 min (1881 s) and requires 5048 MB of memory. In comparison, the hand-written version without PROB's POR takes around 7 min (397 s) and uses 2038 MB of memory. The faster runtime is due to the overhead of the POR as well as the less efficient encoding of the refinement. Reasons for the additional memory usage include a larger refined model and larger states, storage of POR analysis results, etc.

7 Conclusions and Future Work

In this paper, we have identified two idioms in B and Event-B—operation abstraction by parameters and usage of high-level data types—that often hinder

---

[14] https://github.com/pkoerner/train-por/blob/main/train_auto4.mch.

the POR analysis and, henceforth, successful state space reduction. Certainly, there are further patterns that may be uncovered in the future. Thus, our main conclusion is that the usage of high-level constructs prevalent in B are indeed the root cause for our previous unsatisfying experiences with POR and, thus, deeper analysis is required.

We have described three techniques in Sects. 4 and 5, (i.e. unrolling of operations, constraint-based POR analysis of operations based on before-after predicates and/or a precise SAT encoding of finite set variables). Individually, each technique is no universal remedy and brings its own drawbacks to the table. In combination, however, one can exploit their individual advantages and, indeed, we were able to match the two order of magnitude state space reduction of the hand-written version for deadlock checking of the interlocking case study.

Related work is dynamic POR [16] which is especially useful for model checking of concurrent software systems, where possible parameter values are drawn from large or infinite sets such as integer values. It avoids static analysis altogether, tracks information dynamically during execution traces and backtracks later if alternative paths that need to be explored are identified. One main benefit is that one does not need to keep the entire state space in memory but only the execution that is currently considered. While this is quite different from our approach, it still requires precise information on the dependence relation and, thus, cannot yield better reduction alone. Yet, evaluating the dependency relation *lazily*—i.e., considering only combinations of operation instances which are actually encountered—can help where our improvements in Sects. 4 and 5 currently fail, i.e., when parameters are drawn from infinite sets or when sets are statically unbounded.

The constraint-based analysis still has room for improvement: for one, there might be useful heuristics for similar operation pairs to avoid timeouts. If missing information was made more transparent to the user, one might also assist the POR analysis by providing (proven) theorems. Yet, our implementation of SAT encoding is not mature enough for large-scale benchmarking. In the future, we aim to evaluate our new approach in the large.

Finally, the focus of this study lies on deadlock checking—invariant or LTL model checking may require different or additional techniques. In particular, it is often hard to prove that operations preserve the invariant (which is required for operations to be stutter events, which in turn is required for successful reduction during LTL model checking). Thus, work in this direction might benefit from integrating provers to obtain information about invariants that are guaranteed to be preserved by individual operations.

Acknowledgement. The authors thank the anonymous referees for their feedback, Joshua Schmidt for his patience and relentless work on the Z3 interface and Jan Roßbach for his implementation of the SAT encoding of finite sets. Computational infrastructure and support were provided by the Centre for Information and Media Technology at Heinrich Heine University Düsseldorf.

References

1. Abrial, J.R.: The B-Book: Assigning Programs to Meanings. Cambridge University Press, Cambridge (1996)
2. Abrial, J.R.: Modeling in Event-B: System and Software Engineering. Cambridge University Press, Cambridge (2010)
3. Abrial, J.R., Butler, M., Hallerstede, S., Hoang, T.S., Mehta, F., Voisin, L.: Rodin: an open toolset for modelling and reasoning in Event-B. Int. J. Softw. Tools Technol. Transf. 12(6), 447–466 (2010). https://doi.org/10.1007/s10009-010-0145-y
4. Baier, C., Katoen, J.P.: Principles of Model Checking. MIT Press, Cambridge (2008)
5. Bendisposto, J., Leuschel, M.: Proof assisted model checking for B. In: Breitman, K., Cavalcanti, A. (eds.) ICFEM 2009. LNCS, vol. 5885, pp. 504–520. Springer, Heidelberg (2009). https://doi.org/10.1007/978-3-642-10373-5_26
6. Blom, S., van de Pol, J., Weber, M.: LTSMIN: distributed and symbolic reachability. In: Touili, T., Cook, B., Jackson, P. (eds.) CAV 2010. LNCS, vol. 6174, pp. 354–359. Springer, Heidelberg (2010). https://doi.org/10.1007/978-3-642-14295-6_31
7. Bønneland, F.M., Jensen, P.G., Larsen, K.G., Muñiz, M., Srba, J.: Partial order reduction for reachability games. In: Proceedings CONCUR (International Conference on Concurrency Theory). LIPIcs, vol. 140, pp. 23:1–23:15. Schloss Dagstuhl-Leibniz-Zentrum fuer Informatik (2019)
8. Borälv, A.: Interlocking design automation using prover trident. In: Havelund, K., Peleska, J., Roscoe, B., de Vink, E. (eds.) FM 2018. LNCS, vol. 10951, pp. 653–656. Springer, Cham (2018). https://doi.org/10.1007/978-3-319-95582-7_39
9. Butler, M., et al.: The first twenty-five years of industrial use of the B-method. In: ter Beek, M.H., Ničković, D. (eds.) FMICS 2020. LNCS, vol. 12327, pp. 189–209. Springer, Cham (2020). https://doi.org/10.1007/978-3-030-58298-2_8
10. Carlsson, M., Mildner, P.: SICStus Prolog—the first 25 years. Theory Pract. Logic Program. 12, 35–66 (2012)
11. Carlsson, M., Ottosson, G., Carlson, B.: An open-ended finite domain constraint solver. In: Glaser, H., Hartel, P., Kuchen, H. (eds.) PLILP 1997. LNCS, vol. 1292, pp. 191–206. Springer, Heidelberg (1997). https://doi.org/10.1007/BFb0033845
12. Clarke, E., Grumberg, O., Peled, D.: Model Checking. MIT Press, Cambridge (1999)
13. Dobrikov, I., Leuschel, M.: Optimising the ProB model checker for B using partial order reduction. In: Giannakopoulou, D., Salaün, G. (eds.) SEFM 2014. LNCS, vol. 8702, pp. 220–234. Springer, Cham (2014). https://doi.org/10.1007/978-3-319-10431-7_16
14. Dobrikov, I., Leuschel, M.: Optimising the ProB model checker for B using partial order reduction. Form. Asp. Comput. 28(2), 295–323 (2016). https://doi.org/10.1007/s00165-015-0351-1
15. Dobrikov, I.M.: Improving explicit-state model checking for B and Event-B. Ph.D. thesis, Universitäts- und Landesbibliothek der Heinrich-Heine-Universität Düsseldorf (2017)
16. Flanagan, C., Godefroid, P.: Dynamic partial-order reduction for model checking software. In: Proceedings POPL (Symposium on Principles of Programming Languages), pp. 110–121. ACM (2005)
17. Gibson-Robinson, T., Hansen, H., Roscoe, A.W., Wang, X.: Practical partial order reduction for CSP. In: Havelund, K., Holzmann, G., Joshi, R. (eds.) NFM 2015. LNCS, vol. 9058, pp. 188–203. Springer, Cham (2015). https://doi.org/10.1007/978-3-319-17524-9_14

18. Godefroid, P.: Using partial orders to improve automatic verification methods. In: Clarke, E.M., Kurshan, R.P. (eds.) CAV 1990. LNCS, vol. 531, pp. 176–185. Springer, Heidelberg (1991). https://doi.org/10.1007/BFb0023731

19. Holzmann, G.J.: The model checker SPIN. IEEE Trans. Softw. Eng. **23**(5), 279–295 (1997)

20. Krings, S., Leuschel, M.: SMT solvers for validation of B and Event-B models. In: Ábrahám, E., Huisman, M. (eds.) IFM 2016. LNCS, vol. 9681, pp. 361–375. Springer, Cham (2016). https://doi.org/10.1007/978-3-319-33693-0_23

21. Körner, P., Bendisposto, J.: Distributed model checking using PROB. In: Dutle, A., Muñoz, C., Narkawicz, A. (eds.) NFM 2018. LNCS, vol. 10811, pp. 244–260. Springer, Cham (2018). https://doi.org/10.1007/978-3-319-77935-5_18

22. Körner, P., Leuschel, M., Dunkelau, J.: Towards a shared specification repository. In: Raschke, A., Méry, D., Houdek, F. (eds.) ABZ 2020. LNCS, vol. 12071, pp. 266–271. Springer, Cham (2020). https://doi.org/10.1007/978-3-030-48077-6_22

23. Körner, P., Leuschel, M., Meijer, J.: State-of-the-art model checking for B and Event-B using PROB and LTSMIN. In: Furia, C.A., Winter, K. (eds.) IFM 2018. LNCS, vol. 11023, pp. 275–295. Springer, Cham (2018). https://doi.org/10.1007/978-3-319-98938-9_16

24. Kuppe, M.A.: Let TLA+ RiSE. RiSE group all-hands meeting (2018)

25. Laarman, A., Pater, E., van de Pol, J., Hansen, H.: Guard-based partial-order reduction. Int. J. Softw. Tools Technol. Transf. **18**(4), 427–448 (2014). https://doi.org/10.1007/s10009-014-0363-9

26. Lamport, L.: Specifying systems: the TLA+ language and tools for hardware and software engineers. Addison-Wesley (2002)

27. Leuschel, M., Bendisposto, J., Hansen, D.: Unlocking the mysteries of a formal model of an interlocking system. In: Proceedings Rodin Workshop 2014 (2014)

28. Leuschel, M., Butler, M.: ProB: a model checker for B. In: Araki, K., Gnesi, S., Mandrioli, D. (eds.) FME 2003. LNCS, vol. 2805, pp. 855–874. Springer, Heidelberg (2003). https://doi.org/10.1007/978-3-540-45236-2_46

29. Leuschel, M., Butler, M.: ProB: an automated analysis toolset for the B method. Int. J. Softw. Tools Technol. Transf. **10**, 185–203 (2008). https://doi.org/10.1007/s10009-007-0063-9

30. de Moura, L., Bjørner, N.: Z3: an efficient SMT solver. In: Ramakrishnan, C.R., Rehof, J. (eds.) TACAS 2008. LNCS, vol. 4963, pp. 337–340. Springer, Heidelberg (2008). https://doi.org/10.1007/978-3-540-78800-3_24

31. Parillaud, C., Fonteneau, Y., Belmonte, F.: Interlocking formal verification at Alstom signalling. In: Collart-Dutilleul, S., Lecomte, T., Romanovsky, A. (eds.) RSSRail 2019. LNCS, vol. 11495, pp. 215–225. Springer, Cham (2019). https://doi.org/10.1007/978-3-030-18744-6_14

32. Peled, D.: All from one, one for all: on model checking using representatives. In: Courcoubetis, C. (ed.) CAV 1993. LNCS, vol. 697, pp. 409–423. Springer, Heidelberg (1993). https://doi.org/10.1007/3-540-56922-7_34

33. Peled, D.: Combining partial order reductions with on-the-fly model-checking. In: Dill, D.L. (ed.) CAV 1994. LNCS, vol. 818, pp. 377–390. Springer, Heidelberg (1994). https://doi.org/10.1007/3-540-58179-0_69

34. Plagge, D., Leuschel, M.: Validating B,Z and TLA$^+$ using PROB and Kodkod. In: Giannakopoulou, D., Méry, D. (eds.) FM 2012. LNCS, vol. 7436, pp. 372–386. Springer, Heidelberg (2012). https://doi.org/10.1007/978-3-642-32759-9_31

35. Schmidt, J., Leuschel, M.: Improving SMT solver integrations for the validation of B and Event-B models. In: Lluch Lafuente, A., Mavridou, A. (eds.) FMICS 2021. LNCS, vol. 12863, pp. 107–125. Springer, Cham (2021). https://doi.org/10.1007/978-3-030-85248-1_7

36. Siegel, S.F.: What's wrong with on-the-fly partial order reduction. In: Dillig, I., Tasiran, S. (eds.) CAV 2019. LNCS, vol. 11562, pp. 478–495. Springer, Cham (2019). https://doi.org/10.1007/978-3-030-25543-5_27

37. Torlak, E., Jackson, D.: Kodkod: a relational model finder. In: Grumberg, O., Huth, M. (eds.) TACAS 2007. LNCS, vol. 4424, pp. 632–647. Springer, Heidelberg (2007). https://doi.org/10.1007/978-3-540-71209-1_49

38. Valmari, A.: Stubborn sets for reduced state space generation. In: Rozenberg, G. (ed.) ICATPN 1989. LNCS, vol. 483, pp. 491–515. Springer, Heidelberg (1991). https://doi.org/10.1007/3-540-53863-1_36

39. Yu, Y., Manolios, P., Lamport, L.: Model checking TLA$^+$ specifications. In: Pierre, L., Kropf, T. (eds.) CHARME 1999. LNCS, vol. 1703, pp. 54–66. Springer, Heidelberg (1999). https://doi.org/10.1007/3-540-48153-2_6

SMT-Based Verification of Persistency Invariants of Px86 Programs

Iason Marmanis$^{(\boxtimes)}$ and Viktor Vafeiadis

MPI-SWS, Kaiserslautern, Germany
{imarmanis,viktor}@mpi-sws.org

Abstract. While non-volatile memory (NVM) promises to be both performant and durable, the semantics provided by the hardware architectures are rather subtle and significantly complicate reasoning about the possible observed state after a crash.

Starting from recent persistency extension of the x86 model, we present the first automated approach for proving invariants about the persistent state of bounded NVM programs. Our approach works by encoding the program's semantics along with its intended invariants into a compact logical formula and querying an SMT solver for its satisfiability. We propose two alternative encodings, which differ in the way the notion of a crash is encoded. For a collection of small to medium-size benchmarks, our implementation is able to detect or prove absence of persistency bugs in time ranging from a couple of seconds to some minutes.

1 Introduction

Non-volatile memory (NVM) technology can yield large performance improvements in applications that need to persist their data, since they can do so by issuing memory writes to addresses mapped to NVM. Achieving these performance improvements, however, is highly non-trivial because memory writes have rather complex persistency semantics. They are generally persisted neither synchronously nor in program order, unless programmers insert special fence and cache-line flush instructions at the appropriate program points.

Due to the high cost of these instructions, programmers often insert fewer fences than necessary, which can lead to data corruption upon a power failure, thereby negating the benefits of NVM. To date, there are a few tools that can help programmers with fence/flush placements, but sacrifice precision and/or soundness for scalability. JAARU [10] is a stateless model checker that does not explore all program executions exhaustively and so cannot be used to prove absence of bugs. Static analysis approaches assume that all appropriately annotated data is to be flushed, thereby requiring many redundant flush instructions. Dynamic analysis (testing) approaches (e.g., [18,20]) can achieve precision but do not provide any correctness guarantees beyond the executions actually explored, and so they can be used only to find bugs—not to show absence of bugs.

A. Lal and S. Tonetta (Eds.): VSTTE 2022, LNCS 13800, pp. 92–110, 2023.
https://doi.org/10.1007/978-3-031-25803-9_6

In this work, we develop an automated approach for proving invariants about the persistent state of concurrent *bounded* (loop-free) NVM programs, which explores the whole state-space induced by both concurrency and persistency. We employ symbolic model checking: we encode the program, its semantics, and its specification as a logical formula that is satisfiable if and only if the program is incorrect, and use an SMT (Satisfiability Modulo Theories) solver to check for its satisfiability.

The main challenge is to find a suitable encoding so that satisfiability of the constructed formula can be checked in a reasonable amount of time. This is by no means easy because straightforward encodings of the program's semantics generate large formulas (typically, cubic in the size of the program) and checking satisfiability is an NP-hard problem. It is therefore important to optimize the translation because even a small increase in the formula size can quickly lead to an intractable satisfiability problem.

To do so, we first have to choose an appropriate persistency semantics to base our verification upon. Existing semantic models are either operational in terms of a machine with multiple buffers [23,24] or multiple views of the shared state [3], or declarative/axiomatic in terms of a set of constraints over a graph representing a single program execution (e.g., [14,24,25]). We choose the declarative DPTSO$_{syn}$ model [14] for the x86 architecture because it can easily be encoded into propositional logic and is much more suitable for automated verification. Still, however, there are three important challenges that we need to overcome.

First, a large part of the program's state space is typically irrelevant for the specifications we want to prove (invariants about the persisted state). For instance, we do not care whether a write has persisted unless the invariant depends upon the value written by that write. To overcome this challenge, we adopt the idea of a *recovery observer* of Kokologiannakis et al. [15] from stateless model checking setting and model the invariants as an additional thread that reads the relevant memory locations.

Second, DPTSO$_{syn}$, along with the other recent x86 persistency models, places constraints on *partial* program execution graphs (i.e., up until a program crash). Directly encoding these partial graphs (e.g., by introducing variables describing whether each event belongs to the executed prefix of the program) generates a huge state space, which may slow down satisfiability checking. As an alternative, we develop an equivalent reformulation of DPTSO$_{syn}$ on full execution graphs, which leads to a smaller state space without noticeably affecting verification time.

Third, there are a number of places in the DPTSO$_{syn}$ definition containing sequential compositions of relations or where the acyclicity of a relation is checked. A direct encoding of these in propositional logic leads to a formula cubic in the size of the program. While acyclicity can be more effectively encoded using theory of *integer difference logic* (IDL), this is not the case for general sequential compositions of relations. Our solution here is to employ *abstraction refinement* (SCAR) [27,28], i.e., to avoid encoding the constraints related to the memory model in the initial formula and to add clauses on demand to rule out spurious counterexamples. As shown by He et al. [11], SCAR can nicely be integrated with the DPLL(T) framework of SMT solvers as a custom *theory solver*. He et al. [11] address the case of sequential consistency, whose definition contains only one instance of sequential composition. Here, we extend this approach to the weak consistency/persistency x86 model, which contains several instances of sequential composition, and which requires further care to handle TSO program order relaxations and the semantics of cache-line flush operations.

Putting all of this together, we have developed a prototype tool for verifying invariants about the persistent state of C programs against the DPTSO$_{syn}$ memory model. Our tool uses Z3 [19] for solving SMT queries and, following SCAR, implements parts of the encoding natively as a custom theory solver on top of Z3. We have used our tool on a collection of persistency benchmarks and were able to find or prove absence of persistency bugs.

Outline. We start by reviewing the x86 model (Sect. 2). We then give an overview of our approach (Sect. 3) and present our adaptation of DPTSO$_{syn}$ over full execution graphs (Sect. 4). We then discuss the encoding of the program and its semantics as a logical formula (Sect. 5), and our implementation of the theory solver (Sect. 6). We evaluate our tool on a set of benchmarks (Sect. 7), discuss related work (Sect. 8), and conclude (Sect. 9).

2   Preliminaries

In this section, we review the terminology of axiomatic memory models and their extensions to capture the persistency semantics of x86.

2.1   Axiomatic Memory Consistency Models

Axiomatic memory models define the semantics of a program as a set of execution graphs that satisfy a certain consistency predicate. The nodes of these graphs are called *events* and represent the execution of a single memory access or a fence. Formally, an event $e \in$ Event is a tuple of the form $\langle i, t, lab \rangle$, where $i \in \mathbb{N}$ is the unique *event identifier*, $t \in$ Tid is the *thread identifier* of the executing thread, and *lab* is the *event label*. The event label can be one of the following types:

- a *read* label, $R(l, v_R)$, accessing location $l \in$ Loc and reading value $v_R \in$ Val;
- a *write* label, $W(l, v_W)$, writing value $v_W \in$ Val to location $l \in$ Loc;
- a *read-modify-write* (RMW) label $U(l, v_R, v_W)$, updating the value of location l from v_R to v_W;
- a *failed compare-and-swap* (CAS) label $Rex(l, v_R)$, which reads the value v_R at location l, or
- a *memory fence* label MF.

When applicable, the functions tid, loc, val_R, and val_W project the thread identifier, the location (l), the value read (v_R), and the value written (v_W) of an event, respectively. For each type of label, we define the corresponding set of events; the set of read events (R), all write events (W), etc. Let $RU \triangleq R \cup U \cup Rex$ and $WU \triangleq W \cup U$.

An execution graph G also comprises a number of relations on its events, representing the orders in which these events were executed and/or persisted.

Definition 1. *An execution graph G is a tuple $\langle E, I, po, rf, co \rangle$, where:*

- E *is a set of* events.
- $I \subseteq E$ *is a set of* initialization *events, comprising a single write event $w \in W_l$, for each location l.*
- $po \subset E \times E$ *is the* program order, *which totally orders the events of each thread, and the initialization events before all other events: $I \times (E \setminus I) \subseteq po$.*
- $rf \subseteq (E \cap WU) \times (E \cap RU)$ *is the* reads-from *relation, relating events of the same location with matching values, i.e., $\langle a, b \rangle \in rf$ implies that $loc(a) = loc(b)$ and $val_W(a) = val_R(b)$. Additionally, rf matches every read or read-modify-write to exactly on write or read-modify-write.*
- $co \subseteq (E \cap WU) \times (E \cap WU)$ *is the* coherence order, *defined as the disjoint union of relations $\{co_l\}_{l \in Loc}$, where each co_l is a strict total order on $E \cap WU_l$.*

As an example of an execution graph, in Fig. 1 we can see the only execution graph of the program P.

In the sequel, we often call execution graphs simply executions or graphs.

We define the inverse of a relation X, as $X^{-1} \triangleq \{\langle b, a \rangle \mid \langle a, b \rangle \in X\}$. We divide relations into their same-thread (internal) and different thread (external) parts, suffixed i and e respectively. For example, we write rf_i for the relation $rf \cap (po \cup po^{-1})$, and co_e for the relation $co \setminus (po \cup po^{-1})$. Additionally, given a set of events A, we write $[A]$ for the identity relation $\{\langle x, x \rangle \mid x \in A\}$. Given two relations p, q on A, we write $p; q$ for their composition. Finally, we write $rng(p)$ for the codomain of a relation p.

Each memory model defines its own consistency predicate that imposes a number of additional constraints on execution graphs. For example, *sequential consistency* (SC) [16] requires that $po \cup rf \cup co \cup fr$ be acyclic, where $fr \triangleq (rf^{-1}; co) \setminus [E]$ is the *from-reads* relation, ordering a read event r before a write event that is co-later that the write event that r reads-from.

The x86 memory model defines the *preserved program order* $ppo \triangleq po \setminus (W \times R)$ as the largest subset of po that avoids ordering writes with respect to po-later reads. The x86 consistency predicate requires that: 1. $(rf\_i \cup co\_i \cup fr\_i) \subseteq po$, and 2. the *ordered-before* relation $ob \triangleq (ppo \cup rf\_e \cup co\_e \cup fr\_e)^+$ be irreflexive.

2.2 Modeling the Persistency Semantics of x86

To write programs with useful persistency behaviors, we introduce two types of *flush* instructions (flush and flush$_{opt}$), which operate on a given cache line, and the *store fence* instruction, which waits for preceding flush instructions to complete. Accordingly, event labels are extended to also include:

- a *flush* label FL(l) for the cache line containing location l,
- a *flush-opt* label FO(l) for the cache line containing location l, and
- a *store fence* label SF.

To simplify the presentation, we will henceforth elide the handling of flush-opt instructions, and following [14], we assume cache lines contain a single location. Our results extend straightforwardly to cover flush-opt instructions and larger cache lines.

The persistency semantics of x86 is modeled by an additional constraint that describes the values of each location that can be observed after a crash. The precise definition of this constraint is where the various x86 persistency models in the literature differ.

The original persistent x86 model (Px86) [24] designates a subset of the execution's events—which includes the write events—as durable, and keeps track in execution graphs of the *non-volatile-order*, nvo, a total order on the durable events reflecting the order that they persisted. We note that nvo contains information which is frequently irrelevant for verification, as only the last (nvo-maximal) write to each location that persisted in each location is important.

Two additional models, Px86$_{\text{view}}$ [3] and PTSO$_{\text{syn}}$ [14], have been developed for the persistent x86 architecture, both equivalent to the Px86 model in the absence of I/O instructions. Their respective declarative models, Px86$_{\text{axiom}}$ and DPTSO$_{\text{syn}}$[1], avoid the use of the nvo total order, and are defined similarly, with the main difference being that Px86$_{\text{axiom}}$ tracks an additional non-derived relation, thus making it less attractive for model checking. The recent PEx86 model [22], which extends Px86 to account for non-temporal writes and Intel-x86 memory types, also uses this relation to define an execution's consistency.

An important difference in DPTSO$_{\text{syn}}$ is that execution graphs of a program now also include *partial* executions, i.e., executions that crashed before they fully executed. For example, the program P in Fig. 1 contains four executions, depending on which of the instructions were executed before the crash, if any.

DPTSO$_{\text{syn}}$ captures the notion of the recovered write after a crash using a *memory assignment* μ, with $\mu \in \text{Loc} \to (\text{E} \cap \text{WU})$, that maps each location l to the last persisted event of that location. The definition of the execution graph is extended accordingly to include the memory assignment.

To determine an execution's consistency, DPTSO$_{\text{syn}}$ defines the *derived TSO propagation order* dtpo, and extends ob to also include dtpo, i.e.,

$$\text{ob} \triangleq (\text{ppo} \cup \text{rf\_e} \cup \text{co\_e} \cup \text{fr\_e} \cup \text{dtpo})^+$$

The ppo relation is also redefined to reflect the additional allowed reorderings introduced by the new instructions. For example, flush instructions can be reordered w.r.t. to later load instructions.

---

[1] Khyzha et al. [14] actually present two versions of DPTSO$_{\text{syn}}$. Throughout this paper we use the second version, which uses the coherence order to define consistency.

The dtpo orders a flush event before all the write events in the same location that did not persist, i.e., they are co-after the write event that was recovered after the crash. Intuitively, since the flush events are synchronous, every such write must have happened after the flush, otherwise it should have also persisted.

As an example, consider again the program P in Fig. 1 where all the variables are zero-initialized, and assume that after recovery the variable d contains the initial value, while f reads the value one. Then, dtpo would order the flush instruction before the ppo-earlier write instruction to d, leading to an ob loop, which renders the execution inconsistent.

$$\text{dtpo} \triangleq \bigcup_{x \in \text{Loc}} [\text{FL}_x] \times rng(\mu; \text{co}; [\text{WU}_x])$$

3   Overview

Programs that use NVM do not differ from regular volatile-memory programs in the way they access the memory. Programmers, however, have some expectations about the persistent state of their programs, e.g., that some data structure will be in a consistent state even if the program crashes mid-execution.

We formalize such expectations as *persistency invariants*, i.e., assertions which must hold at any post-crash state of the program. We illustrate with the following example. The program in Sect. 3 writes some data to the variable d, flushes the cache-line of d, and finally sets the flag f. The programmer's intention is that after a crash, if the flag f is observed to be set then the write to d will also be observed. This can be made explicit by annotating the program with the persistency invariant $f \Rightarrow d$.

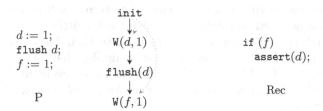

Fig. 1. A program P and its execution graph, along with its recovery routine Rec

3.1   Modeling Recovered Values

It is convenient to think of a persistency invariant as a special routine that runs after the program crashes and checks for any violation of the property of interest. We assume the that such recovery routines do not contain any write instructions. The recovery routine for our previous example is depicted in Fig. 1. Following Kokologiannakis et al. [15], since a crash can occur at any point during the execution of a program, one can model the recovery routine as an additional thread running in parallel to the code, which is subject to somewhat different constraints regarding the possible values it can read.

To encode those constraints, we extend the set of event labels (Sect. 2.1) to include recovery read labels, $\texttt{Rec}(l, v_R)$, which correspond to the read instructions of the recovery routine. We also rewrite the definition of dtpo so that it does not require the memory assignment μ, instead recovering it from the writes that the recovery reads read from. To this end, recall that dtpo orders the flush events on a location x before the writes that happened co-after the last persisted write of x, which are exactly the events in $rng([\texttt{Rec}_x]; \texttt{rf}^{-1}; \texttt{co})$. By introducing a new relation *flush-before* (fb) which orders every flush event with the recovery reads on the same location, we can rewrite dtpo simply as $\texttt{fb}; \texttt{fr}$.

3.2 Symbolic Verification

Symbolic verification requires to construct a logical formula Φ that captures the program, its semantics, and its specification. Here we provide a high-level overview of the construction of Φ leaving the details for Sect. 5 and Sect. 6.

Representing Execution Graphs. To represent the set of possible execution graphs in Φ, we associate with each instruction of the program an event in the execution graph, and introduce variables denoting the various relations between events of the graph. So, for example, for each pair $\langle w, r \rangle$ of a write event w and a read event r, we introduce the variable $rf_{w,r}$ which is set whenever r reads from w.

Since, however, it is possible that not all instructions of the program will be executed, for each instruction n, we associate a formula $\texttt{enabled}(n)$ representing whether the instruction was actually executed, i.e., the control flow reached it. For memory access instructions, we also associate terms such as $\texttt{loc}(n)$ containing the location accessed and $\texttt{val}(n)$ the value read/written.

These variables and terms allow us to express their intended meaning as a number of basic constraints stating, for example, that $rf_{w,r}$ implies that $\texttt{loc}(w) = \texttt{loc}(r)$ and $\texttt{val}(w) = \texttt{val}(r)$, that each read event reads from some write event, and that $\texttt{co}_l$ is a total order for each location l. The exact constraints are shown in Sect. 5.2.

Execution Graph Consistency. Apart from these basic axioms, we also need to encode the specific consistency predicate of the memory model, which is typically an acyclicity constraint on a set of relations including rf, co, and **fr**. Prior work identified that the cubic encoding stemming from the relation composition needed for **fr** dominates the resulting formula [27,28], and proposed *abstraction refinement* to circumvent it [11,27,28].

We adapt the approach of He et al. [11], avoiding completely the encoding of the consistency predicate and delegating consistency checking of the explored execution graph to a custom theory solver, which judges the satisfiability of assignment to the variables concerning the memory model (e.g., *rf* and *co*). We discuss the details of our theory solver for DPTSO$_{\mathrm{syn}}$ in Sect. 6.

Modeling Crashes. The final issue we must address is how to encode the notion of a crash, i.e., the possibility that some instructions were not executed because the program terminated prematurely. This is necessary because the semantics of programs under DPTSO$_{\mathrm{syn}}$ (and similarly in other models) is defined w.r.t. partial execution graphs.

For example, consider the program P in Fig. 1, and a recovery routine that asserts that the value recovered for d is 1. The approach outlined so far would deem this program safe because it would only consider the full execution where the write to d is followed by a flush.

The straightforward approach is to lift our encoding of `enabled`, so that it reflects not only whether control flow reached the corresponding instruction, but also whether the program did not crash until that point. To do so, we need to include one additional boolean variable for each node, capturing whether execution crashed just before the execution of the instruction. We discuss this approach further in Sect. 5.

To partially alleviate the need for these additional variables, we present in Sect. 4 an adaptation of the DPTSO$_{\mathrm{syn}}$ semantics which defines consistent executions only in terms of full execution graphs. We discuss in Sect. 5 the modifications needed in the encoding to support our adaptation.

4   Adapting the DPTSO$_{\mathrm{syn}}$ Model

In this section, we reformulate DPTSO$_{\mathrm{syn}}$ in terms of full execution graphs and show that our reformulated model, DPTSO$_{\mathrm{syn,full}}$, is equivalent to DPTSO$_{\mathrm{syn}}$.

To define DPTSO$_{\mathrm{syn,full}}$, we first have to adapt the definition of `dtpo` concerning the synchronous nature of the execution of flush operations. We can no longer simply assume that all flush operations have executed before any write that was not persisted, because the crash may well have happened much before those flushes. Instead, only on the flushes that are *observed* to have been executed should be ordered before any non-persisted writes. Such flushes are those in the `porf`-prefix of a write that has been observed after the crash, where `porf` $\triangleq$ (po $\cup$ rf)$^+$. Formally, this is:

$$\mathrm{dtpo} \triangleq \bigcup_{x \in \mathsf{Loc}} dom([\mathrm{FL}_x]; \mathrm{porf}; \mu^{-1}) \times rng(\mu; \mathrm{co}; [\mathrm{WU}_x])$$

We illustrate our argument using the example in Fig. 1. The program consists of two write instructions to different locations, separated by a flush instruction to the first location. Under DPTSO$_{\mathrm{syn}}$, it is not consistent to recover the value 1 for f and the initial value for d, since the flush event is `dtpo`-before the `ppo`-later write, thus creating an `ob` cycle. However, it is also not consistent to recover the initial value for d, regardless of the recovered value for f, for the same reason.

If we interpret a graph as any possible execution prefix that resulted from a crash, we would want to still disallow the former behavior, while allowing the latter. Indeed, both executions that crash before the flush instruction permit the behavior in question.

Intuitively, the only reason to rule out these executions is if we can *observe* that the flush instruction indeed happened, i.e., it is in the porf-prefix of a write that was recovered after the crash, and thus the corresponding instruction was executed. This is the case if we recover the write to f after the crash. In this scenario, the flush has executed, and is thus included in dtpo, resulting in a ob cycle.

We next establish the equivalence between the two models with the following two lemmas.

Lemma 1. *If a partial execution G generated by a program P is consistent under* $DPTSO_{syn}$, *then there is a full execution G' generated by P that extends G and is consistent under* $DPTSO_{syn,full}$.

Proof Sketch. We generate G' by repeatedly adding events to G following the program in a way that respects po, and making each event *coherence-maximal* at the point it was added. A write event is coherence-maximal if it is the co-latest event, and a read event is coherence-maximal if it reads from the coherence-maximal write. Observe that this construction avoids adding any edge towards the events of G, as well as any *dtpo* edge that starts from the new events, which leads to G' being $DPTSO_{syn,full}$-consistent. □

Lemma 2. *If a full execution G' generated by a program P is consistent under* $DPTSO_{syn,full}$, *then there is a porf-prefix of G' that is $DPTSO_{syn}$-consistent.*

Proof Sketch. Take $G \triangleq G'|_{dom(porf;\mu^{-1})}$ to be the porf-prefix of the recovered events of G'. Observe that G is $DPTSO_{syn,full}$-consistent and that $DPTSO_{syn}$ and $DPTSO_{syn,full}$ only differ in the definition of dtpo, which, by construction of G, gives rise to the same relation. Therefore G is also $DPTSO_{syn}$-consistent, as required. □

5 Symbolic Encoding

5.1 From Verification to Formula Satisfiability

Following the standard conventions in bounded model checking, we assume that programs are loop-free and in *static single assignment* form (SSA) [4], whereby each variable is assigned to only once. Conversion to such format is possible by bounding the loop iteration depth and standard compiler code transformations (e.g., introducing fresh variable names for each assignment to a variable). From this form, a logical formula Φ_{SSA} is generated, which represents the data and control flow. For shared read memory accesses, the value that is read is left unspecified and is restricted by a formula Φ_{MM} that captures the memory model's semantics. Lastly, the program's specification is encoded in a formula

Φ_{SPEC}, which indicates the violation of some property. The program is deemed safe if $\Phi \triangleq \Phi_{SSA} \wedge \Phi_{MM} \wedge \Phi_{SPEC}$ is unsatisfiable, which can be checked by an SMT solver. Existing techniques differ on how Φ_{MM} is encoded.

5.2 Memory Model Encoding

Along with the SSA form, an *event graph* is constructed, with each node corresponding to a memory event. As discussed in Sect. 3, each node n is associated with formulas $\mathtt{loc}(N), \mathtt{val}(n)$, and $\mathtt{enabled}(n)$. A node also contains an event label, specifying the type of the instruction it corresponds to.

As an example, consider the program *Rec* in Fig. 1. The event graph will contain two events r_f and r_d, for the load instructions to f and d, respectively. The Φ_{SPEC} component of the formula Φ that corresponds to *Rec* is $\mathtt{enabled}(d) \wedge \mathtt{val}(d) = 0$, where $\mathtt{enabled}(d) \triangleq \mathtt{enabled}(f) \wedge \mathtt{val}(f) \neq 0$ and $\mathtt{enabled}(f) \triangleq true$. Both $\mathtt{val}(f) \triangleq u_f$ and $\mathtt{val}(d) \triangleq u_d$ are left unspecified, and will be restricted by Φ_{MM}.

Following He et al. [11], we encode directly into propositional logic only some basic axioms about the memory model (e.g., that every read reads from some write), whose size is at most quadratic in the size of the program.

Specifically, we introduce one boolean variable $rf_{w,r}$ for each pair of write event w and read event r denoting the presence of a rf-edge from w to r, and one boolean variable $co_{w,w'}$ for each pair of write events denoting the presence of a co-edge from w to w'.

Given a read event r and a pair w, w' of write events, we encode the following basic axioms:

$$\mathtt{enabled}(r) \implies \bigvee_{w \in \mathsf{W}} rf_{w,r}$$

$$rf_{w,r} \implies \mathtt{enabled}(w) \wedge \mathtt{enabled}(r) \wedge \mathtt{valw}(w) = \mathtt{valr}(r) \wedge \mathtt{loc}(w) = \mathtt{loc}(r)$$

$$co_{w,w'} \vee co_{w',w} \iff \mathtt{enabled}(w) \wedge \mathtt{enabled}(w') \wedge \mathtt{loc}(w) = \mathtt{loc}(w')$$

The first two axioms state that every enabled read reads from some write, which is also enabled and acts on the same location. The third axiom captures the totality of co for same-location writes.

Note that we do not encode the functionality of rf—that a read cannot read from two different writes—because this constraint does not affect the consistency of a plain execution graph (an rf relation violating functionality can be modified to one satisfying it by removing rf edges).

As an optimization, for events that we can statically determine that they do not access the same location, we avoid introducing new variables and encoding the corresponding constraints.

5.3 Encoding x86 Consistency

To capture the reordering semantics of x86, we also have to add some additional variables that correspond to the ppo edges, instead of relying on the statically predetermined po edges. To this end, for each pair $\langle x, y \rangle$ of ppo-related events, we add a boolean variable $ppo_{x,y}$, and require this variable to be set only when both x and y are enabled.

As an optimization, we avoid encoding the transitive closure of ppo, i.e., we avoid introducing a new variable $ppo_{x,y}$ if it can be derived from a pair of variables $ppo_{x,z}$ and $ppo_{z,y}$.

5.4   Encoding DPTSO$_{syn}$

Finally, to fully encode DPTSO$_{syn}$ we need to account for 1. the additional dtpo edges 2. the fact that, due to a possible crash, a prefix of the program could have been executed.

As discussed in Sect. 3, dtpo can be rewritten as fb; **fr**, where fb is a relation ordering every flush event f on a location x to all the recovery read events r on the same location (Rec$_x$). Thus it suffices to add a new boolean variable $fb_{f,r}$ for each such pair of events, and capture the intended meaning with the following constraint:

$$fb_{f,r} = \texttt{enabled}(f) \wedge \texttt{enabled}(r) \wedge \texttt{loc}(f) = \texttt{loc}(r)$$

A straightforward way to encode the notion of a crash, is to further add a new boolean variable $crash_n$, for each node n of the event graph, reflecting the fact that execution crashed just before the execution of the corresponding memory access. Encapsulating this inside the $\texttt{enabled}(n)$ formula of each node, so that it now signifies that control flow reached the memory accessing instruction without crashing, gives us a full encoding for DPTSO$_{syn}$ without the need of any additional change.

5.5   Alternative Crash Encoding

Alternatively, we can employ our adaptation (DPTSO$_{syn,full}$) of DPTSO$_{syn}$ to partially circumvent the need for these additional *crash* variables.

DPTSO$_{syn,full}$ defines the semantics of x86 programs in terms of full execution graphs, and changes the definition of dtpo to achieve this. Following the same reasoning as in Sect. 3, it is easy to see that dtpo can again be rewritten as fb; **fr**. Now, however, only the flush events that are in the **porf**-prefix of a recovery read event take part in fb.

To capture this, we again introduce a boolean variable *crash* for each flush event f and modify the *fb* constraint to:

$$fb_{f,r} = \texttt{enabled}(f) \wedge \texttt{enabled}(r) \wedge \texttt{loc}(f) = \texttt{loc}(r) \wedge \neg crash_f$$

The intended meaning is that if an enabled node f has its $crash_f$ variable set to true, it is was not executed due to a crash, and thus it cannot be **porf**-before a recovery read event. This is checked and enforced by our custom theory solver (Sect. 6).

6 Theory Solver for DPTSO$_{syn}$

6.1 Preliminaries

Given a formula involving atoms from some first-order theories, DPLL(T) [9] extends DPLL [5,6] by replacing each atom with a new boolean variable, creating its *boolean abstraction*, whose satisfiability is determined by the SAT core of the solver. In case a model is produced, i.e., the boolean abstraction is satisfiable, the theory solvers should be consulted to judge whether the model is also satisfiable in the background theories.

This procedure can also take place *online*, with the theory solvers checking the consistency of *partial* assignments as they are being explored by the SAT solver. In case an inconsistency in detected, a *conflict clause* is generated that captures the inconsistency. The conflict clause is *propagated* to the SAT solver, which initiates a *backjump*, reverting the last N assignments. The conflict clause prevents the same assignment from being explored, and additionally providing some knowledge of the background theory to the SAT solver. The latter is also supported independently of an inconsistency's existence, i.e., the theory solver can propagate additional clauses to assist the SAT solver's exploration.

6.2 Z3 User Propagator

We base our implementation of the theory solver on Z3's user propagator infrastructure, which allows implementing a custom theory solver externally without the need to modify the Z3 codebase.

The user propagator allows the client of Z3's library to track some of its boolean variables, and register a callback that is initiated each time a value is assigned to one of them. The callback's implementation can respond by propagating a logical consequence, whose antecedent is a subset of the set variables, and the consequent is an arbitrary boolean expression. In case the consequent is *false*, the negation of the antecedent corresponds to the conflict clause.

The user propagator's interface provides two additional callbacks to inform the solver about (1) *backtracking* points, and (2) initiation of a backtrack, so that the theory solver reverts all assignments up to the last backtracking point.

6.3 Implementation

Given the event graph (Sect. 2.1) of the program together with its (static) po edges, our theory solver is responsible for judging the satisfiability of the assignments to the rf, co, fb, and $crash$ variables, which corresponds to the consistency of the execution graph that is being explored by the SAT solver.

To detect violations of DPTSO$_{syn}$ consistency, it needs to check for 1. rf_i, co_i, or fr_i edges that contradict po, and 2. cycles consisting of ppo, rf_e, co_e, fr_e, and fb edges. We note that fr edges are derived from their constituent edges ($\text{fr} \triangleq \text{rf}^{-1}; \text{co}$).

Our adaptation DPTSO$_{syn,full}$ additionally requires detecting paths of po and rf edges, which start from a flush event f with $crash_f$ set to true, and end in a recovery read event.

Detecting Inconsistent Assignments. The non-trivial violations (i.e., excluding (rf_i ∪ co_i ∪ fr_i) $\not\subseteq$ po) require an algorithm to detect a cycle or a certain path in the event graph.

These algorithms need to be incremental, in order to quickly rule out inconsistent assignments, and amendable for efficient backtracking, i.e., to revert a suffix of their operations without the need to store a huge amount of state.

To incrementally detect **ob** cycles we use the incremental cycle detection (ICD) on sparse graphs of Bender et al. [2], following He et al. [11]. As noted by the authors, the correctness of the algorithm is preserved in a decremental setting, without the need to revert the changes in the computed order.

To incrementally detect porf paths, we use Italiano [12]'s incremental transitive closure algorithm (Italiano-ITC) on the po and rf edges of the graph, together with the optimizations suggested by Frigioni et al. [8]. Finally, extending the algorithm to support backtracking is trivial, as we only need to revert the value of the matrix's elements to false.

Clearly, the theory for DPTSO$_{syn,full}$ (and DPTSO$_{syn}$) is decidable; the satisfiability of an assignment reduces to the two aforementioned problems.

Explaining Inconsistencies. Apart from detecting inconsistencies, our theory solver needs to succinctly explain them to the SAT core, by generating a conflict clause. To achieve this, we associate each edge with its *reason*, the conjunction of atoms that justify the edge's existence. For the rf, co, fb, and ppo edges, this is just the corresponding atom, set by the SAT core during the construction of model. For **fr**, it is the conjunction of the reasons of the constituent edges. We lift the notion of reasons to paths, defining the reason of a path as the conjunction of the reasons of each constituent edge.

When an **ob** cycle is detected, during the addition of an edge $e = \langle x, y \rangle$, we find the path p from the node y to node x that contains the fewest edges assigned with a reason, i.e., all apart from the static ppo edges, and propagate to the SAT core the contradiction: $reason(p) \wedge reason(e) \implies false$.

Similarly, when a **porf** path p is detected that originates from a node x, whose crash variable $crash_x$ is set to true, and ends in a recovery read r, we propagate to the SAT core that $reason(p) \wedge crash_x \implies false$.

7 Evaluation

In this section, we evaluate the overall performance of an implementation of our approach and compare our two different encodings of the x86 semantics.

To evaluate our approach, we have implemented a prototype verification tool for C programs that use NVM memory. Our tool uses LLVM/clang to transform the input program into SSA form, generates a formula as described in Sect. 5, and calls a version of Z3 [19] containing our custom theory solver to check its satisfiability. If the generated formula is satisfiable, an appropriate error message is reported back to the user.

As benchmarks, we took three recent *durably linearizable* [13] libraries from the literature: the read-write register library of Wei et al. [26] (FLIT), the persistent queue of Friedman et al. [7], and the persistent set of Zuriel et al. [29]. For each library, we constructed several multithreaded client programs that call the various methods of the libraries, In each of these benchmarks, we wrote down a persistency invariant that checks (consequences of) durable linearizability: e.g., if a certain method has been executed, then its effects have persisted. A typical invariant for a program that performs an enqueue operation followed by a write instruction might say that if the write is observed, then the enqueue operation is observed as well.

This way we obtain a set of *safe* benchmarks, i.e., whose invariants hold. Removing some of the flush operations gives us a set of *unsafe* benchmarks, where the invariants are violated.

Experimental Setup. Our experiments are conducted on a Dell OptiPlex 7050 system, running Debian 11, with an Intel(R) Core(TM) i5-6600 CPU and 16 GB of RAM. We used version 4.8.17 of z3.

7.1 Overall Performance

We first evaluate the overall performance of our tool using the $DPTSO_{syn}$ encoding. For this purpose, we consider only the safe benchmarks, which are presented in Table 1. For each benchmark, along with the verification time (in seconds), we report the number of nodes in the event graph, to indicate the size of the benchmark. The name represents the client itself; for example, e3+3dw is a client that uses the queue library, and consists of one thread performing three enqeue operations, and three threads performing a dequeue operation, followed by a write.

The benchmarks are small client programs of persistent libraries with up to 4 threads, each invoking a couple of library operations. The library methods vary in complexity, Flit is the simplest, with each method containing at most 4 memory accesses, while the set library is the most complex, as it can be observed by the large number of nodes even when there are only two executing threads, which is the reason that our tool scales much worse for the client using it. As it can be seen, our tool succeeds in verifying these medium-sized clients, with running time ranging from under 1 s to a bit over 7 min.

We note that we do not compare against any existing tools because, to our knowledge, none is complete for (bounded) NVM programs. While YAT [17] and JAARU [10] can find bugs in NVM programs, they are both incomplete and may miss behaviors arising in multi-threaded programs.

Table 1. Safe benchmarks: flit, queue, set (DPTSO$_{syn}$)

	Time	Nodes
dw	0.35	70
e+d	1.46	145
ee+dw	1.65	205
e+e	3.07	157
ee+d	3.98	213
e+de	6.63	222
ee+ddw	8.54	272
ee+dd	10.99	269
e+e+d	18.16	213
e2+2dw	34.38	332
e+e+d+d	36.70	269
e+e+e	48.88	225
ee+ddw+d	59.62	328
e+de+e	60.94	281
e+de+e+d	227.13	337
e3+3dw	427.54	459

	Time	Nodes
ldld	0.28	29
ww	0.28	24
u+u-w	0.29	33
w+w-w	0.29	30
w+rw-w	0.30	33
u+u+u+u-w	0.39	47
2uu+uu-w	0.46	60
3uu	0.50	53
uu+uu	0.50	39
2uu+2uu-w2	0.87	75
4uu	2.08	67
2uu+2uu-w	2.39	74

	Time	Nodes
iw	10.78	287
i	11.87	286
irw	34.13	471
ir	37.42	469
iw+rw	64.70	472
i+crw	89.31	488
i+i-w	260.89	524
i+i	416.12	505
ii+r	1151.50	688

7.2 Comparison of DPTSO$_{syn}$ and DPTSO$_{syn,full}$ Encodings

We next evaluate the two encodings we proposed to incorporate the notion of crash. The first encoding is based on DPTSO$_{syn}$ and represents partial graphs using an auxiliary `enabled` variable for each program node (Sect. 5). The second encoding is based on DPTSO$_{syn,full}$ (Sect. 4) and partially avoids the need of encoding the possible crashed executions of a program.

Our results are presented in Fig. 2 as a scatter diagram comparing the verification time (in seconds) of each benchmark with the two different encodings. We have also categorized our benchmarks depending on the verification result, i.e., whether the assertion holds (safe) or does not hold (unsafe).

As we observe in Fig. 2, the two encodings yield similar performance, with the relative difference never exceeding an order of magnitude. Sadly, there is no clear trend suggesting that either encoding leads to better performance. In principle, DPTSO$_{syn,full}$ partially eliminates the need for encoding the semantics of a crash, adding only some crash variables for flush events. However, by not fully encoding this, the solver always has to explore a full execution, even though a part of it is irrelevant. In contrast, while the DPTSO$_{syn}$ encoding leads to a larger state space, only the events before the crash take part in the axioms that concern the memory model, and so the basic axioms of Sect. 5.2 are trivially satisfied for crashed events.

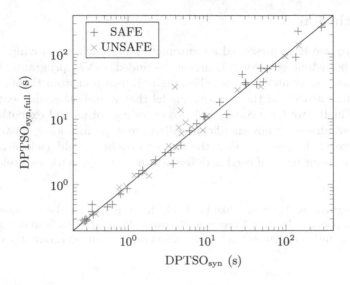

Fig. 2. Comparing the encoding of DPTSO$_{syn}$ and DPTSO$_{syn,full}$

8 Related Work

Several researchers have formalized the persistency semantics of the x86 architecture as an extension of the original x86-TSO memory consistency model [21]. The first such model, Px86 [24], treats flush operations as asynchronous. This is corrected in later models by Khyzha et al. [14] and Cho et al. [3], who treat flush operation as synchronous. More recently, [22] extended those formalizations to cover additional features of the Intel-x86 architecture, such as non-temporal writes and memory types.

There are many verification approaches that deal with multi-threaded programs under various memory consistency models. Among the symbolic techniques, Alglave et al. [1] model program executions as a collection of partial orders and encode acyclicity constraints using integer difference logic. YOGAR-CBMC [27,28] employs abstraction refinement to verify multi-threaded programs under sequential consistency, and weak memory models, accordingly. He et al. [11] propose a new ordering consistency theory for dealing with the concurrency related fragment of the encoding, and a theory solver that incrementally checks for consistency of the explored executions.

In contrast, there is much less work on model checking programs that use persistent memory. We are aware of two such works. YAT [17] eagerly explores post-crash states by injecting crashes in a collected trace, while JAARU [10] explores only the subset of pre-crash states that is relevant in the post-crash execution. Nevertheless, both approaches are not complete for multi-threaded programs since they do not explore the concurrency-induced nondeterminism.

9   Conclusion

In this paper, we have presented an automated approach for proving invariants about the persistent state of concurrent (bounded) NVM programs. Our approach is based on symbolic model checking and uses a custom theory solver to encode certain aspects of the memory model that would otherwise lead to huge formulas. Finally, we have considered two encodings of partial executions without, however, observing any significant difference in performance between them. It may, however, be the case that the two approaches would yield a noticeable difference in performance if used in different contexts, e.g., with a stateless model checker.

Acknowledgments. We would like to thank the reviewers for their comments. This work was supported by the European Research Council (ERC) under the European Union's Horizon 2020 research and innovation programme (grant agreement No. 101003349).

References

1. Alglave, J., Kroening, D., Tautschnig, M.: Partial orders for efficient bounded model checking of concurrent software. In: Sharygina, N., Veith, H. (eds.) CAV 2013. LNCS, vol. 8044, pp. 141–157. Springer, Heidelberg (2013). https://doi.org/10.1007/978-3-642-39799-8_9
2. Bender, M.A., Fineman, J.T., Gilbert, S., Tarjan, R.E.: A new approach to incremental cycle detection and related problems. ACM Trans. Algorithms **12**(2) (2015). https://doi.org/10.1145/2756553. ISSN 1549-6325
3. Cho, K., Lee, S.-H., Raad, A., Kang, J.: Revamping hardware persistency models: view-based and axiomatic persistency models for Intel-X86 and Armv8. In: Proceedings of the 42nd ACM SIGPLAN International Conference on Programming Language Design and Implementation, PLDI 2021. Virtual, Canada, pp. 16–31. Association for Computing Machinery (2021). https://doi.org/10.1145/3453483.3454027. ISBN 9781450383912
4. Cytron, R., Ferrante, J., Rosen, B.K., Wegman, M.N., Kenneth Zadeck, F.: Efficiently computing static single assignment form and the control dependence graph. ACM Trans. Program. Lang. Syst. **13**(4), 451–490 (1991). https://doi.org/10.1145/115372.115320. ISSN 0164-0925
5. Davis, M., Logemann, G., Loveland, D.: A machine program for theorem-proving. Commun. ACM **5**(7), 394–397 (1962). https://doi.org/10.1145/368273.368557. ISSN 0001-0782
6. Davis, M., Putnam, H.: A computing procedure for quantification theory. J. ACM **7**(3), 201–215 (1960). https://doi.org/10.1145/321033.321034. ISSN 0004-5411
7. Friedman, M., Herlihy, M., Marathe, V., Petrank, E.: A persistent lock-free queue for non-volatile memory. In: Proceedings of the 23rd ACM SIGPLAN Symposium on Principles and Practice of Parallel Programming, PPoPP 2018, Vienna, Austria, pp. 28–40. Association for Computing Machinery (2018). https://doi.org/10.1145/3178487.3178490. ISBN 9781450349826
8. Frigioni, D., Miller, T., Nanni, U., Zaroliagis, C.: An experimental study of dynamic algorithms for transitive closure. ACM J. Exp. Algorithmics **6**, 9-es (2002). https://doi.org/10.1145/945394.945403. ISSN 1084-6654

9. Ganzinger, H., Hagen, G., Nieuwenhuis, R., Oliveras, A., Tinelli, C.: DPLL(T): fast decision procedures. In: Alur, R., Peled, D.A. (eds.) CAV 2004. LNCS, vol. 3114, pp. 175–188. Springer, Heidelberg (2004). https://doi.org/10.1007/978-3-540-27813-9_14 ISBN 978-3-540-27813-9

10. Gorjiara, H., Xu, G.H., Demsky, B.: Jaaru: efficiently model checking persistent memory programs. In: Proceedings of the 26th ACM International Conference on Architectural Support for Programming Languages and Operating Systems, pp. 415–428. Association for Computing Machinery, New York (2021). https://doi.org/10.1145/3445814.3446735. ISBN 9781450383172

11. He, F., Sun, Z., Fan, H.: Satisfiability modulo ordering consistency theory for multi-threaded program verification. In: Proceedings of the 42nd CM SIGPLAN International Conference on Programming Language Design and Implementation, PLDI 2021. Virtual, Canada, pp. 1264–1279. Association for Computing Machinery (2021). https://doi.org/10.1145/3453483.3454108. ISBN 9781450383912

12. Italiano, G.F.: Amortized efficiency of a path retrieval data structure. Theor. Comput. Sci. **48**(2-3), 273–281 (1987). ISSN 0304-3975

13. Izraelevitz, J., Mendes, H., Scott, M.L.: Linearizability of persistent memory objects under a full-system-crash failure model. In: Gavoille, C., Ilcinkas, D. (eds.) DISC 2016. LNCS, vol. 9888, pp. 313–327. Springer, Heidelberg (2016). https://doi.org/10.1007/978-3-662-53426-7_23 ISBN 978-3-662-53425-0

14. Khyzha, A., Lahav, O.: Taming X86-TSO persistency. Proc. ACM Program. Lang. **5**(POPL) (2021). https://doi.org/10.1145/3434328

15. Kokologiannakis, M., Kaysin, I., Raad, A., Vafeiadis, V.: PerSeVerE: persistency semantics for verification under ext4. Proc. ACM Program. Lang. **5**(POPL) (2021). https://doi.org/10.1145/3434324

16. Lamport, L.: How to make a multiprocessor computer that correctly executes multiprocess programs. IEEE Trans. Computers **28**(9), 690–691 (1979). https://doi.org/10.1109/TC.1979.1675439

17. Lantz, P., Dulloor, S., Kumar, S., Sankaran, R., Jackson, J.: Yat: a validation framework for persistent memory software. In: Proceedings of the 2014 USENIX Conference on USENIX Annual Technical Conference, USENIX ATC 2014, pp. 433–438. USENIX Association, Philadelphia (2014). ISBN 9781931971102

18. Liu, S., Wei, Y., Zhao, J., Kolli, A., Khan, S.M.: PMTest: a fast and flexible testing framework for persistent memory programs. In: Bahar, I., Herlihy, M., Witchel, E., Lebeck, A.R. (eds.) ASPLOS 2019, pp. 411–425. ACM (2019). https://doi.org/10.1145/3297858.3304015

19. de Moura, L., Bjørner, N.: Z3: an efficient SMT solver. In: Ramakrishnan, C.R., Rehof, J. (eds.) TACAS 2008. LNCS, vol. 4963, pp. 337–340. Springer, Heidelberg (2008). https://doi.org/10.1007/978-3-540-78800-3_24 ISBN 978-3-540-78800-3

20. Oukid, I., Booss, D., Lespinasse, A., Lehner, W.: On testing persistent-memory-based software. In: DaMoN 2016. ACM (2016). https://doi.org/10.1145/2933349.2933354. ISBN 9781450343190

21. Owens, S., Sarkar, S., Sewell, P.: A better x86 memory model: x86-TSO. In: Berghofer, S., Nipkow, T., Urban, C., Wenzel, M. (eds.) TPHOLs 2009. LNCS, vol. 5674, pp. 391–407. Springer, Heidelberg (2009). https://doi.org/10.1007/978-3-642-03359-9_27 ISBN 978-3-642-03358-2

22. Raad, A., Maranget, L., Vafeiadis, V.: Extending Intel-X86 consistency and persistency: formalising the semantics of Intel-X86 memory types and non-temporal stores. Proc. ACM Program. Lang. **6**(POPL) (2022). https://doi.org/10.1145/3498683

23. Raad, A., Vafeiadis, V.: Persistence semantics for weak memory: integrating epoch persistency with the TSO memory model. Proc. ACM Program. Lang. **2**(OOPSLA) (2018). https://doi.org/10.1145/3276507

24. Raad, A., Wickerson, J., Neiger, G., Vafeiadis, V.: Persistency semantics of the Intel-x86 architecture. Proc. ACM Program. Lang. **4**(POPL), 11:1–11:31 (2019). https://doi.org/10.1145/3371079. Accessed 17 June 2020

25. Raad, A., Wickerson, J., Vafeiadis, V.: Weak persistency semantics from the ground up. Proc. ACM Program. Lang. **3**(OOPSLA), 135:1–135:27 (2019). https://doi.org/10.1145/3360561. Accessed 07 Feb 2020

26. Wei, Y., Ben-David, N., Friedman, M., Blelloch, G.E., Petrank, E.: FliT: a library for simple and efficient persistent algorithms. CoRR abs/2108.04202 (2021). arXiv:2108.04202

27. Yin, L., Dong, W., Liu, W., Wang, J.: Scheduling constraint based abstraction refinement for multi-threaded program verification. IEEE Trans. Softw. Eng. (2017). https://doi.org/10.1109/TSE.2018.2864122

28. Yin, L., Dong, W., Liu, W., Wang, J.: Scheduling constraint based abstraction refinement for weak memory models. In: Proceedings of the 33rd ACM/IEEE International Conference on Automated Software Engineering, pp. 645–655. Association for Computing Machinery, New York (2018). https://doi.org/10.1145/3238147.3238223. ISBN 9781450359375

29. Zuriel, Y., Friedman, M., Sheffi, G., Cohen, N., Petrank, E.: Efficient lock-free durable sets. Proc. ACM Program. Lang. **3**(OOPSLA) (2019). https://doi.org/10.1145/3360554

A Formal Semantics for P-Code

Nico Naus[1]([⊠])([iD]), Freek Verbeek[1,2]([iD]), Dale Walker[1], and Binoy Ravindran[1]([iD])

[1] Virginia Tech, Blacksburg, USA
{niconaus,freek,dalewalker,binoy}@vt.edu
[2] Open University of The Netherlands, Heerlen, The Netherlands

Abstract. Decompilation is currently a widely used tool in reverse engineering and exploit detection in binaries. Ghidra, developed by the National Security Agency, is one of the most popular decompilers. It decompiles binaries to high P-Code, from which the final decompilation output in C code is generated. Ghidra allows users to work with P-Code, so users can analyze the intermediate representation directly. Several projects make use of this to build tools that perform verification, decompilation, taint analysis and emulation, to name a few. P-Code lacks a formal semantics, and its documentation is limited. It has a notoriously subtle semantics, which makes it hard to do any sort of analysis on P-Code. We show that P-Code, as-is, cannot be given an executable semantics. In this paper, we augment P-Code and define a complete, executable, formal semantics for it. This is done by looking at the documentation and the decompilation results of binaries with known source code. The development of a formal P-Code semantics uncovered several issues in Ghidra, P-Code, and the documentation. We show that these issues affect projects that rely on Ghidra and P-Code. We evaluate the executability of our semantics by building a P-Code interpreter that directly uses our semantics. Our work uncovered several issues in Ghidra and allows Ghidra users to better leverage P-Code.

Keywords: Decompilation · P-Code · Formal semantics

1 Introduction

After more than 60 years of research, the field of decompilation is currently very mature. A plethora of open source and commercial decompilation tools exist [1,7,11–13]. They are widely used to recover source code from binaries and to detect software vulnerabilities.

Ghidra[1] is one of those tools, developed by the National Security Agency (NSA), and made public and open source a few years ago. Recent comparative studies show that it ranks among the top performing decompilers [5]. At the heart of Ghidra lies P-Code, an intermediate representation that exists at two levels of abstraction. The first is a direct one-to-many translation of the disassembled assembly instructions, called low P-Code. The second is high P-Code,

---

[1] https://ghidra-sre.org/.

© The Author(s) 2023
A. Lal and S. Tonetta (Eds.): VSTTE 2022, LNCS 13800, pp. 111–128, 2023.
https://doi.org/10.1007/978-3-031-25803-9_7

which is the result of various transformations on the low P-Code from Ghidra's decompiler. Since we focus our work on high P-Code, we will simply refer to it as P-Code from now on.

From the P-Code, Ghidra constructs C code, which is the final decompilation result. Users can define their own analyses over high P-Code, customizing the decompilation process or extracting information from it. We have come across several projects that perform a wide range of analyses on P-Code. Verification [6], decompilation [14] and taint analysis [2], to name a few. However, the P-Code documentation is very limited and P-Code lacks any form of formal semantics. On top of that, P-Code has a notoriously subtle semantics, as will become clear in the rest of this paper. This limits the usability of P-Code for formal analysis, since there is no way to know if the analysis that is being performed is correct with respect to the language semantics.

In this paper, we develop a formal semantics for high P-Code. We base our work on Ghidra 10.1.4 released May 2022, which comes with P-Code documentation last updated September 5th, 2019 [9]. Ghidra does come with a P-Code interpreter, but only for low P-Code. This means that there is no ground-truth that we can base our high P-Code semantics on. We therefore start our investigation by looking at the P-Code documentation. Since this is rather limited, we additionally run experiments for P-Code instructions that are unclear. These experiments consist of compiling several C programs to binary, decompiling them using Ghidra, and comparing the high P-Code and decompiled C code to the original source code. During the development of a formal P-Code semantics, we uncover several issues in Ghidra, P-Code and the P-Code documentation. These issues all stem from inconsistencies in documentation, Ghidra's output via UI or API, and in some cases the inability to formulate executable P-Code semantics. As-is, P-Code cannot be given an executable semantics. To overcome the shortcomings of P-Code, we extend the language with additional information. For the extended P-Code semantics, we define a formal operational semantics. We argue that projects relying on P-Code are directly affected by these issues, and could benefit from a formal P-Code semantics. Since there is no interpreter for high P-Code available, we are only able to validate our semantics by writing an interpreter for high P-Code to show that our semantics are executable. We have shared our results with the NSA prior to publication, and they acknowledge all issues identified in this paper.

More specifically, we make the following contributions:

- An extended P-Code language.
- A formal syntax and semantics for extended P-Code.
- A P-Code interpreter written in Haskell.
- An overview of several bugs, issues and inconsistencies in Ghidra, P-Code and documentation.

The P-Code interpreter written in Haskell and the accompanying Ghidra script written in Java are publicly available[2].

---

[2] https://github.com/niconaus/pcode-interpreter
https://github.com/niconaus/PCode-Dump.

Section 2 first gives an introduction to Ghidra, its assembly translator SLEIGH and low & high P-Code. Section 3 describes and motivates our design choices. Section 4 describes the P-Code syntax and Sect. 5 gives its semantics. We list an overview of the bugs, issues and inconsistencies we have found, and a response from the NSA on these, in Sect. 6. Section 7 presents related work and Sect. 8 concludes.

2   Ghidra, SLEIGH and P-Code

Ghidra is an open-source reverse engineering tool, developed by the National Security Agency. It is capable of decompiling binaries of a wide variety of architectures. To do so, it first disassembles the binary using its custom disassembler SLEIGH, and performs several analysis steps. The end result is high-level C code, as well as detailed control flow information. A recent study compared other well known decompilers like IDA-pro [7] and Angr [13] to Ghidra, by evaluating 1760 binaries, using the correctly identified function starts (CFS) metric [5]. They found that Ghidra performs above average.

Address	x86-64	low P-Code	high P-Code
0x100000e70	push rbp	$Uea00:8 = RBP	$Ud100:1 = EDI s< 3:4
		RSP = RSP - 8:8	if $Ud100:1 goto 0x100000e95:1
		*RSP = $Uea00:8	
0x100000e71	mov rbp, rsp	RBP = RSP	
0x100000e74	mov dword ptr [rbp - 8], edi	$U3100:8 = RBP + -8:8	
		$Ubf00:4 = EDI	
		*$U3100:8 = $Ubf00:4	
0x100000e77	cmp dword ptr [rbp - 8], 2	$U3100:8 = RBP + -8:8	
		$Ubf80:4 = *$U3100:8	
		CF = $Ubf80:4 s< 2:4	
		$Ubf80:4 = *$U3100:8	
		OF = sborrow($Ubf80:4, 2:4)	
		$Ubf80:4 = *$U3100:8	
		$U29000:4 = $Ubf80:4 - 2:4	
		SF = $U29000:4 s< 0:4	
		ZF = $U29000:4 == 0:4	
		$U12e80:4 = $U29000:4 & 0xff:4	
		$U12f00:1 = popcount($U12e80:4)	
		$U12f80:1 = $U12f00:1 & 1:1	
		PF = $U12f80:1 == 0:1	
0x100000e7b	jle 20 < _isPrime+0x25>	$Ud000:1 = OF != SF	
		$Ud100:1 = ZF || $Ud000:1	
		if $Ud100:1 goto 0x100000e95:8	

Fig. 1. First few instructions in the decompilation of nearest prime

To illustrate the Ghidra decompilation pipeline, we take a look at the first few instructions of an x86-64 binary. Figure 1 lists the decompilation result for the first few addresses of our example binary. For readability's sake, we have harmonized notation, and simplified in- and output notation. Address 0x100000e70 is the entry point of a function. Ghidra's machine code translator SLEIGH takes the x86-64 assembly instructions as listed in the second column in Intel syntax, and translates them to low P-Code, listed in the third column. The exact meaning of the P-Code instructions will be left for the coming sections, and is not essential to understand at this point. As for notation, the $U prefix indicates local variables. Registers are identified by their name, and are assumed to have a fixed size. Addresses are given in a hexadecimal format, prefixed by

0x. Constants are given either as a decimal or hexadecimal prefixed by 0x. Both addresses and constants have a size indicated by the number after the colon.

P-Code is considered low before decompilation, and is merely a one-to-many translation from assembly instructions to P-Code. The instruction set of P-Code is much smaller than x86, and SLEIGH basically breaks up a complicated assembly instruction into simple P-Code ones. For example, the x86 compare instruction at address 0x100000e77 breaks down into 13 separate P-Code instructions. To break down the instructions, P-Code uses local variables. The x86 `push rbp` instruction at address 0x100000e70 for example, is broken down into three simple assignments, using the variable $Uea00:8 to hold the original value of RBP temporarily, until it has been stored in memory.

After disassembly and translation, Ghidra performs several decompilation analyses. This results in high P-Code, listed in the third column, which uses an instruction set almost identical to low P-Code. The analyses Ghidra performs, remove all instructions that have no effect on execution, resolves the stack and constructs a control flow graph, among other things. A more detailed description of Ghidra's decompilation analyses can be found in other literature [4]. From the high P-Code, Ghidra constructs the final decompilation result in C code.

By example, we have shown how the basic Ghidra pipeline operates. Users can inspect the final decompilation result, but there also exists a plethora of scripts that can be run to further analyse the final or intermediate P-Code result. It is also possible to define custom scripts, through Ghidra's extensive API [10]. Since these analyses can target high P-Code directly, it is important to have a correct semantics for it.

3 Design Choices

As mentioned in Sect. 1, P-Code documentation is limited. On top of that, P-Code as-is cannot be given a formal semantics, because crucial information is not included. To arrive at an executable P-Code semantics, we had to make the following design choices.

Conditional Branches. We observed that the P-Code generated for conditional branches is often incorrect. Three different situations occur. One, the conditional branch is correct. Two, the conditional branch incorrectly jumps to the fall-through address in the True case. Three, the conditional branch should jump to a different address than the fall-through in the False case. The control flow API always returned the correct out addresses in our experiments. We use this fact later on when we build our interpreter.

Phi-nodes. P-Code has a MULTIEQUAL instruction, which is better known as a phi-node in literature [3]. A phi-node's value depends on the address of the previous block that was executed. In other SSA languages using phi-nodes, like LLVM IR [8], every alternative value is guarded by an address, which is compared to the address of the previous block. You compare the address to the alternatives in the phi-node, to know which value will be selected. This is not the case in P-Code. Here, only the alternative values are listed. Looking at the documentation, no additional information is provided about the ordering of the alternatives.

To determine which alternative belongs to which control flow, we have ran several experiments. From these experiments, we know that the order of the alternatives coincides with the inbound edge ordering when requesting these though Ghidra's control flow API.

Varnodes. Inputs and outputs are encoded by the so called varnodes. They represent the arguments and destination of the instructions. The P-Code manual states that varnodes are either a register or a memory location, and that they consist of three components: address space, offset and size.

We use a slightly different view of varnodes, and regard the "address space" as a varnode type. We have come across six different types, and they consist of two components: a value and a size. Of those six, we can bring it down to four essential types of varnodes.

$(\mathbf{R}\, r, l)$ register, identified by a register address r and size l.

$(\mathbf{A}\, a, l)$ memory, with a the starting address and l the size of the memory region.

$(\mathbf{C}\, c, l)$ constant value, with c the value and l the size.

(v, l) local variable, with v the identifier and l its size.

In the case where P-Code models a Harvard architecture binary instead of the more common von Neumann architecture, the memory varnode is split up into a data varnode and a code varnode, to model the dedicated addresses in this architecture.

$(\mathbf{A_C}\, a, l)$ memory containing code, with a the starting address and l the size of the memory region.

$(\mathbf{A_D}\, a, l)$ memory containing data, with a the starting address and l the size of the memory region.

The register notation differs from the previous P-Code example, as listed in Fig. 1. Instead of listing register names, an address in the register space is used, together with a size. Using register addresses and sizes has the advantage that we do not explicitly have to take care of register aliasing.

Call & Return. For the CALL instruction, P-Code documentation lists:

"This instruction is semantically equivalent to the BRANCH instruction. (...) The P-Code instruction does not implement the full semantics of the call itself; it only implements the final branch."

Looking at P-Code programs, it is immediately clear that this cannot be true. A function can have arguments and return a value, and this behavior is certainly not captured by a basic BRANCH instruction. What is more, not all varnode address spaces will be in scope when dispatching a function call. Local variables are cleared when a new function context is entered. Arguments are passed through the registers, and these registers are cleaned up when P-Code returns from a call. How this is done exactly depends on the calling convention that the original binary relies on, more on this later.

For the indirect call and return, documentation lists a similar description. They are both said to be equivalent to BRANCHIND. For indirect call, this is false, for the reasons described above. For return, we see that this cannot hold for two reasons. One, in high P-Code, a return instruction can hold a return value that is to be the result of calling the function. Furthermore, no address to return to is included in the instruction; we do not have a branch destination.

Fall-through. The P-Code outputted by Ghidra performs fall-through in a non-uniform way. Looking at the P-Code output for several decompiled binaries, there is no pattern to be found in the way fall-through is performed. The most natural way to perform fall-through is to let control flow jump to the next block listed in the output, but this is not always true. It can occur that control flow jumps to a later or earlier block instead. The addresses of those blocks are not logical either. In some cases, the address of the fall-through block is higher than the current block, in some cases it is lower. We therefore do away with fall-through all-together, instead requiring that every block ends in a branching instruction.

User defined instructions. P-Code allows the use of the so called "USERDE-FINED" instruction. The goal of this instruction is to capture very complicated behavior that cannot be described in terms of existing P-Code instructions. Since the semantics are user-provided, we consider this instruction to be out of scope for this paper.

Indirect instruction. One final tricky aspect of P-Code is the use of the indirect instruction. We will denote an indirect instruction as $out = in_0 \hookleftarrow in_1$. The intuition of this instruction is that the value of in_0 should be assigned to out, but may be influenced indirectly by an instruction elsewhere, which is described by in_1. If there was an indirect influence, this means that potentially any value may be assigned to out. This can happen for example when calling external functions, so there is no way of knowing what the value will be.

4   P-Code Syntax

This section lists the syntax of P-Code programs. We base the syntax on the notation used in the P-Code documentation. P-Code features some instructions that do not have a defined syntax. For those instructions, we have taken the liberty of choosing an appropriate representation ourselves. On top of that, there are several minor changes that we needed to make, in accordance with the design choices from Sect. 3.

Figures 2 and 3 lists our P-Code syntax and P-Code operators. We model a program as a mapping from addresses a to code blocks b.

Inputs and outputs are modeled by four different varnodes. Registers, memory, constants and variables. For registers, addresses are used instead of names. To give an example, (0x18,8), (0x18,4) and (0x19,1) refer to RBX, EBX and BH respectively.

Program

$p ::= a \mapsto b$ Mapping from address to block

Block

$b ::= i; b \mid t$ Sequence, terminator

Instruction

$i ::= \text{out} = (o \mid s) \mid s$ Assignment, call

$\quad \mid \ast\,\text{out} = \text{in} \mid \text{out} = \ast\,\text{in}$ Store, load

$\quad \mid \text{out} = \mathbf{zext}(\text{in}) \mid \text{out} = \mathbf{sext}(\text{in})$ Zero-extend, sign-extend

$\quad \mid \text{out} = \mathbf{float2float}\,\text{in}$ Float size conversion

$\quad \mid \text{out} = \mathbf{trunc}(\text{in})$ Float truncation

$s ::= \mathbf{call}\,[\text{in}_0]\,\text{in}_1 \ldots \text{in}_n$ (Indirect) function call

Operation

$o ::= \text{in} \mid \text{in}\,((c,s)) \mid \ominus\,\text{in} \mid \text{in}_0 \oplus \text{in}_1$ Copy, subpiece, Unary, binary operation

$\quad \mid \phi(a_0, \text{in}_0) \ldots (a_n, \text{in}_n) \mid \text{in}_0 \hookleftarrow \text{in}_1$ Phi node (multiequal), indirect

$\quad \mid \text{in}_0 +_p \text{in}_1 \times_p \text{in}_2 \mid \text{in}_0 +_p \text{in}_1$ Pointer calculation, simple pointer calc

$\quad \mid \text{out}((c_0, l_0), (c_1, l_0)) = \text{in}$ Bit insert

$\quad \mid \text{out} = \text{in}((c_0, l_0), (c_1, l_0))$ Bit extract

Terminator

$t ::= \mathbf{goto}\,\text{in} \mid \mathbf{if}\,\text{in}_0\,\mathbf{goto}\,\text{in}_1\,\mathbf{else}\,\text{in}_2$ (In)direct branch, conditional branch

$\quad \mid \mathbf{return}\,[\text{in}_0]\,\text{in}_1$ Function return

Varnode

$\text{in}, \text{out} ::= (\text{R}\,r, l) \mid (\text{A}\,a, l) \mid (\text{C}\,c, l) \mid (v, l)$ Register, ram, constant, variable

$a, r, c, l \in \mathbb{N}$ Address, register, constant, length

$v \quad \in \text{set of names}$

Fig. 2. P-Code language syntax definition

A P-Code block must be non-empty, can have zero or more instructions i, and must end in a terminator instruction t. This does not adhere to documentation or Ghidra produced P-Code, but is required to correct the fall-through issues that occur, as mentioned in Sect. 3. We distinguish between regular instructions and terminator instructions, to make it easier to construct a semantics later on.

Instructions i are either basic operations on data, that are assigned to an output, or a function call that may or may not return some value. The instruction $\text{out} = (o \mid s)$ represents basic operations o that are assigned to the output out, or a function call s with a return value. In some cases, the data operation depends on the size of the output, like sign-extend. These instructions are added at this level for that reason.

A function call is denoted by $\mathbf{call}\,[\text{in}_0]\,\text{in}_1 \ldots \text{in}_n$, where in_0 is either a constant, for direct calls, or a register, memory location or variable, which indicates that this is an indirect function call. This notation is identical to the P-Code documentation, but differs from the P-Code that Ghidra produces. Instead, Ghidra explicitly differentiates between direct and indirect function calls using different instructions, and uses a memory-varnode in the case of a direct function call, instead of a constant value.

Operators

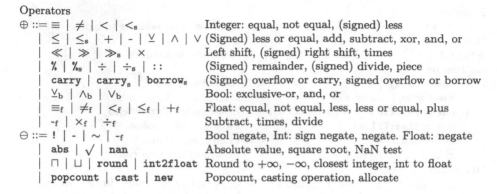

Fig. 3. P-Code language operator syntax definition

Basic operations o are all data operations that are independent of the output. Most of them are straight forward binary or unary operations. We will discuss two non-standard operations.

The P-Code documentation does not list a syntax for the phi-node, so we have chosen one ourselves. We enhance the phi-node to include the address that guards the value alternative.

Indirect ($in_0 \hookleftarrow in_1$) is the second non-standard operation. This instruction indicates that either the value of in_0 will be returned, or the value is unknown, because an instruction pointed to by in_1 has altered it. A typical use case of this is when an external function is called with a pointer.

Finally, we have terminator instructions. These instructions are not singled out by the P-Code documentation, but as mentioned, by separating them, constructing a semantics becomes easier.

The conditional branch is an interesting case. We have seen that Ghidra does not produces consistent P-Code for this instruction. To work around this issue, we replaced the conditional branch instruction with our own, so we can later use the Ghidra API to get a hold of the correct addresses, and explicitly state both the true and false branch. This works since conditional branches are terminators and can thus only appear at the end of a block.

Lastly, the return instruction. This instruction includes an offset, and may hold a value to be returned. Looking at large pieces of P-Code, we found that the offset is not actually used in performing the return. For completeness sake we include this parameter in the syntax, but we will not give it any semantics. The same is true for the **cast** and **new** unary operators, these are merely placeholders to indicate that a value has been cast or new memory has been allocated. This information can then be used by subsequent analyses.

For space reasons, we omit a description of all basic operations, as well as unary and binary operators.

5   P-Code Semantics

This section presents a big-step semantics for P-Code. As described in the previous sections, defining a semantics for P-Code is not trivial. Based on our experiments and observations so far, we assume that the following holds for programs written in P-Code.

Local variables do not overlap. We assume that local variables do not overlap in the local variable address space. In other words, local variables occupy separate memory locations. This property of P-Code has been verified by decompiling large binaries and checking that no variables overlap.

No global variables. We assume that all declared variables are local. Strictly speaking, the P-Code documentation does not prohibit an address space that serves as global variables, but after running several experiments, this behaviour has not been observed. Programs can and do have global variables, but they are confined to memory and registers.

Call and Branch on constant. We assume that direct calls and direct branches are encoded by having a constant varnode as an argument. In all other cases, the call and branch will be interpreted as indirect.

Terminators only at block's end. We assume that terminator instructions like branch and return only occur at the end of a block. This assumption already shows up in the syntax listed in the previous section, but for completeness sake, we reiterate this fact here.

$$\sigma = (\mathcal{M}, \mathcal{R}, \mathcal{V}) \qquad \text{State, containing the address of the previous block,}$$
$$\text{the current block, memory, registers and variables}$$
$$\mathcal{M} = (\mathrm{A}\,a, l) \mapsto (\mathrm{C}\,c, l) \;\; \text{Memory}$$
$$\mathcal{R} = (\mathrm{R}\,r, l) \mapsto (\mathrm{C}\,c, l) \;\; \text{Register mapping}$$
$$\mathcal{V} = v \mapsto (\mathrm{C}\,c, l) \qquad \text{Variable mapping}$$

Fig. 4. Semantic objects

Figure 4 lists the semantic objects needed for evaluation; state, memory, registers and variable mapping. The memory mapping $\mathcal{M}$ takes an address a and size l and returns a constant varnode $(\mathrm{C}c, l)$. The register mapping $\mathcal{R}$ takes a register address r and a size l and returns a constant varnode $(\mathrm{C}c, l)$. Just a register identifier is not sufficient, since registers can alias. Three special registers are used to keep track of function return value, the address of the previous block and the address of the current block. These registers are denoted by "Ret", "Prev" and "Cur", assuming that a varnode representation that is separate from registers used by the program exists. Variable mapping $\mathcal{V}$ takes a variable identifier v and returns a constant varnode $(\mathrm{C}c, l)$. Figures 7 through 11 list the rules for the different semantic judgements we use. These rules use two auxiliary judgements, namely the evaluation of varnodes and state update, listed in Fig. 5 and 6 respectively.

$$\text{V-MEM } (\mathcal{M}, \mathcal{R}, \mathcal{V}), (A\,a, l) \downarrow \mathcal{M}[(A\,a, l)] \quad \text{V-REG } (\mathcal{M}, \mathcal{R}, \mathcal{V}), (R\,r, l) \downarrow \mathcal{R}[(R\,r, l)]$$

$$\text{V-CONST } \sigma, (C\,c, l) \downarrow (C\,c, l) \quad \text{V-UNIQUE } (\mathcal{M}, \mathcal{R}, \mathcal{V}), (v, l) \downarrow (\mathcal{V}[v], l)$$

Fig. 5. Evaluation of varnodes to values

$$\text{U-REG} \quad \frac{(\mathcal{M}, \mathcal{R}, \mathcal{V}), (x, l_2) \downarrow \text{val} \qquad l_1 \equiv l_2 \qquad \mathcal{R}' = \mathcal{R}[(R\,r, l_1) \mapsto \text{val}]}{(\mathcal{M}, \mathcal{R}, \mathcal{V}), (R\,r, l_1), (x, l_2) \uparrow (\mathcal{M}, \mathcal{R}', \mathcal{V})}$$

$$\text{U-MEM} \quad \frac{(\mathcal{M}, \mathcal{R}, \mathcal{V}), (x, l_2) \downarrow \text{val} \qquad l_1 \equiv l_2 \qquad \mathcal{M}' = \mathcal{M}[(A\,a, l_1) \mapsto \text{val}]}{(\mathcal{M}, \mathcal{R}, \mathcal{V}), (A\,a, l_1), (x, l_2) \uparrow (\mathcal{M}', \mathcal{R}, \mathcal{V})}$$

$$\text{U-VAR} \quad \frac{(\mathcal{M}, \mathcal{R}, \mathcal{V}), (x, l_2) \downarrow \text{val} \qquad l_1 \equiv l_2}{(\mathcal{M}, \mathcal{R}, \mathcal{V}), (v, l_1), (x, l_2) \uparrow (\mathcal{M}, \mathcal{R}, \mathcal{V}[v \mapsto \text{val}])}$$

Fig. 6. State update semantics

Varnodes are evaluated by judgements of the form σ, in $\downarrow$ val, taking a state σ and varnode in, and returning the resulting value val, as listed in Fig. 5. The resulting value is again a varnode, of the form $(C\,c, l)$, where c is a constant and l the size. Depending on the type of the varnode, this value is retrieved from memory, register mapping or variable mapping.

Updates to memory are handled by judgements of the form σ, out, in $\uparrow \sigma'$, taking a state σ, destination out and source in, returning the updated state σ', as listed in Fig. 6. The type of the destination is used to select the correct rule, and ultimately which part of the state to update. In general, P-Code always requires that destination and source size is equal. This is ensured by the update semantics.

At the top-level, we evaluate a block using the judgement $p, \sigma, b \longrightarrow_b \sigma'$, which takes a program p, state σ and entry block b and returns a new state σ', which is the result of completely executing the program. Figure 7 lists the semantic rules for block evaluation.

B-SEQ first evaluates the instruction i, and uses the resulting state to evaluate the remainder of the block, b.

B-TERM evaluates a block ending in a terminator, using the terminator semantics.

The terminator semantics is given in Fig. 8. It uses judgements of the form $p, \sigma, t \longrightarrow_t \sigma'$, taking a program p, state σ and terminator t as input and producing a resulting state σ'.

The terminator semantics is pretty straight forward. T-BRANCH evaluates its varnode in and looks up the next block in p, and then use the block semantics to evaluate it. These rules make use of the varnode evaluation semantics $\downarrow$ listed in Fig. 5. In the case of a conditional branch, in_0 is evaluated. If the condition returns decimal 1, of any size, we go to the true-branch. All other return values are regarded as false. Branching instructions also perform some bookkeeping on what the current and previous block addresses are.

$$\text{B-Seq} \frac{p, \sigma, i \longrightarrow_i \sigma' \quad p, \sigma', b \longrightarrow_b \sigma''}{p, \sigma, i; b \longrightarrow_b \sigma''} \qquad \text{B-Term} \frac{p, \sigma, t \longrightarrow_t \sigma'}{p, \sigma, t \longrightarrow_b \sigma'}$$

Fig. 7. Block evaluation semantics

$$\text{T-CBranch-T} \frac{\begin{array}{c} (\mathcal{M}, \mathcal{R}, \mathcal{V}), \text{in}_0 \downarrow (C\,1, l_0) \\ \mathcal{R}' = \mathcal{R}[\text{Prev} \mapsto \mathcal{R}(\text{Cur}), \text{Cur} \mapsto (C\,a_1, l_1)] \\ p, (\mathcal{M}, \mathcal{R}', \mathcal{V}), p(a_1) \longrightarrow_b \sigma' \end{array}}{p, (\mathcal{M}, \mathcal{R}, \mathcal{V}), \text{if in}_0 \text{ goto } (a_1, l_1) \text{ else } (a_2, l_2) \longrightarrow_t \sigma'}$$

$$\text{T-CBranch-F} \frac{\begin{array}{c} (\mathcal{M}, \mathcal{R}, \mathcal{V}), \text{in}_0 \downarrow (C\,c, l_0) \\ c \neq 1 \quad \mathcal{R}' = \mathcal{R}[\text{Prev} \mapsto \mathcal{R}(\text{Cur}), \text{Cur} \mapsto (C\,a_2, l_2)] \\ p, (\mathcal{M}, \mathcal{R}, \mathcal{V}), p(a_2) \longrightarrow_b \sigma' \end{array}}{p, (\mathcal{M}, \mathcal{R}', \mathcal{V}), \text{if in}_0 \text{ goto } (a_1, l_1) \text{ else } (a_2, l_2) \longrightarrow_t \sigma'}$$

$$\text{T-Branch} \frac{\begin{array}{c} (\mathcal{M}, \mathcal{R}, \mathcal{V}), \text{in} \downarrow (C\,c, l) \\ \mathcal{R}' = \mathcal{R}[\text{Prev} \mapsto \mathcal{R}(\text{Cur}), \text{Cur} \mapsto (C\,c, l_1)] \\ p, (\mathcal{M}, \mathcal{R}, \mathcal{V}), p(c) \longrightarrow_b \sigma' \end{array}}{p, (\mathcal{M}, \mathcal{R}, \mathcal{V}), \text{goto in} \longrightarrow_t \sigma'} \qquad \text{T-Return} \frac{\sigma, (\text{Ret}, s), (x, s) \uparrow \sigma'}{p, \sigma, \text{return } [\text{in}](x, s) \longrightarrow_t \sigma'}$$

Fig. 8. Terminator evaluation semantics

T-Return handles a return statement. To pass the return value to the caller, we use the Ret register. Updating the state as such is taken care of by the memory update function $\uparrow$.

Figure 9 lists the partial instruction semantics. Judgements have the form $p, \sigma, i \longrightarrow_i \sigma'$, taking a program p, state σ and instruction i, and returning the resulting state σ'. For space reasons, we only list I-Assign, I-AssCall, I-Store and I-Load here.

I-Assign uses the operation semantics to evaluate o, which returns the value that should be assigned to out. The output out is updated by $\uparrow$, depending on the type of varnode that out is; memory, register or variable.

I-AssCall relies on the call semantics to perform the call, and the resulting value is again used to update out, and the final state is returned.

I-Store evaluates the destination, converts it to a varnode of type address, and updates accordingly.

I-Load evaluates the input and then treats it as a memory address, and looks up the final value in memory. The number of bytes to be retrieved from memory is dictated by the output varnode.

The calling semantics is one of the more perculiar aspects of P-Code. All arguments that are passed though registers in the original binary, are now passed

I-Assign
$$\frac{\sigma, o \longrightarrow_o \text{val} \qquad \sigma, \text{out}, \text{val} \uparrow \sigma'}{p, \sigma, \text{out} = o \longrightarrow_i \sigma'}$$

I-AssCall
$$\frac{p, \sigma, s \longrightarrow_s \sigma', \text{val} \qquad \sigma', \text{out}, \text{val} \uparrow \sigma''}{p, \sigma, \text{out} = s \longrightarrow_i \sigma''}$$

I-Store
$$\frac{\sigma, \text{out} \downarrow (C\, c, l) \qquad \sigma, (A\, c, l), \text{in} \uparrow \sigma'}{p, \sigma, *\text{out} = \text{in} \longrightarrow_i \sigma'}$$

I-Load
$$\frac{\sigma, \text{in} \downarrow (A\, a, l') \qquad \sigma, (A\, a, l) \downarrow \text{val}' \qquad \sigma, (x, l), \text{val}' \uparrow \sigma'}{p, \sigma, (x, l) = *\text{in} \longrightarrow_i \sigma'}$$

Fig. 9. Partial instruction evaluation semantics

Call-AMD64-ABI
$$\frac{\begin{array}{c}(\mathcal{M}, \mathcal{R}, \mathcal{V}), \text{in} \downarrow (C\, c, l) \qquad (\mathcal{M}, \mathcal{R}, \mathcal{V}), \text{in}_i \downarrow (C\, c_i, l_i) \\ \mathcal{R}' = \mathcal{R} \left[\begin{smallmatrix} (0x38, l_0) \mapsto (C\, c_0, l_0), (0x30, l_1) \mapsto (C\, c_1, l_1), (0x10, l_2) \mapsto (C\, c_2, l_2), (0x8, l_3) \mapsto (C\, c_3, l_3) \\ , (0x80, s_4) \mapsto (C\, c_4, l_4), (0x88, l_5) \mapsto (C\, c_5, l_5), \text{Prev} \mapsto \mathcal{R}(\text{Cur}), \text{Cur} \mapsto (C\, c, l) \end{smallmatrix} \right] \\ p, (\mathcal{M}, \mathcal{R}', \emptyset), p(c) \longrightarrow_b \mathcal{M}', \mathcal{R}'', \mathcal{V}') \\ \mathcal{R}''' = \mathcal{R}'' \left[\begin{smallmatrix} (0x38, l_0) \mapsto \mathcal{R}[(0x38, l_0)], (0x30, l_1) \mapsto \mathcal{R}[(0x30, l_1)], (0x10, l_2) \mapsto \mathcal{R}[(0x10, l_2)], (0x8, l_3) \mapsto \mathcal{R}[(0x8, l_3)] \\ , (0x80, l_4) \mapsto \mathcal{R}[(0x80, l_4)], (0x88, l_5) \mapsto \mathcal{R}[(0x88, l_5)], \text{Prev} \mapsto \mathcal{R}(\text{Prev}), \text{Cur} \mapsto \mathcal{R}(\text{Cur}) \end{smallmatrix} \right] \\ \sigma = (\mathcal{M}', \mathcal{R}''', \mathcal{V}) \end{array}}{p, (\mathcal{M}, \mathcal{R}, \mathcal{V}), \texttt{call} \ [\text{in}] \ \text{in}_0 \ \text{in}_1 \ \text{in}_2 \ \text{in}_3 \ \text{in}_4 \ \text{in}_5 \longrightarrow_s \sigma, \mathcal{R}''[\text{Return}]}$$

Fig. 10. Example of a function call evaluation rule

as function arguments in the call instruction. However, the called function does still retrieve them from registers. How this is done precicely depends on the original calling convention. Figure 10 lists an example of a call rule for a binary that uses the AMD64-ABI calling convention.

Judgements are of the form $p, \sigma, s \longrightarrow_s \sigma', \text{val}$, taking a program p, state σ, call statement s and returning the resulting state σ' and value val. In this case, a call can have at most six arguments, adhering to the specific calling convention.

The semantics completely deviates from the P-Code documentation. Section 3 discusses this issue, here we stick to a description of the semantics.

The Call-rule first resolves the address of the function to be called. As mentioned in Sect. 4, if in is a constant, we have a direct call. In all other cases, we have an indirect call, and the varnode evaluation semantics takes care of resolving the address. We evaluate all arguments to the call, which are then assigned to the appropriate registers. To execute the called function, the block semantics is used. We look up the block, and evaluate it under the current memory, the registers containing the arguments, and an empty local variable mapping $\emptyset$. Returning from the call, the local variable mapping is disregarded, registers are cleaned up, and the return value is retrieved from the registers. This value, along with the new state are then returned.

Figure 11 lists a few of the operation evaluation rules. Judgements are of the form $\sigma, o \longrightarrow_o \text{val}$, taking a state σ and operation o, returning the resulting value

$$\text{O-Copy} \; \frac{\sigma, \text{in} \downarrow \text{val}}{\sigma, \text{in} \longrightarrow_o \text{val}} \qquad \text{O-Phi} \; \frac{a_i \equiv \mathcal{R}(\text{Prev}) \qquad (\mathcal{M}, \mathcal{R}, \mathcal{V}), \text{in}_i \downarrow \text{val}}{(\mathcal{M}, \mathcal{R}, \mathcal{V}), \phi(a_1, \text{in}_1) \ldots (a_n, \text{in}_n) \longrightarrow_o \text{val}}$$

$$\text{O-Indirect-val} \; \frac{\sigma, \text{in}_0 \downarrow \text{val}}{\sigma, \text{in}_0 \hookleftarrow \text{in}_1 \longrightarrow_o \text{val}} \qquad \text{O-Indirect-ND} \; \frac{c, l \in \mathbb{N}}{\sigma, \text{in}_0 \hookleftarrow \text{in}_1 \longrightarrow_o (C\,c, l)}$$

Fig. 11. Partial operation evaluation semantics

val. For space reasons, we omit all basic operations, as well as unary and binary operations. These operations are all straight-forward and standard.

O-Copy evaluates the varnode and return its value.

O-phi evaluates the phi-node by finding the address a_i that is equal to the address of the last block. The selected input is evaluated and its value returned.

O-Indirect-val and -ND rules handle the indirect instruction. Here, we basically have two options. Either the value is unaffected, and we can return it, or the instruction pointed to by the second argument has altered the first in some way, in which case any value of any size can be returned.

The above syntax and semantics assume that the P-Code models the von Neumann architecture. Extending them to deal with Harvard architecture that has dedicated code and data memory sections is straight-forward, but omitted from the description here for space reasons.

5.1   P-Code Interpreter

To validate that the semantics above are executable, we have built a P-Code interpreter in Haskell. The source code is publicly available, and consists of a parser, type definitions and the interpreter itself[3]. Ghidra does not come with a script to dump P-Code, so we have created a script with that functionality[4]. The interpreter is intended to be used in combination with this Ghidra script, since it corrects the P-Code output of Ghidra with respect to the conditional branch, fall-through and phi-nodes.

We encountered several interesting issues in order to get to a working interpreter. First of all, we had to bridge the gap between what we think the syntax and semantics of P-Code should be, ideally, and what Ghidra actually produces for us. We assumed that both call and indirect call use the same instruction, and we merged the branch and indirect branch instruction. In the P-Code produced by Ghidra, these are all separate instructions. The direct call and direct branch use a memory varnode where we prefer to use a constant. For the MULTI-EQUAL (phi-node), conditional branch instruction and the fall-through mechanism, Ghidra's output does not contain enough information to come to an executable semantics, as described above. We augment the P-Code dumping

---

[3] https://github.com/niconaus/pcode-interpreter.
[4] https://github.com/niconaus/PCode-Dump.

script to include the additional information required. Second, we assumed several properties to hold for P-Code programs, as outlined in the beginning of this section.

Finally, it is important to note that although the semantics is executable, it is not practical to do so. Any realistic program will produce many INDIRECT instructions, which introduces non-determinism into the program. Execution of P-Code containing these instructions will therefore return many different alternative outcomes, and may be propagating unknown values, not returning a meaningful result. The point of the P-Code interpreter is merely to validate the property of our semantics that it is in fact executable. In our interpreter, we have chosen to regard INDIRECT instructions as deterministic, assuming that their value has not been changed by the indicated side-effect.

6 Changes to Ghidra and P-Code

Based on our findings, we recommend the following changes to be made to Ghidra, P-Code and its documentation.

6.1 P-Code

Currently, the phi-node, or MULTIEQUAL as P-Code calls it, is incomplete. It only contains a list of alternative values, but not the control flow address that guards it. We suggest to adopt the definition introduced in Sect. 4, which includes both the address of the previous block and the value associated.

6.2 Ghidra/SLEIGH

We recommend the following changes to be made to Ghidra and its machine code translator SLEIGH.

CBRANCH Our experiments show that Ghidra can return erroneous destinations for the CBRANCH instruction. It does have the correct information available, as we have validated by requesting the true-branch and false-branch destination via the Ghidra API instead of P-Code. It is clear that there is a bug in the way Ghidra produces P-Code. As mentioned before, one of three situations occur. The conditional branch is correct, and so is the fall-through. The conditional branch is incorrect, either the true-address or the fall-through branches to the wrong address.

Fall-through The P-Code outputted by Ghidra performs fall-through in a non-standard way in certain cases. For assembly languages, the fall-through address is the next instruction listed, or in our case, the next block listed. The P-Code that Ghidra returns sometimes breaks with this standard, and fall-through goes to the next block listed, which might have a completely different address, or in some rare cases, to a completely different block all together.

P-Code rendering The P-Code displayed in Ghidra's GUI uses a different syntax than the one given in the P-Code documentation. The low P-Code in the listing view uses the capital letters notation, where tools like the graph AST do use the regular syntax. Readability would be greatly improved if the same, preferably the regular, syntax is used.

6.3   Documentation

The P-Code documentation included with Ghidra has not been updated for several years. We suggest to make the following changes to greatly improve the quality of the documentation, both in correctness and completeness.

High and Low P-Code The P-Code Reference Manual attempts to cover both low and high P-Code with one description for each instruction, and then tagging on extra information for the high P-Code case. We recommend splitting up documentation in high and low P-Code.

Varnodes In documentation, varnodes are described as containing three elements: address space, address and size. From our experiments, we see that this view does not work in practice. Constants are also encoded as varnodes, where the address is used as a constant value instead. When performing a call (also see below), some address spaces are preserved, some are reset for the scope of the call. In this paper we have used the address space field as the type of the varnode, and this seems to be a better fit. We suggest one of two things to be done. One, this view is adopted by documentation, including a list of the different types of varnodes and how they behave in for example a function call. Or two, the CALL and RETURN instructions are updated to include address space scoping.

CALL, CALLIND, RETURN As mentioned in Sect. 3, documentation states that CALL, CALLIND and RETURN are equivalent to BRANCH, BRANCHIND and BRANCHIND respectively. From our experimental results, we see that this is not the case. Function arguments are transferred via registers, local variables are reset, a value can be returned, and after a call, register cleanup is performed and local variables restored. We don't see an issue with these instructions themselves, more with the way they are explained. This also ties in with the first point made on the difference between low and high P-Code. Call, indirect call and return behave completely different in low and high P-Code, and deserve a better documentation.

Small inconsistencies The documentation contains many small inconsistencies which should be cleared up. For example, the syntax reference introduces two different notations for SUBPIECE that are not in the P-Code Operation reference, and that we have not found in our experiments.

6.4   Response from Ghidra Developers

We have reached out to the Ghidra development team at NSA with our findings and the above recommendations. They have confirmed our findings and acknowledged all issues we found. As for the conditional branch, they refer to a GitHub issue where this problem is also identified[5]. Their stance is that although it is semantically incorrect, they do not consider this to be a bug. The destination of the conditional jump is preserved from low to high P-Code, which they deem more important than the correctness of the instruction itself.

7   Related Work

Research that makes use of Ghidra's results is scarce, due to the fact that Ghidra has only been publicly available for a few years. Below is a survey of several interesting projects that use Ghidra and P-Code to perform program analysis.

GhiHorn is an SMT based path analysis tool that uses Ghidra and P-Code [6]. Their goal is to determine if a path exists to a certain program point, and how the program should be instantiated to reach this point. Their approach relies on Ghidra's control flow API to construct flow from block to block. For the individual blocks, they use a custom made transformer from P-Code to Z3 expressions. The documentation provided is limited, and GhiHorn does not seem to deal with the more intricate details of P-Code, such as phi-nodes, indirect and the call/return mechanism. It would be interesting to see where this approach leads in the future, when the tool matures further.

A recent master thesis describes work on decompiling binaries into LLVM IR using Ghidra [14]. The binary is loaded into Ghidra, and the decompiled P-Code is then translated to LLVM IR. Although this work does not provide a semantics for P-Code, it does relate LLVM IR's semantics to that of P-Code. We've looked though the source code for this project, and compared the relational semantics to our P-Code semantics. In most cases, translation to LLVM IR seems to be a more straight-forward affair, since issues like the call/return mechanism carry over directly. One big limitation of this work is again that more difficult P-Code concepts like phi-nodes, the nondeterministic indirect instruction, floating point operations and pointer calculations are not supported. Looking at the translation for conditional branches, we see that this work is susceptible to the error that we discovered in Ghidra.

Ghidra has also been used to develop a static taint analysis [2]. The author uses external lists containing sources and sinks, and uses a taint policy that defines how a taint is introduced and propagated. Unfortunately, source code for this project is no longer available. The group is working on a new version and has pulled the code in the mean time. It would have been very interesting to see what P-Code semantics they employ.

A caveat of all of these approaches is the fact that none of them do any kind of verification or have any formal theory on their approaches. As we have seen from our experiments, the P-Code semantics is not straight-forward. Having a formal semantics has the potential to improve these and future efforts on decompilation and binary analysis.

---

[5] https://github.com/NationalSecurityAgency/ghidra/issues/2736.

8   Conclusion

We have presented a formal semantics for Ghidra's P-Code. By developing this semantics, we have uncovered several undocumented properties of P-Code, as well as some inconsistencies and one serious bug in the way that Ghidra builds the conditional branch instruction. To arrive at an executable P-Code semantics, we have made several extensions to the language. We have validated that our semantics is executable by building an interpreter for P-Code in Haskell. The semantics and issues described have been acknowledged by the NSA. We have performed a survey of binary analysis projects that leverage Ghidra and P-Code, and have seen several that are directly affected by the issues we uncovered.

Acknowledgements. We would like to thank the anonymous reviewers for their insightful comments and suggestions, which helped to greatly improve the paper.

This material is based upon work supported by the Defense Advanced Research Projects Agency (DARPA) and Naval Information Warfare Center Pacific (NIWC Pacific) under contract N6600121C4028 and Agreement No. HR.00112090028, and the US Office of Naval Research (ONR) under grant N00014-17-1-2297.

Any opinions, findings and conclusions or recommendations expressed in this material are those of the author(s) and do not necessarily reflect the views of DARPA or NIWC Pacific, or ONR.

References

1. Brumley, D., Jager, I., Avgerinos, T., Schwartz, E.J.: BAP: a binary analysis platform. In: Computer Aided Verification–23rd International Conference, CAV 2011, Snowbird, UT, USA, 14–20 July 2011. Proceedings, pp. 463–469 (2011)
2. Cole, E.: Static taint analysis of binary executables using architecture-neutral intermediate representation (2019)
3. Cytron, R., Ferrante, J., Rosen, B.K., Wegman, M.N., Zadeck, F.K.: Efficiently computing static single assignment form and the control dependence graph. ACM Trans. Program. Lang. Syst. **13**(4), 451–490 (1991)
4. Eagle, C., Nance, K.: The Ghidra Book: The Definitive Guide. No Starch Press, California (2020)
5. Shaila, S., Darki, A., Faloutsos, M., Abu-Ghazaleh, N., Sridharan, M.: Disco: combining disassemblers for improved performance. In: RAID 2021: 24th International Symposium on Research in Attacks, Intrusions and Defenses, San Sebastian, Spain, 6–8 October 2021, pp. 148–161 (2021)
6. Gennari, J.: Ghihorn: Path analysis in Ghidra using smt solvers. Carnegie Mellon University's Software Engineering Institute Blog, 18 October 2021. http://insights. sei.cmu.edu/blog/ghihorn-path-analysis-in-ghidra-using-smt-solvers/
7. Hex-Rays, S.: Ida pro disassembler (2022)
8. Lattner, C., Adve, V.S.: LLVM: a compilation framework for lifelong program analysis & transformation. In: 2nd IEEE/ACM International Symposium on Code Generation and Optimization (CGO 2004), 20–24 March 2004, San Jose, CA, USA, pp. 75–88 (2004)
9. National Security Agency: P-Code Reference Manual, September 2019
10. National Security Agency: Ghidra API help (2021)

11. PNF Software: Jeb decompiler (2022). https://www.pnfsoftware.com
12. Radare org: Radare2 (2022). https://github.com/radareorg/radare2
13. Shoshitaishvili, Y., et al.: SOK: (state of) the art of war: offensive techniques in binary analysis. In: IEEE Symposium on Security and Privacy, SP 2016, San Jose, CA, USA, 22–26 May 2016, pp. 138–157. IEEE Computer Society (2016)
14. Toor, T.: Decompilation of Binaries into LLVM IR for Automated Analysis. Master's thesis, University of Waterloo (2022)

Separating Separation Logic – Modular Verification of Red-Black Trees

Gerhard Schellhorn, Stefan Bodenmüller[✉], Martin Bitterlich,
and Wolfgang Reif

Institute for Software and Systems Engineering, University of Augsburg,
Augsburg, Germany
{schellhorn,stefan.bodenmueller,
martin.bitterlich,reif}@informatik.uni-augsburg.de

Abstract. Interactive theorem provers typically use abstract algebraic data structures to focus on algorithmic correctness. Verification of programs in real programming languages also has to deal with pointer structures, aliasing and, in the case of C, memory management. While progress has been made by using Separation Logic, direct verification of code still has to deal with both aspects at once. In this paper, we show a refinement-based approach that separates the two issues by using a suitable modular structure.

We exemplify the approach with a correctness proof for red-black trees, demonstrating that our approach can generate efficient C code that uses parent pointers and avoids recursion. The proof is split into a large part almost identical to high-level algebraic proofs and a separate small part that uses Separation Logic to verify primitive operations on pointer structures.

Keywords: Hierarchical components · Refinement · Verification · Separation logic · Efficient C code · Red-Black trees

1 Introduction

Interactive theorem provers typically use high-level algebraic data structures like lists, sets, or trees to verify the correctness of algorithms conceptually. Code generated from such algorithms is typically purely functional and often not very efficient. Side effects, aliasing, or memory allocation are absent, except when a heap with allocation and deallocation is explicitly modeled, which is rarely done when studying algorithmic correctness.

However, verification of programs in real programming languages has to deal with the fact that all non-primitive data types are represented as pointer structures, and destructive operations are often used to improve efficiency. The most popular concept to handle these issues is to use Separation Logic, which moves

Partly supported by the Deutsche Forschungsgemeinschaft (DFG), "Verifikation von Flash-Dateisystemen" (grants RE828/13-1 and RE828/13-2).

A. Lal and S. Tonetta (Eds.): VSTTE 2022, LNCS 13800, pp. 129–147, 2023.
https://doi.org/10.1007/978-3-031-25803-9_8

the specification of a heap structure into the semantics of the logic. Provers that target the verification of C, Java, or Rust programs like VeriFast [20] or Viper [26] are directly based on it. Many interactive theorem provers now support a library for Separation Logic similar to the one we give in Sect. 3.2.

However, direct verification of algorithms given e.g. in C still suffers from the complexity of conceptual correctness arguments being intertwined with questions about pointer aliasing and side effects.

This paper contributes an approach that modularizes the verification effort of a library implementation of sets by red-black trees into two independent parts: a bigger one that deals with functional correctness on an algebraic level, and a smaller part that is independent of the first and deals with mapping small operations (like removing a leaf or rotating at a path) on abstract data structures to operations on pointer structures. The approach separates the use of Separation Logic from the proof of conceptual correctness by restricting it to the latter part. It is based on components with sequential programs linked by data refinement, supported natively in our theorem prover KIV.

We have chosen red-black trees as they offer good worst-case guarantees for the operations search, insert and remove. Their verification on an algebraic level is already non-trivial. However, our goal was to verify an efficient version such that the resulting code is on par with standard C code implementations. This mandates that our final implementation uses parent-pointers and avoids recursion to be as efficient as possible. Our implementation is based on the pseudocode given in [9].

Red-black trees are also useful in the Flashix project [5], where we have implemented and verified a realistic file system for flash memory which can be used as a kernel module in Linux. There, red-black are used to balance erase counts of raw flash blocks in the wear leveling algorithm. Since verification there is also based on the concept of components connected by refinement, we could replace an unverified external C library with the verified implementation described here.

This paper is organized as follows. Section 2 introduces characteristic features of our theorem prover KIV that comprises both a specification and programming language. Section 3 presents the algebraic data types to describe a red-black tree and the explicit heap that is used to reason about pointer-based programs. Section 4 explains how a software system can be broken down into hierarchical components that refine an abstract system description to a realistic implementation.

Section 5 highlights the implementation split into a common part and elementary operations that can also be performed on a pointer structure. Section 6 follows with an overview of some key properties for verification. Section 7 presents existing approaches and draws a comparison to them.

2   Background

To develop the necessary formal specifications and prove that our implementation follows them, we use the theorem prover KIV, which provides interactive verification using a sequent calculus with explicit proof trees. The basic logic of the specification language is higher order logic (HOL), recently extended from monomorphic to polymorphic types. KIV supports an imperative programming language with recursive procedures and nondeterminism. Details on the syntax can be found in [34], Fig. 4 shows a procedure definition. The arguments of a procedure **proc**#(in; ref; out) are grouped into sequences of input, reference, and output parameters. KIV does not support global variables, these must be added explicitly as reference parameters.

Reasoning about sequential programs in KIV is done with a weakest precondition calculus, borrowing notation from Dynamic Logic (DL) [18], including its two standard modalities: the formula $[\alpha]\varphi$ (*box*) denotes that, for every terminating run of α, the final state must satisfy φ, corresponding to the weakest liberal precondition $wlp(\alpha, \varphi)$. The formula $\langle\alpha\rangle\varphi$ (*diamond*) guarantees that there is a terminating execution of α that establishes φ. Finally, the formula $\langle\!|\alpha|\!\rangle\,\varphi$ (*strong diamond*) states that all runs of α terminate with a final state satisfying φ (weakest precondition $wp(\alpha, \varphi)$). Partial and total correctness of a program α with respect to pre-/post-conditions $pre/post$ is written $pre \rightarrow [\alpha]\ post$ and $pre \rightarrow \langle\!|\alpha|\!\rangle\,post$, respectively. The calculus is more expressive than standard Hoare-like program logics since it allows to combine and nest program formulas. This allows e.g. to establish a relation between two programs, which will be useful in defining proof obligations for refinement, cf. Sect. 4.

The main proof technique for verifying program correctness in KIV is *symbolic execution*. Each symbolic execution step calculates the strongest postconditions of the first program statement from the preconditions. When the symbolic execution of the program is completed, the goal is reduced to predicate logic, where proof automation is achieved via rewrite rules and heuristics, see [34].

3   Structured Specifications of Algebraic Data Types

In KIV, structured algebraic specifications are used to build a hierarchy of data type definitions. Primitive data types may be generated freely or non-freely. Specifications can be augmented by additional functions and combined using standard structuring operations like enrichment, union, and renaming. It is also possible to specify parameterized data types that can be instantiated explicitly.

3.1   Algebraic Red Black Tree Definition

The standard approach for proving the correctness of algorithms using complex data structures is to specify the data structures algebraically. Red-black trees [17,35] can be defined as a polymorphic free data type $rbtree('a)$, using a constant constructor SENTINEL (representing the leaves of the tree) and a non-constant constructor Node.

$$rbtree('a) := \text{SENTINEL} \mid \text{Node}(.\text{elem}: \text{ } 'a\text{ };\text{ }.\text{color}: \text{ } rbcolor\text{ };$$
$$.\text{left}: rbtree('a)\text{ };\text{ }.\text{right}: rbtree('a))$$

Nodes have a color (either RED or BLACK, defined by the enumeration type $rbcolor$), a left and a right subtree, and an element of generic type $'a$. These fields can be accessed via the postfix selector functions .elem, .color, .left, and .right. A type variable $'a$ for the type of elements stored in the tree is used in the definition. So in principle, the data type can be used with any element type. However, to express the properties of binary search trees, a generic, totally ordered elements type *tord* (with $<$) is used. The resulting tree type is written *rbtree(tord)*. The specification can be instantiated later as needed by suitable types, e.g. natural numbers or integers. When such a parameter is instantiated, KIV generates proof obligations to ensure that the instantiated type satisfies the assumed properties (in this case, a total order over the type).

For a free data type specification, KIV generates all necessary axioms, as well as update functions (written e.g. $rbt.\texttt{color}:= newcol$), including their definitions. Note that selector (and update) functions are not given axioms for all arguments: SENTINEL.color is left unspecified. The semantic function in a model is still total, and SENTINEL.color may be any value, following the standard loose approach to semantics. However, KIV attaches a *domain* to the function for use in programs. Calling .color outside of its domain in a program (here: with SENTINEL, where it is "undefined") will raise an exception. Therefore, proving the correct use of the data type in programs includes showing the absence of such exceptions, i.e. one has to prove that all operations are called with arguments within their respective domain.

3.2   Modeling the Heap and Separation Logic

Reasoning about destructive pointer algorithms requires to model the heap, either implicitly as part of the semantics of formulas or explicitly as an algebraic data type. In KIV, the latter approach is realized: heaps are specified as a polymorphic non-free data type $heap('a)$. A heap can be considered a partial function mapping references r (of type $ref('a)$) to objects obj of a generic type $'a$, where allocation of references is explicit and the reference type contains a distinguished element null that is never allocated (representing the null pointer).

The $heap('a)$ data type is inductively generated by the constant $\emptyset$ representing the empty heap, allocating a new reference r (written h ++ r), or updating an allocated location r with a new object obj (written $h[r := obj]$). Again, the object type is not specified further so that the heap specification can be used with any concrete object type (for red-black trees, the type *rbnode* represents individual nodes of the tree, see Sect. 5).

A predicate $r \in h$ checks whether a reference is allocated in a heap, and a function $h[r]$ is used to lookup objects in a heap (this corresponds to dereferencing a pointer). References can also be deallocated by the function h -- r.

Similar to the selector functions of free data types, the constructor functions as well as lookup and deallocation are partial functions in order to specify valid accesses to the heap: accesses to the heap with the null reference are always undefined ($r \neq$ null), allocation is allowed with a new reference ($\neg\ r \in h$) only. Lookup, update, and deallocation require an allocated reference $r \in h$.

In KIV, all parameters of procedures are explicit. Hence, when reasoning about pointer-based programs, the heap must be an explicit parameter of the program as well. To facilitate the verification of such programs, we built a simple library for Separation Logic (SL) [32] in KIV, similar to the libraries of Isabelle [24] and Coq [8]. We give some information, to explain the notation used in the following. SL formulas are encoded using heap predicates $hP : heap('a) \to bool$. A heap predicate describes the structure of a heap h. At its simplest, h is the empty heap emp:

$$emp(h) \leftrightarrow h = \emptyset$$

The maplet $r \mapsto obj$ describes a singleton heap containing only one reference r mapping to an object obj. It is defined as a higher-order function of type $(ref('a) \times 'a) \to heap('a) \to bool$:

$$(r \mapsto obj)(h) \leftrightarrow h = (\emptyset \texttt{ ++ } r)[r := obj] \wedge r \neq \texttt{null}$$

More complex heaps can be described using the separating conjunction $hP_0 * hP_1$ asserting that the heap consists of two disjoint parts, one satisfying hP_0 and one satisfying hP_1, respectively. Since it connects two heap predicates, it is defined as a function with type $(heap('a) \to bool) \times (heap('a) \to bool) \to (heap('a) \to bool)$:

$$(hP_0 * hP_1)(h) \leftrightarrow \exists h_0, h_1.\ h_0 \perp h_1 \wedge h = h_0 \cup h_1 \wedge hP_0(h_0) \wedge hP_1(h_1)$$

Besides the basic SL definitions, the KIV library contains various abstractions of commonly used pointer data structures like singly-/doubly-linked lists or binary trees. These abstractions allow to prove the functional correctness (incl. memory safety) of algorithms on pointer structures against their algebraic counterparts. We will demonstrate this approach for a red-black tree implementation.

4   Modular Software Systems

For the development of complex software systems in KIV, we use the concept of hierarchical components combined with the contract approach to data refinement [10]. A component is an abstract data type $(ST, \texttt{Init}, (\texttt{Op}_j)_{j \in J})$ consisting of a set of states ST, a set of initial states $\texttt{Init} \subseteq ST$, and a set of operations $\texttt{Op}_j \subseteq In_j \times ST \times ST \times Out_j$. An operation $\texttt{Op}_j$ takes inputs In_i and outputs Out_j and modifies the state of the component. Operations are specified with contracts using the operational approach of ASMs [6]: for an operation $\texttt{Op}_j$, we give a precondition pre_j and a program α_j in the form of a procedure declaration $\texttt{op}_j\#(in_j; st; out_j)$ **pre** pre_j $\{\alpha_j\}$. The program α_j is given in KIV's imperative programming language and establishes the postcondition of the operation. Instead of defining initial states directly, we also give a procedure declaration $\texttt{init}\#(in_{init}; st; out_{init})$ $\{\alpha_{init}\}$.

Components are distinguished between specifications and implementations. The former are used to model the functional requirements of a (sub-)system and are typically kept as simple as possible by heavily utilizing algebraic functions and non-determinism. The approach is as general as specifying pre- and post-conditions since the program **choose** st', out' **with** $post(st', out')$ **in** $st, out := st', out'$ can be used to establish any postcondition $post$ over state st and output *out.* Implementations are typically deterministic and use constructs only that allow generating executable Scala or C code from them with our code generator.

The functional correctness of implementation components is then proven by a data refinement of the corresponding specification components (we write $C \leq A$ if $C = (ST^C, \texttt{Init}^C, (\texttt{Op}_j^C)_{j \in J})$ is a refinement of $A = (ST^A, \texttt{Init}^A, (\texttt{Op}_j^A)_{j \in J})$ where C and A have the same set of operations J). Proofs for such a refinement are done with a forward simulation $R \subseteq ST^A \times ST^C$ using commuting diagrams. This results in correctness proof obligations for all $j \in J$ (an extra obligation ensures that $\texttt{Init}^A$ and $\texttt{Init}^C$ establish matching states).

$$R(st^A, st^C) \wedge pre_j^A(st^A)$$
$$\rightarrow \langle\!| \mathbf{op}_j^C \# (in_j; st^C; out_j) |\!\rangle \langle \mathbf{op}_j^A \# (in_j; st^A; out_j') \rangle (R(st^A, st^C) \wedge out_j = out_j')$$

Note that the obligation refers to two procedure runs ($\mathbf{op}_j^C \#$ and $\mathbf{op}_j^A \#$), stringing together a *strong diamond* and a *diamond* program formula. Thus, st^A and st^C in the postcondition of the obligation refer to the changed states after the runs of $\mathbf{op}_j^A \#$ and $\mathbf{op}_j^C \#$, respectively. Informally, one has to prove that, when starting in R-related states, for each run of an operation $\mathbf{op}_j^C \#$ of C, there must be a matching run of $\mathbf{op}_j^A \#$ of A that maintains $R(st^A, st^C)$ with the same inputs and outputs. The obligation also requires to show that the precondition $pre_j^A(st^A)$ is strong enough to establish the precondition $pre_j^C(st^C)$ if $R(st^A, st^C)$ holds. This obligation is implicit as the call rule creates this premise for a procedure with a precondition.

For each component, invariant formulas $inv(st)$ over the state st can be given, which must be maintained by all $(\texttt{Op}_j)_{j \in J}$. This simplifies (or even makes it possible in the first place) to prove the correctness proof obligations of a refinement as invariants $inv^A(st^A)$ and $inv^C(st^C)$ are added as assumptions. If an invariant is given for a component, additional proof obligations for all its operations are generated that ensure that the invariant holds. Additionally, one can give an individual postcondition $post_j(st)$ for an operation, which extends its invariant contract.

$$pre_j(st) \wedge inv(st) \rightarrow \langle\!| \mathbf{op}_j \# (in_j; st; out_j) |\!\rangle (inv(st) \wedge post_j(st))$$

These invariant contracts can be applied when proving the refinement proof obligations and may further simplify the proofs since symbolic execution of the operation can be avoided.

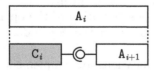

Fig. 1. Data refinement with subcomponents.

To facilitate the development of larger systems, we introduced a concept of modularization in the form of *subcomponents*. A component (usually an implementation) can use one or more components as subcomponents (usually specifications). The client component cannot access the state of its subcomponents directly but only via calls to the interface operations of the subcomponents. Using subcomponents, a refinement hierarchy is

state $rbs : set(tord)$

init#()
   initialization
{ $rbs := \emptyset$ }

insert#($elem$; ; $exists$)
   interface
{ $exists := elem \in rbs$, $rbs := rbs \cup \{elem\}$ }

remove#($elem$; ; $exists$)
   interface
{ $exists := elem \in rbs$, $rbs := rbs \setminus \{elem\}$ }

isEmpty#(; ; $empty$)
   interface
{ $empty := rbs = \emptyset$ }

lookup#($elem$; ; $exists$)
   interface
{ $exists := elem \in rbs$ }

getMin#(; ; $elem$)
   interface
   pre $rbs \neq \emptyset$
{ $elem := rbs.\min$ }

Fig. 2. Abstract representation of red-black trees: the component RBSET.

composed of multiple refinements like in Fig. 1. A specification component A_i is refined by an implementation C_i (dotted lines in Fig. 1) that uses a specification A_{i+1} as a subcomponent (—◉— in Fig. 1, we write $C_i(A_{i+1})$ for this subcomponent relation). This pattern then repeats in the sense that A_{i+1} is refined further by an implementation C_{i+1} that again uses a subcomponent A_{i+2} and so on. If it is not the top-level specification, A_i may also be used as a subcomponent of an implementation C_{i-1}. The complete implementation of the system then results from composing all individual implementation components $C_0(C_1(C_2(...)))$. In [13] we have shown that $C \leq A$ implies $M(C) \leq M(A)$ for a client component M which ensures that the composed implementation is a correct refinement of its top-level specification A_0, i.e. $C_0(C_1(C_2(...))) \leq A_0$. This allows us to divide a complex refinement task into multiple, more manageable ones, as demonstrated in the following sections for a red-black tree implementation.

5 Implementation of Destructive Red-Black Trees

Red-black trees are typically used as an efficient data structure for ordered sets (or multisets). In order to abstract from the complex implementation details of red-black trees (traversal, rotations, ...), the simple specification component RBSET given in Fig. 2 can be used. Other components then can use RBSET as a subcomponent, which simplifies formal reasoning about the client component while the resulting system still uses an efficient heap implementation.

The state of RBSET is just a set of elements that are totally ordered. It is determined by a state variable rbs of type $set(tord)$, where set is a polymorphic non-free data type (cf. Sect. 3.2), and a strict total order is given over elements of type $tord$. Initially, rbs is empty ($\emptyset$), and it can be modified by inserting or removing elements $elem$ (by **insert**# and

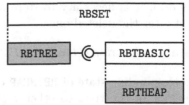

Fig. 3. The refinement hierarchy for red-black trees.

remove#). Additional interface procedures check whether the set is empty and whether an element is in the set. The minimal element can be selected. In Fig. 2 and below, state variables are omitted from the parameters of operation declarations but are implicitly added as reference arguments.

This component is refined by a pointer-based implementation of red-black trees. However, this refinement is split into two parts to reduce the complexity of the necessary reasoning about the heap done with Separation Logic. The result is the refinement hierarchy shown in Fig. 3. In the first refinement step RBTREE(RBTBASIC) ≤ RBSET, we show that the a red-black tree can implement the set abstraction and that this implementation maintains all red-black tree properties (cf. Sect. 6). But instead of using a heap data structure, we do this using the algebraic datatype *rbtree* presented in Sect. 3.1.

The second refinement step RBTHEAP ≤ RBTBASIC proves that a heap implementation conforms to this algebraic datatype. The goal of this separation is to keep the operations of RBTBASIC (and hence those of RBTHEAP) as simple as possible. The more complex algorithmic parts are handled in RBTREE while RBTBASIC only provides an interface for primitive manipulations of *rbtree*. This includes for example the insertion of an element at a given point within the tree, or a single left- or right-rotation of one particular subtree. To specify a location in the tree on the abstract level, we simply use paths, i.e. lists of an enumeration type *lrdesc* := LEFT | RIGHT, and define functions like $p \in rbt$, $rbt[p]$ and $rbt[p := rbt']$ that check a path p to be in a tree rbt, select the subtree at a path p, or update the subtree at a path p with a new tree rbt', respectively.

When used directly, these operations are inefficient since RBTBASIC has to traverse the paths at every access. However, note that we can already generate Scala code from RBTREE(RBTBASIC): the resulting code can be used for testing invariants and results of example runs, which often avoids unsuccessful proof attempts of properties that do not hold in the first place.

Since the algorithms on red-black trees use at most two paths and data refinement can refine state only (not input/output), we place two paths in the state of RBTBASIC. The implementation in RBTHEAP replaces these paths with two references that point to a heap storing individual tree nodes. The nodes of the implementation use parent pointers, so shortening or lengthening one of the two paths by one (which are operations of RBTBASIC) can be implemented by simply dereferencing a pointer. Hence, the state of the component RBTBASIC consists of an algebraic red-black-tree *rbt* using totally ordered elements *tord* and two paths *curPath* and *auxPath*. Most of the time *curPath* is used only, but for removal, it is necessary to store a second path *auxPath* that points to the element after the deleted one.

state $rbt : rbtree(tord),$ $curPath : list(lrdesc),$ $auxPath : list(lrdesc)$

The corresponding state of RBTHEAP contains a heap *rbh* and a pointer *rootRef* to the root of the tree, together with pointers *curRef* and *auxRef* matching *curPath* and *auxPath*, respectively.

```
     remove#(elem; ; exists)
       interface
       post elems(rbt) = elems(rbt') -- elem ∧ (exists ↔ elem ∈ elems(rbt'));
     {
  1      rbtbasic_reset#(); // curPath := [], auxPath := []
  2      search#(elem); // sets curPath to position of elem or to a leaf
  3      rbtbasic_isLeaf#(; ; exists); // exists := (rbt[curPath] = SENTINEL)
  4      if ¬ exists then {
  5        let doFix = ?, isLeftChild = ?, cond = ? in {
  6          rbtbasic_hasLeft#(; ; cond); // cond := curPath + LEFT' ∈ rbt;
  7          if ¬ cond then {
  8            rbtbasic_replRight#(; ; doFix, isLeftChild);
  9            // replace node at curPath with its right child
 10            // and move curPath up one node
 11          } else {
 12            rbtbasic_hasRight#(; ; cond); // analogous to hasLeft
 13            if ¬ cond then {
 14              rbtbasic_replLeft#(; ; doFix, isLeftChild);
 15            } else {
 16              rbtbasic_initD#(); // auxPath := curPath
 17              rbtbasic_right#(); // curPath := curPath + RIGHT
 18              leftMost# // extend curPath to leftmost inner node
 19              rbtbasic_getElem#(; ; elem); // elem := rbt[curPath].elem
 20              rbtbasic_replRight#(; ; doFix, isLeftChild);
 21              rbtbasic_setElemD#(elem); // rbt[auxPath].elem := elem
 22        } };
 23          if doFix then removeFixup#(isLeftChild);
 24          // restore balance and red-black tree properties
 25          exists := true; }
 26      } else exists := false // element was not found
     }
```

Fig. 4. RBTREE procedure for removing an element *elem* from the tree.

state   *rbh* : *heap(rbnode)*, *rootRef* : *ref(rbnode)*,
          curRef : *ref(rbnode)*, *auxRef* : *ref(rbnode)*

The heap stores nodes of type *rbnode*, which contain an element and a color like the Nodes of *rbtree* but use references that point to their left and right subtrees. A parent pointer is added to allow efficient traversal upwards in the tree.

rbnode := Node(.elem : *tord*; .color : *rbcolor*; .parent : *ref(rbnode)*;
          .left : *ref(rbnode)*; .right : *ref(rbnode)*)

Figure 4 lists the implementation of **remove#** in the RBTREE component as an example of how this state is modified via the interface of RBTBASIC. For primitive RBTBASIC operations, the comments in green show their implementation. All operations start by resetting the paths to point to the root (line 1, [] denotes an empty list). Then the tree is traversed to an element of interest by performing a binary search in the procedure **search#**(*elem*). For removal, the element to be removed (*elem*) is searched and *curPath* will be updated to point to *elem* if it is found. When a SENTINEL is reached (checked in line 3), the search is stopped and the removal is aborted with *exists* := false (line 26). If *elem* was found, the element must be replaced in order to restore the red-black tree properties. In case the node has a SENTINEL as left or right child (line 8 resp. 14), substitution of the node is performed simply by replacing it with the other child. Otherwise, *curPath* is stored in *auxPath* (line 16) and is then updated by **rbtbasic_right#** and **leftMost#** to point to the next greater element. This element is the minimal element of the right subtree of *elem* and thus cannot have a left child (*curPath* + LEFT points to a SENTINEL). Therefore, the element can be moved to *auxPath* (line 21) and the tree at *curPath* can be replaced with its right child (line 20). Finally, the routine **removeFixup#** is called to fix up the tree starting at *curPath* since the removal may have broken the red-black tree properties and the tree may need to be rebalanced.

The RBTHEAP operations work similar to RBTBASIC but on the pointer structure. So instead of selecting a subtree at *curPath*, which requires a traversal of the complete path, the node at *curRef* is accessed simply by dereferencing the pointer (*rbh*[*curRef*]). Analogously, instead of adjusting the paths, e.g. with *curPath* := *curPath* + RIGHT, pointers are updated by following the references of the current node, e.g. with *curRef* := *rbh*[*curRef*].right.

The algorithm is essentially the same as the one in [9]. However, we implement SENTINEL nodes as null pointers instead of using a dummy node that would be necessary to get the parent of a leaf. This does not change the *insert* algorithm, but results in *remove* working on the parent of the deleted node. Our algorithm therefore has to explicitly pass the information whether the left or right child was deleted (*isLeftChild* in Fig. 4). On the other hand, our **removeFixup#** is not called when *curPath* points to a leaf (and only when there is something to fix), so the loop test in the original **removeFixup#** that checks for a leaf or the root (which can only be true in the first iteration) is removed. Otherwise the various cases and rotations are identical to [9].

6   Verification of Destructive Red-Black Trees

For verification, the functional properties must be specified as invariants of RBTREE. In between interface calls, *rbt* must be a valid red-black tree (expressed by isRbtree(*rbt*)) and must be a valid search tree, i.e. its elements must be ordered (described by the predicate isOrdered(*rbt*)).

A non-empty red-black tree is characterized by three main properties: the root of the tree is BLACK, both children of a RED node have to be BLACK, and each path of any node to a leaf must contain the same number of BLACK nodes.

$$\text{isRbtree}(rbt) \leftrightarrow \big(rbt = \text{SENTINEL} \vee$$
$$(rbt.\text{color} = \text{BLACK} \wedge \text{redCorrect}(rbt, \text{RED}) \wedge \text{sameBlacks}(rbt))\big)$$

The predicate redCorrect($rbt, parCol$) ($parCol$ is the color of the parent node) specifies the first two properties, sameBlacks(rbt) the last. Both are defined recursively over the structure of the tree, as is isOrdered(rbt). As an example, the axiom for a RED node for redCorrect is

$$redCorrect(\texttt{Node}(e, \texttt{RED}, left, right), parCol) \leftrightarrow$$
$$parCol = \texttt{BLACK} \wedge redCorrect(left, \texttt{RED}) \wedge redCorrect(right, \texttt{RED})$$

For the deletion of a node, additional predicates must be defined that allow the properties to be violated at a specific path in the tree (we indicate them by attaching D). They allow the tree to be characterized during the procedure **remove#**. For instance, the following definition describes the violation of redCorrect at the current node ($path = \texttt{[]}$).

$$redCorrectD(\texttt{Node}(e, col, left, right), parCol, \texttt{[]}) \leftrightarrow$$
$$redCorrect(left, col) \wedge redCorrect(right, col)$$

While isOrdered(rbt) is maintained quite easily by the operations of RBTREE, e.g. **insert#** adds the new element directly at a position that maintains the order property, complex fixing mechanisms are necessary to re-establish isRbtree(rbt). The main proof effort is to show that these mechanisms are actually correct. To keep proof size manageable, we split the procedures into several subroutines, and formulated and proved contracts for these separately. We will not go into details of the verification of the routines (**insertFixup#** for insertion and **removeFixup#** for removal), the KIV code and proofs can be found online [23].

The refinement RBTREE(RBTBASIC) ≤ RBSET is proven by the following forward simulation, where elems calculates the set of elements stored in the tree.

abstraction relation $rbs = \texttt{elems}(rbt)$

This simple abstraction allows to encode the set modifications of RBSET into the contracts of RBTREE. For example, the contract of **remove#** in Fig. 4 states that *elem* is removed from the tree (elems(rbt) = elems(rbt') -- *elem* where rbt' denotes the value of rbt just before the execution of the procedure). This modification happens within **rbtbasic_replRight#** and **rbtbasic_replLeft#**, the contracts of all other modifying auxiliary procedures, e.g. **removeFixup#**, ensure that they do not change the set of elements stored in the tree (elems(rbt) = elems(rbt')). Similar contracts are given for the other interface procedures, so the refinement is proven mainly by applying these contracts. Note that the refinement proofs do not require the invariant isRbtree(rbt) (an unbalanced tree would also refine a set correctly). However, they do require isOrdered(rbt) since otherwise tree search is not correct (and thus correctness of **remove#**, **lookup#**, and **getMin#** could not be shown).

For none of these proofs, it is necessary to reason about the heap implementation. In particular, the main invariant properties isOrdered and isRbtree are

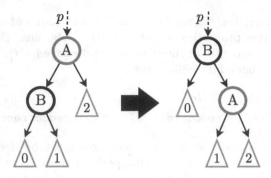

Fig. 5. Exemplary right-rotation at a path p.

rotateRight#(p)
    auxiliary
    pre $p + \text{LEFT} \in rbt$;
{
1   **let** $rbt_0 = rbt[p]$ **in**
2   **let** $rbt_1 = rbt_0.\texttt{left}$ **in**
3   **let** $rbt_2 = \texttt{Node}(rbt_0.\texttt{elem}, rbt_0.\texttt{color}, rbt_1.\texttt{right}, rbt_0.\texttt{right})$ **in**
4       $rbt[p] := \texttt{Node}(rbt_1.\texttt{elem}, rbt_1.\texttt{color}, rbt_1.\texttt{left}, rbt_2)$
}

Fig. 6. Procedure for right-rotations at a path p of component RBTBASIC.

proved solely over algebraic trees. What remains to prove is that the pointer-based implementation in RBTHEAP is a correct refinement of RBTBASIC.

Most of the operations of RBTBASIC are just single assignments, for example recolorings of the node at *curPath* or one of its relatives, or changes of *curPath* or *auxPath*. RBTHEAP implements these operations analogously with lookups at *curRef* and updates of *curRef* or *auxRef* by following the parent- or child-pointers. The only more complex operations are rotations used in the fixing routines. For example, Fig. 5 shows the effect of a right-rotation at some location within the tree, i.e. at some path p (note that the left child B of A must be an actual Node for a valid right-rotation, while the subtrees 0, 1, and 2 can be SENTINELs). In RBTBASIC, such rotations are performed using the auxiliary procedure **rotateRight**# listed in Fig. 6 (or a symmetric version **rotateLeft**# for left-rotations). The operation takes a path p as an argument and performs a right-rotation at the corresponding location. It selects the subtree at p, builds the rotated subtree, and then inserts it at p again (the program $rbt[p] := rbt_0$ is an abbreviation for $rbt := rbt[p := rbt_0]$ which replaces $rbt[p]$ with rbt_0 in rbt). The RBTBASIC interface then provides operations for rotations at different locations (at *curPath*, *auxPath*, or one of their relatives), all of which use one of the two auxiliary procedures with respective arguments.

Figure 7 shows the corresponding implementation of RBTHEAP. Instead of a path, it takes a reference *ref* as an input. The heap implementation performs

rotateRight#(*ref*)
  auxiliary
  pre *ref* ∈ *rbh* ∧ *rbh*[*ref*].left ∈ *rbh*;
{
1   **let** *lRef* = *rbh*[*ref*].left **in** {
2   *rbh*[*ref*].left := *rbh*[*lRef*].right;
3   **if** *rbh*[*lRef*].right ≠ null **then** *rbh*[*rbh*[*lRef*].right].parent := *ref*;
4   **if** *lRef* ≠ null **then** *rbh*[*lRef*].parent := *rbh*[*ref*].parent;
5   **if** *rbh*[*ref*].parent ≠ null **then** {
6   **if** *ref* = *rbh*[*rbh*[*ref*].parent].right
7   **then** *rbh*[*rbh*[*ref*].parent].right := *lRef*;
8   **else** *rbh*[*rbh*[*ref*].parent].left := *lRef*;
9   } **else** *rootRef* := *lRef*;
10   *rbh*[*lRef*].right := *ref*;
11   **if** *ref* ≠ null **then** *rbh*[*ref*].parent := *lRef*;
}}

Fig. 7. Procedure for right-rotations at a reference *ref* of component RBTHEAP.

the rotation by updating the pointers of the node at *ref* as well as those of its parent and left child. First, the link between the node at *ref* and its new left child is established (lines 2 and 3). Then the link between the new root of the subtree (*lRef*) and its new parent is created (lines 5–8). Finally, *ref* is linked to *lRef* as its new right child (lines 10 and 11). In contrast to the algebraic variant in Fig. 6 (the assignment in line 4 would copy the whole tree *rbt*), all updates are destructive. For example in C, the assignment in line 2 corresponds to a statement **ref->left = lRef->right** where both **ref** and **lRef** as well as the fields **left** and **right** are pointers to a struct **rbnode**.

The refinement is proven using Separation Logic (see Sect. 3.2) and the following abstraction that does not refer to any red-black tree properties.

abstraction relation   *rbh*[*rootRef*, *curPath*] = *curRef*
$$\land \; rbh[rootRef,\, auxPath] = auxRef$$
$$\land \; \textbf{abs}(rootRef,\, \text{null},\, rbt)(rbh)$$

The first two formulas assert that the references *curRef* and *auxRef* correspond to the paths *curPath* and *auxPath*, respectively, i.e. they point to the same locations in the tree. Here, the function *rbh*[*r*, *p*] yields the reference reached when traversing the heap *rbh* along the path *p*, starting at *r*. The heap predicate **abs** : (*ref*(*rbnode*) × *ref*(*rbnode*) × *rbtree*(*tord*)) → *heap*(*rbnode*) → *bool* abstracts the pointer tree in *rbh* starting at *rootRef* to the algebraic tree *rbt*. The second *ref* (*rbnode*) argument specifies the parent of the root, for the complete tree it is null. **abs** is defined recursively over the structure of *rbt*:

$$\text{abs}(rootRef, \ pRef, \ \text{SENTINEL})(rbh) \leftrightarrow rootRef = \texttt{null} \land rbh = \emptyset$$

$$\text{abs}(rootRef, \ pRef, \ \text{Node}(elem, \ col, \ l, \ r))(rbh) \leftrightarrow$$
$$\exists \ lRef, \ rRef. \ (\quad (rootRef \mapsto \text{Node}(elem, \ col, \ pRef, \ lRef, \ rRef))$$
$$* \ \text{abs}(lRef, \ rootRef, \ l)$$
$$* \ \text{abs}(rRef, \ rootRef, \ r))(rbh)$$

For a SENTINEL, the heap rbh must be empty. This ensures the absence of memory leaks since one has to prove that all nodes have been deallocated when they are removed from the tree. For a Node, the heap is separated into three disjoint parts: a root node containing the same element and color as the algebraic node and two trees that abstract to the left and right algebraic subtree.

The abstraction relation uses ordinary conjunction, and we found it easy to support updating the first and second conjunct on heap updates via suitable rewrite rules: modifications happen either at one of the two paths or below them (in the latter case no update is necessary at all). Most Separation Logic based provers (e.g. [20, 26]) support separating conjunction only, which would require to define several versions of abs with additional paths and references as arguments, depending on which of them is contained in a subtree.

The proof exploits that each operation modifies at most one location inside the tree. This allows to split up the abstraction at this location, prove that the operation has the expected local behavior (e.g. that it rotates the referenced subtree correctly), and then merge the abstraction again with the updated subtree. For this, two fundamental theorems were formulated. The first theorem splits the abstraction of a tree rbt at a path p.

$$p \in rbt \rightarrow (\text{abs}(rootRef, \ pRef, \ rbt)(rbh) \leftrightarrow$$
$$\exists \ pthRef, \ pPthRef.$$
$$(\text{abspath}(rootRef, \ pRef, \ rbt, \ p, \ pthRef, \ pPthRef)$$
$$* \ \text{abs}(pthRef, \ pPthRef, \ rbt[p]))(rbh))$$

The heap predicate abspath is a weaker version of abs: the tree represented in rbh must match rbt except for the subtree starting at p. The references $pthRef$ and $pPthRef$ are used to fix the references of the root of the subtree and its parent. Thus, the split-off subtree $rbt[p]$ can be abstracted separately using abs with $pthRef$ as root and $pPthRef$ as parent reference. Conversely, reconnecting a detached subtree rbt_0 at path p with the original tree rbt is done via

$$(\text{abspath}(rootRef, \ pRef, \ rbt, \ p, \ pthRef, \ pPthRef)$$
$$* \ \text{abs}(pthRef, \ pPthRef, \ rbt_0))(rbh)$$
$$\rightarrow \text{abs}(rootRef, \ pRef, \ rbt[p := rbt_0])(rbh)$$

The theorem allows to attach an arbitrary tree rbt_0 (that is not necessarily related to the originally separated subtree $rbt[p]$). In practice, rbt_0 typically results from a simple modification of $rbt[p]$ like a recoloration or a rotation.

7 Related Work

Our concept with components (machines) and subcomponents is similar to the 'include' of B machines into others (see [1], chapter 7), although our individual operations (called events in B) are not assumed to be atomic (B disallows recursion, loops and sequential composition in operations).

Our approach is related but goes beyond the standard technique to use an abstraction relation (or function) that maps the pointer structure to a (free) algebraic structure, which is e.g. supported by Verifast [20] or was used e.g. in Automath [30]. We use such an abstraction function, but only to verify the core refinement from RBTBASIC to RBTHEAP.

We are aware of two alternatives to our approach. First, there is Cogent [28] which restricts programs by using a linear type system to propagate data structures linearly. This allows to generate destructive code immediately but places severe limitations on the programming language.

Another alternative is to optimize code with a code generator that transforms algebraic types into pointer structures and tries to optimize non-destructive operations to destructive ones using checks for linear use. The approach developed in [25] follows this idea. It additionally generates proof obligations showing that the destructive implementation behaves the same way as the abstract one. It may be possible to encode our approach into this approach, as it is also based on data refinement, though the approach seems to be targeted towards individual algorithms, not (state-based) abstract data types.

Our code generator in KIV works similarly: it would transform trees into a tree-shaped pointer structure and use destructive updates on the pointer structure whenever a data flow analysis suggests this is possible (current work is to optimize this). However, we currently do not verify the correctness of these transformations; this is up to future work. The strategy is often sufficient to get efficient code. However, without the refinement of RBTBASIC to RBTHEAP, paths would be represented as doubly- linked lists, which would still be inefficient.

We are aware of several other works that verify red-black trees. Partial verifications, where the emphasis is on automation, are [7] (proving insertion without establishing that on every path to a leaf the number of black nodes must be equal) and [27] (just proving the ordering property). [2,3,16,29] are complete verifications of algebraic implementations that produce functional (nondestructive) code. Our approach follows that idea but expands it to refine the functional to an imperative (destructive) implementation.

There are two complete verifications of destructive code we are aware of. One is described in the recent paper [4] using VerCors. The implementation is directly in Java, and the main routines use recursion and no parent pointers. But typical C implementations of red-black trees do without a recursion stack, so they are somewhat more efficient. Recursion simplifies the proofs considerably, as then a recursive call transforms a red-black subtree into another one and an invariant that combines isRbtreeD on our upper level with *abspath* from the lower level can be avoided. With VerCors being an automatic verifier backed by an SMT solver, proofs are guided by adding suitable annotations to the programs instead of directly interacting with a GUI during a proof as in KIV. Overall, the user input necessary for the final proof seems somewhat smaller in VerCors than in KIV, but we expect that finding why a proof fails to be significantly harder since SMT solvers do not give a reason why a goal is not provable, while KIV's proof trees allow inspecting residual goals that have been maximally simplified.

From the data given, the effort seems to have been somewhat higher than with our approach. The case study described also includes the verification of an extra concurrent operation that merges two red-black trees using lists as an intermediate representation. Verification of our case study took two regular students of computer science (who had done a KIV course) two months each under the mentoring of one of the authors.

The other complete verification of a pointer-implementation of red-black trees we are aware of is mentioned in [36] and can be found in Isabelle's AFP library. The version verified is derived from [22], which is a version of red-black trees intended to be used in a functional language with garbage collection, originally Haskell (the Scala-Library also uses it to implement *immutable* sets). This version of the algorithm uses recursion and no parent pointers. For verification, it has been modified to use destructive updates instead of copying the modified branch. The algorithm has a simpler, different rebalancing strategy than the original algorithm, making it less efficient than the original algorithm: when backing out of the recursion, a check for rebalancing is necessary on every level, resulting in logarithmic effort for fixing the tree. The original algorithm however has only one of four cases, where fixing a leaf after an insert (one in six cases for delete) has to traverse upwards to fix the parent. The resulting geometric series $(1 + 1/4 + 1/16 + \ldots = 4/3$ nodes are traversed upwards on average) results in *constant* average complexity for fixing the tree (see also [21], Chapter 7.4ff). That a full traversal upwards is unnecessary is the main reason, why red-black trees are more efficient than other versions of search trees like AVL trees, that need rebalancing checks on every level. We were unable to get a figure on the proof effort spent for the verification in [36], the automation using an automated saturation prover called auto2 implemented on top of Isabelle however is quite impressive. Apart from specific setup instructions for the prover, the proof seems to be fully automated requiring just a few lemmas.

Partial verification of destructive code can also be found in [12] (C code) and [11] (SPARKS, a subset of Ada). Both have analyzed insertion only and left away the `sameBlacks` property. The last approach is interesting since it uses an array-representation of red-black trees that would be suitable for real-time use (the array needs to be large enough to hold all tree nodes). It should not be too difficult to replace our heap-based representation in the lower refinement with their array-based one, exploiting that we do not have to re-verify any of the invariants of red-black trees to do this.

8   Conclusion

In this paper, we have demonstrated a refinement-based approach that allows to separate considerations of algorithmic correctness and of using destructive updates, aliasing and memory allocation into two individual refinements. The two core ideas are to abstract pointers as used by the algorithm to paths over an algebraic structure, and to use an interface that encapsulates primitive manipulations on abstract structures and paths. Verification is then split into functional correctness of the relevant algorithms on a purely algebraic level and a small part that shows that primitive operations can be correctly refined to pointer updates.

Our approach is not intended to compete with the best-automated techniques but to demonstrate that a clean separation of functional and pointer correctness is possible without compromising the final algorithm's efficiency. Our approach also should enable using one of the many techniques that automate proofs, e.g. [31] for Separation Logic used in the lower refinement, or [15] for the algebraic trees of the upper refinement.

KIV's code generator generates C code from this implementation that is available together with all KIV specifications and proofs online [23].

The approach is successful in generating optimal code: it runs as fast (within a margin of ±5%) of the code in stdc++ library when elements are inserted, looked up, or deleted randomly (the code also uses the rotations as given in [9] to fix red-black trees after inserting/deleting elements). For comparison, we also programmed the recursive red-black algorithms verified in [36] in KIV (without any modular structure or verification) and generated C code from them. The resulting code runs ca. 10% slower than our code. The KIV programs, resulting C code, and the benchmarks are included in the Web presentation [23] too.

There are two features we have not implemented compared to this code: one is to have an additional pointer to the minimal and maximal element. As a consequence accessing the maximum skips traversing the tree to the rightmost leaf, so inserting (or removing) elements in ascending order is still 10–20% faster. The algorithm in the library also has the option to cache deleted nodes to avoid deallocation and reallocation. We have not used this option in the comparison. Our current modularization, however, is certainly able to add these features.

We currently work on applying the approach to other data structures, namely (wandering) B+ Trees [19], which are the last not yet verified component of our flash filesystem [5], where we so far have achieved partial results [14] only.

Though we have defined an extension of the component concept to concurrency [33], it is future work to research how the approach given here could be extended to concurrent data structures.

Acknowledgement. We would like to thank our students Nikolai Glaab and Felix Pribyl, who have done large parts of the verification of red-black trees.

References

1. Abrial, J.R., Hoare, A., Chapron, P.: The B-Book: Assigning Programs to Meanings. Cambridge University Press, Cambridge (1996)

2. Affeldt, R., Garrigue, J., Qi, X., Tanaka, K.: Proving tree algorithms for succinct data structures. In: 10th International Conference on Interactive Theorem Proving (ITP 2019). Leibniz International Proceedings in Informatics (LIPIcs), vol. 141, pp. 5:1–5:19 (2019)
3. Appel, A.: Efficient Verified Red-Black Trees (2011)
4. Armborst, L., Huisman, M.: Permission-based verification of red-black trees and their merging. In: Proceedings of FormaliSE, vol. 21, pp. 111–123 (2021)
5. Bodenmüller, S., Schellhorn, G., Bitterlich, M., Reif, W.: Flashix: modular verification of a concurrent and crash-safe flash file system. In: Raschke, A., Riccobene, E., Schewe, K.-D. (eds.) Logic, Computation and Rigorous Methods. LNCS, vol. 12750, pp. 239–265. Springer, Cham (2021). https://doi.org/10.1007/978-3-030-76020-5_14
6. Börger, E.: The ASM refinement method. Formal Aspects Comput. **15**(1–2), 237–257 (2003)
7. Charguéraud, A.: Program verification through characteristic formulae. In: Proceedings of ACM SIGPLAN International Conference on Functional Programming (ICFP), pp. 321–332. Association for Computing Machinery (2010)
8. Charguéraud, A.: Higher-order representation predicates in separation logic. In: Proceedings of ACM SIGPLAN Conference on Certified Programs and Proofs (CPP), pp. 3–14. Association for Computing Machinery (2016)
9. Cormen, T., Leiserson, C., Rivest, R., Stein, C.: Introduction to Algorithms, 3rd edn. The MIT Press, Cambridge (2009)
10. Derrick, J., Boiten, E.: Refinement in Z and in Object-Z: Foundations and Advanced Applications. FACIT. Springer, Cham (2001). Second, Revised Edition (2014)
11. Dross, C., Moy, Y.: Auto-active proof of red-black trees in SPARK. In: Barrett, C., Davies, M., Kahsai, T. (eds.) NFM 2017. LNCS, vol. 10227, pp. 68–83. Springer, Cham (2017). https://doi.org/10.1007/978-3-319-57288-8_5
12. Elgaard, J., Møller, A., Schwartzbach, M.I.: Compile-time debugging of C programs working on trees. In: Smolka, G. (ed.) ESOP 2000. LNCS, vol. 1782, pp. 119–134. Springer, Heidelberg (2000). https://doi.org/10.1007/3-540-46425-5_8
13. Ernst, G., Pfähler, J., Schellhorn, G., Reif, W.: Modular, crash-safe refinement for ASMs with submachines. Sci. Comput. Program. **131**, 3–21 (2016). Abstract State Machines, Alloy, B, TLA, VDM and Z (ABZ 2014)
14. Ernst, G., Schellhorn, G., Reif, W.: Verification of B^+ trees: an experiment combining shape analysis and interactive theorem proving. In: Barthe, G., Pardo, A., Schneider, G. (eds.) SEFM 2011. LNCS, vol. 7041, pp. 188–203. Springer, Heidelberg (2011). https://doi.org/10.1007/978-3-642-24690-6_14
15. Faella, M., Parlato, G.: Reasoning about data trees using CHCs. In: Shoham, S., Vizel, Y. (eds.) CAV 2022. LNCS, vol. 13372, pp. 249–271. Springer, Cham (2022). https://doi.org/10.1007/978-3-031-13188-2_13
16. Filliâtre, J.-C., Letouzey, P.: Functors for proofs and programs. In: Schmidt, D. (ed.) ESOP 2004. LNCS, vol. 2986, pp. 370–384. Springer, Heidelberg (2004). https://doi.org/10.1007/978-3-540-24725-8_26
17. Guibas, L.J., Sedgewick, R.: A dichromatic framework for balanced trees. In: Proceedings of the 19th Symposium on Foundations of Computer Science (SFCS), pp. 8–21. IEEE (1978)
18. Harel, D., Tiuryn, J., Kozen, D.: Dynamic Logic. MIT Press, Cambridge (2000)
19. Havasi, F.: An improved B+ tree for flash file systems. In: Černá, I., et al. (eds.) SOFSEM 2011. LNCS, vol. 6543, pp. 297–307. Springer, Heidelberg (2011). https://doi.org/10.1007/978-3-642-18381-2_25

20. Jacobs, B., Smans, J., Philippaerts, P., Vogels, F., Penninckx, W., Piessens, F.: VeriFast: a powerful, sound, predictable, fast verifier for C and Java. In: Bobaru, M., Havelund, K., Holzmann, G.J., Joshi, R. (eds.) NFM 2011. LNCS, vol. 6617, pp. 41–55. Springer, Heidelberg (2011). https://doi.org/10.1007/978-3-642-20398-5_4

21. Sanders, P., Mehlhorn, K.: Algorithms and Data Structures - The Basic Toolbox. Springer, Heidelberg (2008)

22. Kahrs, S.: Red-black trees with types. J. Funct. Program. **11**(4), 182–196 (2001)

23. KIV Proofs for the Correctness of Red-Black Trees (2022). https://kiv.isse.de/projects/RBtree.html

24. Lammich, P.: Refinement to imperative/HOL. In: Urban, C., Zhang, X. (eds.) ITP 2015. LNCS, vol. 9236, pp. 253–269. Springer, Cham (2015). https://doi.org/10.1007/978-3-319-22102-1_17

25. Lammich, P.: Efficient verified implementation of Introsort and Pdqsort. In: Peltier, N., Sofronie-Stokkermans, V. (eds.) IJCAR 2020. LNCS (LNAI), vol. 12167, pp. 307–323. Springer, Cham (2020). https://doi.org/10.1007/978-3-030-51054-1_18

26. Müller, P., Schwerhoff, M., Summers, A.J.: Viper: a verification infrastructure for permission-based reasoning. In: Jobstmann, B., Leino, K.R.M. (eds.) VMCAI 2016. LNCS, vol. 9583, pp. 41–62. Springer, Heidelberg (2016). https://doi.org/10.1007/978-3-662-49122-5_2

27. Nipkow, T.: Automatic functional correctness proofs for functional search trees. In: Blanchette, J.C., Merz, S. (eds.) ITP 2016. LNCS, vol. 9807, pp. 307–322. Springer, Cham (2016). https://doi.org/10.1007/978-3-319-43144-4_19

28. O'Connor, L., et al.: Cogent: uniqueness types and certifying compilation. J. Funct. Program. **31**, 25 (2021)

29. Peña, R.: An assertional proof of red–black trees using Dafny. J. Autom. Reason. **64**(4), 767–791 (2019). https://doi.org/10.1007/s10817-019-09534-y

30. Polikarpova, N., Tschannen, J., Furia, C.A.: A fully verified container library. In: Bjørner, N., de Boer, F. (eds.) FM 2015. LNCS, vol. 9109, pp. 414–434. Springer, Cham (2015). https://doi.org/10.1007/978-3-319-19249-9_26

31. Reynolds, A., Iosif, R., Serban, C., King, T.: A decision procedure for separation logic in SMT. In: Artho, C., Legay, A., Peled, D. (eds.) ATVA 2016. LNCS, vol. 9938, pp. 244–261. Springer, Cham (2016). https://doi.org/10.1007/978-3-319-46520-3_16

32. Reynolds, J.C.: Separation logic: a logic for shared mutable data structures. In: Proceedings of the 17th Annual IEEE Symposium on Logic in Computer Science, pp. 55–74. IEEE (2002)

33. Schellhorn, G., Bodenmüller, S., Pfähler, J., Reif, W.: Adding concurrency to a sequential refinement tower. In: Raschke, A., Méry, D., Houdek, F. (eds.) ABZ 2020. LNCS, vol. 12071, pp. 6–23. Springer, Cham (2020). https://doi.org/10.1007/978-3-030-48077-6_2

34. Schellhorn, G., Bodenmüller, S., Bitterlich, M., Reif, W.: Software & system verification with KIV. In: Ahrendt, W., Beckert, B., Bubel, R., Johnsen, E.B. (eds.) The Logic of Software. A Tasting Menu of Formal Methods. LNCS, vol. 13360, pp. 408–436. Springer, Cham (2022). https://doi.org/10.1007/978-3-031-08166-8_20

35. Sedgewick, R., Wayne, K.: Algorithms, 4th edn. Addison-Wesley (2011)

36. Zhan, B.: Efficient verification of imperative programs using auto2. In: Beyer, D., Huisman, M. (eds.) TACAS 2018. LNCS, vol. 10805, pp. 23–40. Springer, Cham (2018). https://doi.org/10.1007/978-3-319-89960-2_2

Residual Runtime Verification via Reachability Analysis

Chukri Soueidi[✉][iD] and Yliès Falcone[iD]

Univ. Grenoble Alpes, Inria, CNRS, Grenoble INP, LIG, 38000 Grenoble, France
{chukri.a.soueidi,ylies.falcone}@inria.fr

Abstract. We leverage static verification to reduce monitoring overhead when runtime verifying a property. We present a sound and efficient analysis to statically find safe execution paths in the control flow at the intra-procedural level of programs. Such paths are guaranteed to preserve the monitored property and thus can be ignored at runtime. Our analysis guides an instrumentation tool to select program points that should be observed at runtime. The monitor is left to perform residual runtime verification for parts of the program that the analysis could not statically prove safe. Our approach does not depend on dataflow analysis, thus separating the task of residual analysis from static analysis; allowing for seamless integration with many RV frameworks and development pipelines. We implement our approach within BISM, which is a recent tool for bytecode-level instrumentation of Java programs. Our experiments on the DaCapo benchmark show a reduction in instrumentation points by a factor of 2.5 on average (reaching 9), and accordingly, a reduction in the number of runtime events by a factor of 1.8 on average (reaching 6).

Keywords: Residual runtime verification · Instrumentation · Parametric monitoring · Control flow · Runtime overhead · Bad prefix

1 Introduction

Runtime verification (RV) [6,17–19,26] is a formal method that allows checking whether a run of a system respects a specification. The specification usually formalizes a correctness property and is written in a suitable formalism based for instance on temporal logic or finite-state machines. There are still many challenges in runtime verification, see [27] for a survey. One of the most prominent and fundamental ones, hindering its wide applicability in application domains, is the runtime overhead introduced when augmenting a system with runtime verification. Overhead is caused by the instrumentation code inserted in the program to generate traces. In the case of online monitoring, overhead also comprises the evaluation of traces by the monitors.

RV can complement and has been used in combination with other formal static verification methods such as model checking [25], deductive verification [12] and static analysis [4,9,12,15], as well as informal dynamic methods such as testing [13] and debugging [22]. While a complete *a priori* verification is ideally desirable for verifying program correctness, proving the correctness of many properties is fundamentally undecidable statically. However, static verification often relies on conservative approximations that produce sound results while sacrificing completeness. Combining static and runtime verification for a more complete verification scheme seems natural. The

ⓒ The Author(s), under exclusive license to Springer Nature Switzerland AG 2023
A. Lal and S. Tonetta (Eds.): VSTTE 2022, LNCS 13800, pp. 148–166, 2023.
https://doi.org/10.1007/978-3-031-25803-9_9

combination is useful in the two complementary directions. For static verification, it improves completeness by deferring verification of undecidable fragments for some properties until runtime. For RV, it reduces the overhead of monitoring by pruning parts of the program that can be statically analyzed. In this paper, we pursue the second direction.

We follow the terminology of [15] and refer to the introduced technique as *residual runtime verification*. Our work is directed to handle properties that can be expressed by finite-state automata, such as typestate [30] errors, supporting different formalisms and monitoring approaches that allow specifications with data. In such approaches, a parametric monitor receives a parametrized trace and spawns multiple monitors for different trace slices corresponding to sets of related objects [20]. We see our contributions as follows. We present a *sound and efficient* technique to statically find "safe" execution paths in the control flow at the intra-procedural level of programs. Such paths are guaranteed to preserve the monitored property and thus can be ignored at runtime. As a result, the monitor is left to perform verification for residual parts of the program that the analysis failed to prove safe statically. Our approach, at its core, does not depend on data-flow analysis nor on a static construction of the full call graph of the program, which might be difficult and expensive to produce in practice. Thus, we separate the problem of static analysis from the residual analysis, allowing for seamless integration with the RV workflow. Instead, we analyze the control-flow graphs of single methods and rely on over-approximations of the behavior of the program. We assume that the variables generating events within one method *may-alias* and our analysis reasons about all possible projections of traces. We also handle instructions that may allow references to escape from methods by including them in the analysis to guarantee soundness. We demonstrate the effectiveness of our analysis when we reduce the number of instrumentation points by a factor of 2.5 on average (reaching 9), and accordingly, the number of generated events at runtime by a factor of 1.8 on average (reaching 6). Our approach is fully implemented as an extension of the instrumentation tool BISM [29], and [28] where we presented the *control-flow graph automaton*, a model to abstract the program behavior at the intra-procedural level.

The rest of this paper is structured as follows. Section 2 motivates our approach with a running example. Section 3 reviews background notions. Section 4 defines the requirements for residual analysis. Section 5 describes our instantiation of residual analysis at the interprocedural level. Section 6 briefly overviews our implementation. Section 7 reports on our experiments. Section 8 reviews the related research focusing on residual analysis. Section 9 concludes and presents perspectives.

2   Motivating Example and Approach Overview

We first introduce our running example. We are interested in monitoring the **SafeIterator** property which specifies that "*A collection should not be updated when an iterator associated with it is created and being used*". Figure 1, shows a contrived Java method m along with its control-flow graph (CFG). It retrieves 2 lists (lines 3,4), updates them (lines 6,10,11), creates iterators (lines 7,15), and calls the "next" method on the iterator (line 14). We are interested in answering the following questions:

```
1  void m()
2  {
3      List l1 = ... ;
4      List l2 = ... ;

6      l1.add(..); // event u
7      Iterator it = l1.iterator();// event c

9      if(someflag) {
10         l2.add(..); // event u
11         l2.add(..); // event u
12     }

14     Object o = it.next(); // event n
15     it = l1.iterator(); // event c
16     l2.add(..); // event u
17 }
```

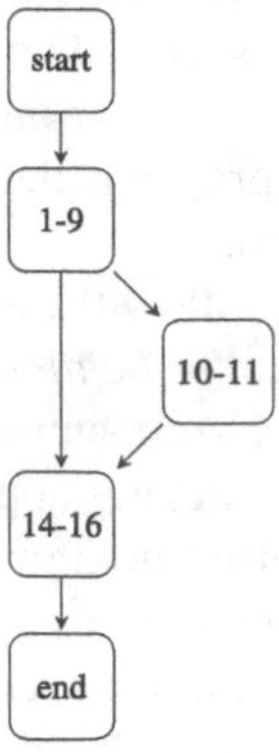

start

1-9

10-11

14-16

end

Fig. 1. A method using Iterators in Java, and its CFG.

- **Q1:** Can we fully verify this program statically? If yes, then there is no need to instrument and runtime monitor it.
- **Q2:** If not, can we statically verify some parts of it? If yes, how can we find them so that we only monitor the *residual* parts?

By manually inspecting the program and its control-flow graph we see that, at runtime, it may violate the property if the execution enters the if block, labeled (10–11) in the graph. More precisely, a violation can occur if both of the following conditions are met: **(1)** someflag evaluates to *true*; and **(2)** if the variables l1 and l2 alias each other i.e., they refer to the same object in memory. Let us consider that Condition **(1)** is only decidable at runtime. To generally decide Condition **(2)** statically, we need to perform pointer analysis on the program that checks all calling contexts m and return whether l1 and l2 alias. In practice, we may get one of the following results about our query: the two objects *must-alias*, *may-alias*, or *must-not-alias*. Moreover, pointer analysis often times out and never returns a result. However, to answer **Q1**, we need to get the result that l1 and l2 *must-not-alias*, i.e., they refer to different objects in memory. This is a sufficient condition to statically ensure that m will behave correctly at runtime regardless of the control flow since the update actions on Lines 10–11 are not on the list iterated by iterator it. To answer **Q2**, by observing Lines 15–16, we can see that, regardless of what happens at execution, these two instructions are safe and their execution does not need to be monitored. Also, in Line 6, the instruction is safe since it updates the list before the creation of the iterator.

Pointer analysis may not always conclude with a result, especially for Java programs. In addition to the inability to construct the full static call graph of the program, Java allows for dynamic class loading and reflection which often cause additional problems to pointer analysis. Our work relies on the idea that when statically analyzing cases such as the one of Condition (2), one can safely assume that such two variables *may-alias*, even without performing pointer-analysis. Also, we analyze methods separately and thus need to handle escaping references. Objects in the program that are relevant to the property may escape from the method to a subroutine or a return statement and produce events there. As such, we handle all instructions that may allow references to escape, such as method calls, with special *escape events*.

Our over-approximation might miss some positive answers to **Q1**, therefore missing some optimization opportunities. However, based on our observation (such as the experiments in Sect. 7), cases where one needs to perform pointer analysis such as in Condition (2) are less frequent in many Java programs. As such, our approach mainly addresses **Q2** while it is also capable of answering **Q1** but, in certain cases, less effectively.

3 Background

We recall concepts related to monitoring in general and our verification approach in particular. We assume basic familiarity with automata theory such as the definitions of a finite-state machine, words, runs, and acceptance, and refer to [21] for more details.

3.1 Monitoring

Let Σ be a set of events, Σ^* and Σ^ω are the sets of all finite and infinite traces over Σ, respectively. A finite trace is a sequence of events, a word in Σ, that can be modeled by a function $t : [1, n] \rightarrow \Sigma$ for a trace of length n. We say that an event belongs to the trace, noted $e \in t$, when $e \in \mathrm{codom}(t)$. A property φ is a *language* over Σ which is a subset of Σ^*. Given a trace t in Σ^*, the set of prefixes of t, noted $pre(t)$, is defined as: $pre(t) = \{p \in \Sigma^* \mid \exists s \in \Sigma^* : t = ps\}$. The set of matching prefixes is the set of prefixes of a trace within a given language L.

Definition 1 (Matching prefixes [10]). *Given a language $L \subseteq \Sigma^*$ and a trace $t \in \Sigma^*$, the matching prefixes of t in L is given by: $match_L(t) = pre(t) \cap L$.*

Many monitoring techniques and approaches essentially rely on the detection of *bad and good prefixes*, which are intuitively the witnessing sequences allowing a monitor to conclude about monitoring the program based on the trace observed so far.

Definition 2 (Bad/Good prefixes [24]). *Given a language $L \subseteq \Sigma^*$ of finite traces over Σ (or of infinite traces, $L \subseteq \Sigma^\omega$). A finite trace $u \in \Sigma^*$ is a bad prefix for L, if $\forall w \in \Sigma^* : uw \notin L$ (or $\forall w \in \Sigma^\omega : uw \notin L$, if L is over infinite traces). Moreover, u is a good prefix for L, if $\forall w \in \Sigma^* : uw \in L$ (or $\forall w \in \Sigma^\omega : uw \in L$, if L is over infinite traces).*

The languages of bad and good prefixes are extension-closed; since every continuation of a bad or a good prefix for a language, L, by a finite word is also a bad (good) prefix for L. When monitoring at runtime, we are interested in reporting a violation/satisfaction of a property from a trace as early as possible. Matching a *bad* (alternatively *good*) prefix is sufficient to produce a final verdict since every continuation of the trace will produce the same result. For instance, the techniques in [7, 16] synthesize a monitor (as a finite-state automaton) that recognizes the good and bad prefixes of the language denoted by a temporal-logic formula or by an automaton over infinite traces.

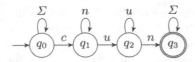

Fig. 2. Monitor recognizing the language of bad prefixes for the *SafeIterator* property.

Example 1 (SafeIterator monitor). Figure 2 shows the monitor that checks for the violation of the property from Sect. 2. Event c denotes a creation of an iterator associated with a list by calling `list.iterator()`, event u denotes an update on a list by calling `list.add(..)`, and event n denotes calling the next method `iterator.next()` on an iterator. The monitor recognizes the bad prefixes in the traces received from a running program. Note that the monitor reaches the accepting state when seeing the pattern $c.n^*.u^+.n$, as it suffices to conclude that the whole run violates the property.

Definition 3 (Property satisfaction). *We say that a trace $t \in \Sigma^*$, satisfies a property $\varphi \subseteq \Sigma^*$ denoted by $t \models \varphi$ iff $t \in \varphi$. Alternatively, for a safety property φ with its language of bad-prefixes L, $t \models \varphi$ iff $match_L(t) = \emptyset$. And, for a co-safety property φ' with its language of good-prefixes L', $t \models \varphi$ iff $match_{L'}(t) \neq \emptyset$.*

3.2 Parametric Monitoring

Monitoring is in practice performed on parametric monitors that receive events accompanied by runtime information about the objects producing them, allowing to monitor each related set of objects in the program separately. There is a myriad of different approaches to parametric monitoring that differ in the manner they interpret events with runtime information and project these to instances of monitors. See [5,11] for example approaches and [18,20] for overviews. Here, we sketch a simple and general approach to parametric monitoring that can be adapted to several existing approaches.

We denote the set of variables defined by a parametric monitor by X, and the set of values that these variables can take by V. These values usually correspond to objects in the memory of the execution environment of the program. A variable binding $\theta : X \rightarrow V$ maps monitor parameters to their values and $\mathcal{B}$ is the set of all possible bindings in a program. A parametric event $e\langle\theta\rangle$ is then a pair $(e, \theta) \in \Sigma \times \mathcal{B}$. We denote the set of all parametric events as $\Sigma\langle X\rangle$ and a parametric trace as a word in $\Sigma\langle X\rangle^*$.

Example 2 (Parametric traces). One trace that the program from Fig. 1 may generate at runtime is the following: $\tau = (u, [l \mapsto o(l1)]) (c, [l \mapsto o(l1), i \mapsto o(it)]) (u, [l \mapsto o(l2)]) (u, [l \mapsto o(l2)]) (n, [l \mapsto o(l1), i \mapsto o(it)]) (c, [l \mapsto o(l1), i \mapsto o(it)]) (u, [l \mapsto o(l2)])$. The event $(c, [l \mapsto o(l1), i \mapsto o(it)])$ denotes the creation of an iterator, event c, where the variable l, representing the associated list, is bound to the runtime object of $l1$ denoted by $o(l1)$ and the variable i, representing the created iterator, is bound to the runtime object of it denoted by $o(it)$.

A parametric property $\Lambda X.\varphi$ (notation borrowed from [11]) is then defined over traces of parametric events such that $\Lambda X.\varphi \subseteq \Sigma\langle X\rangle^*$. To monitor each group of related objects separately, a parametric monitor slices a parametric trace according to the values bound to the monitor parameters carried within events. Slicing is achieved by projecting a trace τ on all seen bindings using a projection function denoted by $\tau\downarrow_\theta$. We omit the formal details here for brevity. The projection results in a set of traces, we refer to as *projected traces*, where each trace contains non-parametric events that correspond to related objects in the program and is sent to a monitor that was spawned specifically for that slice.

Definition 4 (Projected traces). *Given a parametric trace τ in $\Sigma\langle X\rangle^*$, the set of projected traces is denoted by $Proj(\tau) \subseteq \Sigma^*$, and is defined as:*

$$Proj(\tau) = \bigcup_{\theta \in \mathcal{B}} \tau\downarrow_\theta$$

Example 3 (Projected traces). Consider τ from Example 2. A parametric monitor will check at runtime the relation between $o(l1)$ and $o(l2)$[1] then accordingly produce $Proj(\tau) = \{ucuuncu\}$ if $o(l1) = o(l2)$ or $Proj(\tau) = \{ucnc, uuu\}$ if $o(l1) \neq o(l2)$.

Definition 5 (Parametric property satisfaction). *A parametric trace $\tau \in \Sigma\langle X\rangle^*$ satisfies a parametric property $\Lambda X.\varphi$ denoted by:*

$$\tau \models \Lambda X.\varphi \overset{\text{def}}{=} \forall t \in Proj(\tau) : t \models \varphi$$

3.3 Upward Closure

We recall the notions for subwords and their closures for regular languages. We refer to [23] for full details and borrow their definitions. For a word $x \in \Sigma^*$, the length of x is denoted by $|x|$, and for $1 \leq i \leq |x|$, let x_i denote the i-th letter of x. We denote the empty word by ϵ. A *subword* is obtained by removing certain letters from a word at arbitrary positions, and, a *superword* is obtained by inserting any number of letters into a word at arbitrary positions. We say that a word x is a subword of y, denoted by $x \sqsubseteq y$, equivalently y is a superword of x when there are positions $0 < p_1 < p_2 < \ldots p_l \leq |y|$ such that $x[i] = y[p_i]$ for all $1 \leq i \leq l = |x|$. For $\Sigma = \{a, b, c\}$, we have $\varepsilon \sqsubseteq ab \sqsubseteq acba$.

Definition 6 (Upward closure of a language). *For a language $L \subseteq \Sigma^*$, the upward closure of L, is denoted by $\uparrow L$ and defined as $\{x \in \Sigma^* \mid \exists y \in L : y \sqsubseteq x\}$.*

For any language $L \subseteq \Sigma^*$, we have $L \subseteq \uparrow L$. Moreover, a language L is *upward-closed* if $L = \uparrow L$. For a regular language L recognized by a non-deterministic finite-state automaton (NFA), we can obtain an NFA recognizing $\uparrow L$ by simply adding transitions without increasing the number of states. More precisely, given an automaton $A = (\Sigma, Q, \delta, Q_0, F)$ recognizing L, the NFA $A^\uparrow = (\Sigma, Q, \delta', Q_0, F)$ recognizing $\uparrow L$ is obtained by adding a self loop on every state $q \in Q$ and every letter $s \in \Sigma$ such that $\delta' = \delta \cup \{\langle q, s, q\rangle \mid q \in Q, s \in \Sigma\}$.

---

[1] This can checked with == in Java.

3.4   Programs, CFG and Instrumentation

Given a program P, let $Methods$ be the set of all its methods, $Instructions$ the set of all byte-code instructions, and $Instructions_m$ all instructions of a method m. The $CFG_m = \langle B_m, E_m \rangle$ of m is a directed graph, where B_m is the set of nodes such that each instruction is a node, and $E_m \subseteq B_m \times B_m$ are edges that connect nodes to their successors. The instruction in a node b is denoted by $b.instr$, and $b.entry$ (resp. $b.exit$) is a Boolean which holds if b is the entry node (resp. is an exit node) for the method. To monitor a program, we abstract its execution in a trace of events extracted at runtime. This is achieved by instrumentation, which can be modeled by the function $instrument : Instructions^* \rightharpoonup \Sigma\langle X \rangle^*$.

4   Residual Analysis of Parametric Properties

We aim to verify a program P against some parametric property $\Lambda X.\varphi$. The behavior of a program is abstracted by the set of parametric event traces that it can produce at runtime. Let $[P] \subseteq \Sigma\langle X \rangle^*$ be such set for a program P. The verification problem can then be stated as checking if all the traces of the program satisfy the property:

$$P \models \Lambda X.\varphi \overset{\text{def}}{=} \forall \tau \in [P] : \tau \models \Lambda X.\varphi$$

Any verification technique aiming to verify the program should then be able to explore all the parametric traces that the program can generate. Moreover, the technique should also be able to explore for each parametric trace τ the set of projected traces $Proj(\tau)$ (see Sect. 3.2). However, statically, exploring the parametric traces requires full knowledge of the call graph of the program, whereas exploring projected traces requires knowledge of the aliasing relations between objects producing them. We know that obtaining such information is generally undecidable statically. Meanwhile, at runtime, this information is completely available. Yet, runtime verification incurs overhead on the execution of the program where this overhead is typically positively correlated with the size of traces. Our interest is then to statically verify parts of the program and leave a residual part for runtime verification.

Our proposed residual analysis *statically* identifies a set of instructions in the program, $\mathcal{S}_P$, that can be safely silenced/ignored at runtime from the monitor side without affecting verification. Ignoring an instruction means that there is no need to produce an event when it executes. As such, we aim to construct the *residual instrumentation* function $residual : Instructions^* \rightarrow (\mathcal{S}_P \rightarrow \Sigma\langle X \rangle^*)$. Let us note $Runs \subseteq Instructions^*$ the set of all the possible runs of a program P. Instrumenting the program with residual should ideally produce shorter traces than instrument, however, for both, we should get the same monitoring verdict. We can state the condition that should be met by the residual analysis as follows:

$$\forall r \in Runs : |\text{residual}(r)| \leq |\text{instrument}(r)|$$
$$\wedge\ \text{residual}(r) \models \Lambda X.\varphi \iff \text{instrument}(r) \models \Lambda X.\varphi$$

To perform the residual analysis statically and produce the set $\mathcal{S}_P$, we can over-approximate the program behavior by constructing a set $[\widehat{P}] \supseteq [P]$. This allows us to explore all the parametric traces that the program can produce but also traces that the program might never produce. A residual analysis should then check whether silencing some instructions does not affect the verification verdict of any trace in $[\widehat{P}]$, and safely assumes the same effect in $[P]$. Yet, given that $[\widehat{P}]$ is an over-approximation, the analysis may suffer from false positives, which are instructions that can indeed be silenced however the analysis found the opposite. In what follows, we consider a subset $[\widehat{P_m}] \subseteq [\widehat{P}]$ for our residual analysis, these are traces that are fully produced in single methods.

5   Residual Analysis via Intraprocedural Reachability Analysis

We demonstrate our instantiation of the residual analysis at the intraprocedural level using reachability analysis. Recall that we avoid dataflow and pointer analysis, as such, we do not have a static call graph for the program nor the variable aliasing relation. In Sect. 5.1, we capture the behavior of a method by using its control-flow graph to construct a representative model that allows us to explore the parametric traces a method can generate. In Sect. 5.2, we deal with the over-approximations by extending the bad-prefix automaton to handle different projections that might be produced by a parametric trace. In Sect. 5.3, we then present the reachability analysis algorithm that finds *safe* and *violating* paths in the control-flow graph; by cutting the behavior in a model-based checking approach. Finally, in Sect. 5.4, we discuss the soundness of our analysis.

5.1   Capturing the Behavior

Our analysis treats methods separately, however, we need to be careful. If a method receives as an argument an object which is a type that is capable of producing events in the alphabet of the property, then we cannot assume any previous behavior. As such, we exclude such methods from the analysis. For the same reason, we exclude all methods that operate on static instances of the types involved.

For each method m, we map two types of instructions to events and discard all other instructions as they are irrelevant to our analysis. We keep instructions that produce events in Σ, given by the property specification. We also keep instructions that may allow any object reference to escape from the context of method m; we introduce the new *escape* event ($\#$) for such instructions. Escape events are assignments to class fields, method calls that pass objects by references, in addition, to return statements that return objects [14]. However, our analysis allows the user to specify a safe list of instructions, denoted by the set $SafeList$, defined over the compile type information such as method names, package and type names, and opcodes. For instance, calling `System.out.print(11.toString())` is a safe instruction. All instructions that are escape events and are not in $SafeList$ are added to the set Esc_m.

Given the alphabet of a property Σ and the control-flow graph of a method m, $CFG_m = \langle B_m, E_m \rangle$, we replace each block b in B_m with b' and map its instruction to an event, and construct the CFG Automaton as follows.

$$b'.instr = b.instr.\mathrm{map}\left(i \mapsto \begin{cases} i \text{ if } i \in \Sigma, \\ \# \text{ else if } i \in Esc_m \\ \epsilon \text{ otherwise} \end{cases} \right)$$

Definition 7 (CFG Automaton). *Given the mapped CFG_m, the CFG Automaton is the non-deterministic finite-state automaton $\mathcal{A}_m^c = (\Sigma \cup \{\#\}, Q, \delta, q_0, F)$ constructed as follows:*

$$Q = \{q_b \mid b \in B_m\} \qquad q_0 = \{q_b \mid b \in B_m \wedge b.entry = true\}$$
$$F = Q \qquad \delta = \{\langle q_b, s, q_{b'} \rangle \mid \langle b, b' \rangle \in E_m \wedge b.\text{instr} = s\}$$

Each node in the control-flow graph is now represented as a state in the CFG Automaton. We make all states accepting states and merge states connected with ϵ transitions. Now, by traversing the CFG Automaton, we can explore the paths that method m can take at runtime and thus the parametric traces it can produce.

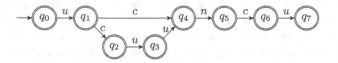

Fig. 3. The constructed CFG Automaton $\mathcal{A}_m^c$

Example 4 (CFG Automaton). Figure 3, shows the CFG Automaton constructed from the method in Sect. 2. Each state corresponds to an instruction that we are interested in the program. Two traces can be explored from the automaton in Fig. 3, $t_1 = ucuuncu$, which corresponds to the parametric trace τ from Example 2, and $t_2 = ucncu$.

5.2 Extending the Automaton of Bad Prefixes

We now describe how our analysis handles the over-approximations and extends the bad prefix automaton.

Handling Variables May-alias. Recall from Sect. 3.2, that a parametric trace τ in $\Sigma\langle X \rangle^*$ at runtime is projected into $Proj(\tau)$ to possibly multiple traces in Σ^*, depending on the aliasing relationship between the objects carried in the events. At runtime, this aliasing relationship is available for the parametric monitor to do the projection. However, statically for our residual analysis this information is not available. Our central idea in this paper is to avoid performing data-flow analysis and assume that the objects producing events in a method may-alias. For two events, our analysis should then consider the case when the objects bound to them *must-alias* and the case when they *must-not-alias*. In the former case, both events will be projected into the same trace, and in the latter, they will be projected into different traces.

Example 5 (Projected traces approximation with may-alias). Consider the trace t_1 which can be explored with the CFG Automaton from Example 4. At runtime, if the program takes such a control flow path, it emits a parametric trace that produces either of the projected traces from Example 3 depending on whether $l1$ and $l2$ alias. Since we avoid producing the aliasing relation statically and assume that $l1$ and $l2$ may alias, we should then consider in our residual analysis the disjunction of both cases. Thus the traces $pt_1 = \{ucuuncu, ucnc, uuu\}$ should be checked by our residual analysis. As for t_2 from Example 4, by the same reasoning, the traces to be checked are $pt_2 = \{ucncu, ucnc, u\}$. Hence for method m, the set of traces that should be checked is $pt_1 \cup pt_2$.

The CFG Automaton allows us to explore the different paths that the program can take at runtime, however, its traces are too coarse. They may be *polluted* with events that do not correspond to the same trace at runtime. We notice from above that this is equivalent to generating and considering all the subwords of a trace, where the real trace can be any subword of a trace that can be explored with the automaton. Thus, to safely handle the different projections, we use the upward closure, from Sect. 3.3, of the language of bad prefixes L. By using the upward closure $\uparrow L$, we can recognize a bad prefix in a full trace or any subword of it since $L \subseteq \uparrow L$, allowing us to find bad prefixes in all possible projected traces. However, we restrict the closure by removing the Σ self-loops from the initial and final states as we want to find the shortest paths that match a bad prefix.

Handling Escape Events. In Sect. 5.1, when constructing the CFG automaton, we introduced the escape $\#$ events. Since our analysis analyzes each method separately, we are oblivious to what might be happening in $\#$-transitions. We have to assume that they might produce events untracked by the method under analysis. To handle them safely, we add a $\#$-transition in the bad prefixes automaton from each state to all of its reachable states. Intuitively, this means when $\#$ event is encountered in a path, we assume that the path is not safe anymore and that it might match a bad prefix.

Extending the Bad Prefixes Automaton. We proceed to show how we extend the automaton of bad prefixes to handle the multiple projected traces and the escape events.

Definition 8 (Extended automaton of bad prefixes). *Given the language of bad prefixes* $\mathcal{L}(bad_\varphi)$ *recognized by automaton* $\mathcal{A}^{bad_\varphi} = (\Sigma, Q, \delta, Q_0, F)$ *with its extended transition function* $\hat{\delta}$. *The extended automaton of bad prefixes is defined as* $\mathcal{A}^{\uparrow bad_\varphi} = (\Sigma \cup \{\#\}, Q, \delta', Q_0, F)$ *where:*

$$\begin{align}
\delta' = \quad & \delta \setminus \{ \langle q, s, q \rangle \mid s \in \Sigma \wedge (q \in F \vee q \in Q_0) \} \tag{1} \\
\cup \quad & \{ \langle q, s, q \rangle \mid s \in \Sigma \cup \{\#\} \wedge q \in Q \wedge q \notin Q_0 \wedge q \notin F \} \tag{2} \\
\cup \quad & \{ \langle q, \#, q' \rangle \mid q, q' \in Q \wedge \exists w \in \Sigma^* : \hat{\delta}(q, w) = q' \wedge q' \notin F \} \tag{3}
\end{align}$$

The extended automaton has the same states. We remove the self-loops from initial and final states, as we want to find the shortest paths that match a bad prefix (1). We add the upward closure by adding Σ and $\#$ self-loops on all other states (2). We add $\#$-transitions from each state to the reachable states from it (3).

Example 6 ($\mathcal{A}^{\uparrow bad_\varphi}$ for the SafeIterator property). Figure 4, shows a construction of automaton $\mathcal{A}^{\uparrow bad_\varphi}$. Recall the pattern $c.n^*.u^+.n$ from Example 1, the new automaton will now recognize such a pattern while also handling the two over-approximations above.

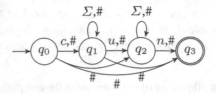

Fig. 4. The constructed automaton $\mathcal{A}^{\uparrow bad_\varphi}$.

5.3   Cutting the Behavior

We now proceed to describe how we find violating paths in the method. The idea is to traverse the constructed CFG automaton $\mathcal{A}_m^c$ state by state and check whether there is a path, starting from the visited state, that makes the extended bad prefixes automaton reach a final state. We limit the discussion here to matching bad prefixes, nevertheless, the same analysis works for matching good prefixes. However, when finding paths that match good prefixes, these will be the safe paths.

Given an automaton, $\mathcal{A}$, $\mathcal{A}(q)$ denotes $\mathcal{A}$ where q is set to be the initial state. Recall that, given a finite state machine $\mathcal{A}(q)$ with its extended transition function $\hat{\delta}$ [21], a state q is coreachable if there exists a word $s \in \Sigma^*$ such that $\hat{\delta}(q, s) \in F$. State q is reachable if there exists a word $s \in \Sigma^*$ such that $\hat{\delta}(q_0, s) = q$ and q_0 is an initial state.

Algorithm 1: Marking violating and safe paths

---

1 Given $\mathcal{A}_m^c = (\Sigma \cup \{\#\}, Q, \delta, q_0, F)$, $\mathcal{A}^{\uparrow bad_\varphi}$
2 $\mathcal{V}_m = \emptyset$ // represents all states in a violating path
3 $\mathcal{S}_m = Q$ // represents all states in a safe path

4 $work := q_0$ // represents a worklist stack
5 $visited = \emptyset$

6 **while** $work$ not $empty$ **do**
7 $\quad$ $q = work.pop()$
8 $\quad$ **if** $q \notin visited$ **then**
9 $\quad\quad$ $visited = visited \cup q$
10 $\quad\quad$ **if** $q \notin \mathcal{V}_m$ **then**
11 $\quad\quad\quad$ $\hat{A} = \mathcal{A}_m^c(q) \times \mathcal{A}^{\uparrow bad_\varphi}$
12 $\quad\quad\quad$ **if** $\mathcal{L}(\hat{A}) \neq \emptyset$ **then**
13 $\quad\quad\quad\quad$ $\mathcal{V}_m = \mathcal{V}_m \cup \{\{q' \mid (q', -) \in \text{coreachable}(\hat{A})\} \cap \text{reachable}(\mathcal{A}_m^c(q))\}$
14 $\quad\quad$ **foreach** q'' in $\{q'' \mid \langle q, s, q'' \rangle \in \delta\}$ **do**
15 $\quad\quad\quad$ $work.push(q'')$
16 $\quad\quad$ **end**
17 **end**
18 $\mathcal{S}_m = \mathcal{S}_m \setminus \mathcal{V}_m$

Algorithm 1, shows how to mark all states in $\mathcal{A}_m^c$ as either safe (in $\mathcal{S}_m$) or violating (in $\mathcal{V}_m$). The algorithm implements a depth-first search starting from the initial node of $\mathcal{A}_m^c$. We maintain a *work* stack and *visited* set, in lines (4,5,7,9,15), to hold automaton states to be visited and states that were already visited, respectively. For each state q we visit, we set q as the initial node and find the intersection with the $\mathcal{A}^{\uparrow bad_\varphi}$, line (11). If the intersection is not empty (line 12), we find the set of all co-reachable states in the intersection automaton. Each state in the intersection automaton $\hat{\mathcal{A}}$ corresponds to a state in $\mathcal{A}_m^c$ and $\mathcal{A}^{\uparrow bad_\varphi}$. For each coreachable state in $\hat{\mathcal{A}}$, we add its corresponding state in $\mathcal{A}_m^c$ to the set $\mathcal{V}_m$, (line 13). We do not revisit states that are already in $\mathcal{V}_m$ (line 10) since paths leading to a final state in $\mathcal{A}^{\uparrow bad_\varphi}$ are already explored by the intersection.

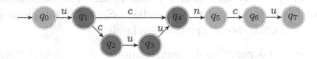

Fig. 5. Marking property violating paths in red, and safe in green. (Color figure online)

Example 7 (Property violating states). Figure 5, shows the CFG Automaton constructed from the program from Fig. 1, where states marked in red exist in a property-violating path. The red states in the automaton are the states that we need to instrument, and the green states are hidden from instrumentation. We can see that instead of instrumenting at 8 different locations, we only have to instrument at 4 locations.

For our residual analysis, for each method m we analyze, we add the instructions corresponding to the states in $\mathcal{S}_m$ to the set $\mathcal{S}_P$. As for the other states in $\mathcal{V}_m$, their corresponding instructions will be instrumented for runtime monitoring.

5.4 Scope and Soundness of the Analysis

We first argue that our analysis only affects the traces that are fully produced in one method. Recall from Sect. 5.1, that the nodes of CFG automaton $\mathcal{A}_m^c$ correspond to instructions in method m that produce events. We use the notation $ev(q)$ to denote the corresponding event from an automaton state, and $events(t)$ to denote all events from a trace t. If some trace t contains events produced by instructions outside of m, then no instruction in m that produced events in t was marked safe.

Proposition 1 (Scope of the analysis). *Given a parametric trace τ in $[P]$:*

$$\forall t \in Proj(\tau), \forall m \in Methods:$$
$$(\exists i \in Instructions \backslash Instructions_m : \text{instrument}(i) \in t)$$
$$\implies \{ ev(q) \mid q \in \mathcal{S}_m \} \cap events(t) = \emptyset$$

Proof. Assume that there exists some trace t that has events produced outside of m i.e. $\exists i \in Instructions \backslash Instructions_m$: instrument(i) $\in t$ is true. Such traces can be split into two types. Traces that contained events before the execution of m at runtime (1), and traces that start from m but have some events that are produced outside of m at runtime (2). We will show that for both types of traces, the analysis would result in $S_m = \emptyset$. Since we exclude from the analysis any method that receives a parameter of a type that generates events. Traces from (1), will not be affected by analysis. For that to happen, method m should receive the objects generating the events. Therefore, m will be excluded from the analysis resulting in $S_m = \emptyset$. As for (2), any escape of an object, which might produce events outside m, is captured by the $\#$ transitions. From the construction of the bad-prefixes automaton and Algorithm 1, such transitions will result in reaching a final state from any state in the CFG automaton, resulting in $S_m = \emptyset$. Hence for both types of traces we have $S_m = \emptyset$, therefore $\{ev(q) \mid q \in S_m\} \cap \text{events}(t) = \emptyset$ holds, and the proposition holds.   □

Proposition 1 in fact depends on the specification of the *SafeList* from Sect. 5.1. If some method was added by the user that is not safe, i.e. allows references to escape, then the proposition will not hold. From the above, we also see that our analysis only affects instructions that produce events only in traces that are collected fully in the method itself since otherwise $S_m = \emptyset$. For soundness, we need to guarantee that at any run of the program, an event that we marked safe in our residual analysis does not have any effect on deciding the violation/satisfaction of the property for any projected trace at runtime. As we showed that the analysis only affects projected traces that are fully produced in one method, we only reason about single methods when discussing soundness.

Theorem 1 (Soundness of the analysis). *Given a language $L \subseteq \Sigma^*$ and S_m resulting from the analysis on method m, the analysis is sound iff*

$$\forall a_1 \cdots a_i \cdots a_n \in \Sigma^+, \forall i \in \mathbb{N} :$$
$$match_L(a_1 \cdots a_i \cdots a_n) \neq match_L(a_1 \cdots a_{i-1}a_{i+1} \cdots a_n)$$
$$\implies a_i \notin \{ ev(q) \mid q \in S_m \}$$

The condition states that given a projected trace at runtime, if we remove an event a_i from it and get a different match from the new trace i.e. $match_L(a_1 \cdots a_i \cdots a_n) \neq match_L(a_1 \cdots a_{i-1}a_{i+1} \cdots a_n)$, then our analysis must have not statically marked a_i as safe ($a_i \notin \{ ev(q) \mid q \in S_m \}$).

Proof. The proof follows from the definition of Algorithm 1. Assume that when our analysis removes a_i, then $match_L(a_1 \cdots a_i \cdots a_n) \neq match_L(a_1 \cdots a_{i-1}a_{i+1} \cdots a_n)$. This means that a_i is in an extension of $a_1 \cdots a_{i-1}$ that leads to a final state in the monitor of the bad-prefixes of L, or else $match_L(a_1 \cdots a_i \cdots a_n) = match_L(a_1 \cdots a_{i-1}a_{i+1} \cdots a_n)$. However, if a_i is in such a path, then it will be added to V_m as per Line 7 of Algorithm 1 since the algorithm finds any path from a state in the CFG that reaches the final state of the automaton of bad-prefixes. Then a_i is not in S_m and $a_i \notin \{ ev(q) \mid q \in S_m \}$ holds.   □

6   Implementation

We implement our work as a plugin to the BISM [29] Java byte-code instrumentation tool. Instrumentation directives in BISM are given with *transformers*, which resemble aspects of aspect-oriented programming. BISM provides a mechanism to compose multiple transformers. Transformers, in composition, are capable of controlling the visibility of instructions. For each property, we then apply two transformers to the program: the static analyzer, which performs the residual analysis with a single pass over the code of methods and hides safe instructions, and the second one to instrument the residual part for runtime monitoring. We extend BISM with a module that enables performing the residual analysis and provides automata operations. The module is used to generate the CFG automata of methods, extend the automaton for bad prefixes, and detect the property-violating execution paths.

7   Evaluation

We report on our evaluation of the effectiveness of our approach[2].

Experimental Setup. We compare the instrumentation overhead with our residual analysis, denoted by **RRV**, and without the analysis, denoted by **RV**. We instrument with BISM the programs, in the DaCapo suite [8], for the monitoring of the classical SafeListIterator (P1), SafeMapIterator (P2), and SafeHasNext (P3) properties. (P2) is similar to (P1) from Sect. 2 but is concerned with Java maps. (P3) specifies that a program does not call the next method before calling the hasNext method of an iterator. We include as *escape* events (#) all assignments to class fields, all method calls that pass objects by references, and in addition, return statements that return objects [14]. We include in the *SafeList* all calls to methods of Java classes. Other than the method calls relevant to the property and captured by instrumentation, these calls do not produce events. We note that *fop* is the only single-threaded benchmark, however, we can use the multi-threaded benchmarks as we checked that for the properties all the events in the projected traces are being produced within the same thread. We consider 100 runs and then calculate the mean and the standard deviation[3].

Evaluation Metrics. We consider the number of affected instructions, methods, and classes by our residual analysis (RRV) and without it (RV). We also consider the improvement factor. We are also interested in evaluating the runtime overhead, that is, the performance degradation caused by instrumentation for monitoring. For runtime, we measure the execution time of the instrumented program. For used memory, we measure the used heap and non-heap memory after a forced garbage collection.

---

[2] Implementation details and experiments can be found at https://gitlab.inria.fr/monitoring/residual-runtime-verification-with-bism.

[3] We use Java JDK 8u251 with 16 GB maximum heap size on an Intel Core i9-9980HK (2.4 GHz. 16 GB RAM). We use the DaCapo version 9.12-bach.

Table 1. For each program (Bench), and property (P1), (P2), and (P3), we report # of relevant classes, methods, and instructions (Rel) producing events, number proved safe statically by our technique (Nop), # of events produced at runtime (RV) and after our analysis (RRV), improvement factor for # of instructions instrumented and events produced (Imp). $K = 10^3$, $M = 10^6$.

Bench	Property	# Classes		# Methods		# Instructions			# Events		
		Rel	Nop	Rel	Nop	Rel	Nop	Imp	RV	RRV	Imp
avrora	P1	41	14	99	56	165	86	2.09	1.36M	1.36M	1.00
fop	P1	123	33	275	103	700	210	1.43	729K	490K	1.49
sunflow	P1	11	2	35	15	50	15	1.43	2.55M	1.27M	2.00
pmd	P1	86	27	200	95	420	146	1.53	4.77M	778K	6.13
avrora	P2	41	19	111	78	160	117	3.72	353K	246K	1.43
fop	P2	100	28	206	85	2.9K	2.6K	9.19	545K	351K	1.55
sunflow	P2	11	6	32	24	40	26	2.86	2.55M	1.27M	2.00
pmd	P2	81	27	168	70	392	211	2.17	3.01M	2.6M	1.16
avrora	P3	32	11	76	33	160	79	1.98	1.5M	1.29M	1.16
fop	P3	70	7	145	31	376	67	1.22	1.07M	882K	1.21
sunflow	P3	8	2	12	3	29	3	1.12	3.93M	2.65M	1.48
pmd	P3	65	21	126	48	343	115	1.50	5.64M	5.23M	1.08

Results. In Table 1, we report the results. The table demonstrates the effectiveness of the residual analysis as it reduces the number of instrumentation points by a factor of 2.5 on average (reaching 9.19), and accordingly, a reduction in the number of generated events at runtime by a factor of 1.8 on average (reaching 6.13). We notice that the reduction of instrumentation points does not always result in a reduction of runtime events for instance with *avrora* with (P1), where we find methods that produce most of the events that we could not prove safe statically. We also notice that most of our missed optimizations are due to escape # events (see Sect. 5.1). The more diverse operations between events, the more missed optimization. However, the *SafeList* can be improved with the help of escape analysis to include more instructions that we can guarantee are safe for our analysis and accordingly reduce the number of escape events. We leave that for future work as we envision adding plugins to incorporate static analysis. We also note that many of the events generated under classical instrumentation (RV) are irrelevant; they occur in methods that do not produce enough events to reach a final state in the monitor. As such, our analysis is effective in removing those from instrumentation. Figures 6 report the execution time and the memory usage for the benchmarks with all three properties combined. The figures show that **RRV** results in better performance in all benchmarks than classical instrumentation **RV**.

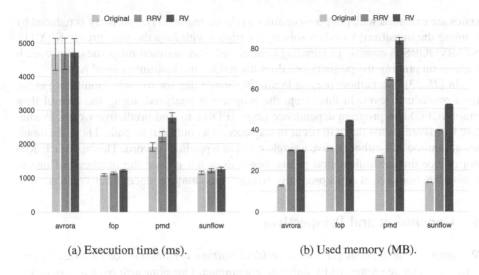

(a) Execution time (ms).   (b) Used memory (MB).

Fig. 6. Evaluation for the three properties.

8 Related Work

Many research approaches combine static and runtime verification. We focus here on some influential and most recent tools devised for verifying general behavioral parametric properties in sequential programs via residual analysis.

CLARA [9, 10] handles properties that can be expressed by finite-state automata by partially evaluating the runtime monitors at compile time and reducing the instrumentation points. It performs three-staged phases of analysis with increasing precision. The more precise phase uses a demand-driven pointer analysis and handles intra-procedural analysis. The first two phases of its analysis can be easily applied within our framework. However, unfortunately, CLARA is no longer maintained and so is its underlying instrumentation tool the abc compiler [3]. In [32], the authors present two optimizations for [10]. One optimization identifies changeless configurations during the backward analysis; the other one uses local object information to refine the forward analysis and backward analysis of the *nop-shadow* analysis. CLARVA [4] extends CLARA [10] to handle properties expressed by DATEs (Dynamic Automata with Events and Timers [2]) where events are guarded by runtime conditions and timers. Similar to our approach, it transforms Java code into an automaton-based model and allows for the incorporation of control-flow analyses. CLARVA is capable of reducing the instrumentation points as well as reasoning about and pruning the property itself. However, the analysis relies on constructing the callgraph of the full program and on pointer analysis using Soot [31]. Our approach is still capable of producing optimizations with a single pass on the program and without any dependence on static analysis, separating the limitations of static analysis from the residual analysis.

STARVOORS [12] combines deductive theorem proving with control-flow reachability analysis allowing to target control and data-oriented properties. The formalism used for property specification is ppDATE (an extension of DATE) where the automaton states are extended with pre/post-conditions (*Hoare triples*). The property is reduced by pruning the transitions based on solving the triples with Java theorem prover KEY [1]. STARVOORS is capable of handling control and data-oriented properties, however, it focuses on pruning the property and does not reduce the instrumentation points.

In [25,33], the authors present Predictive Semantics for runtime monitoring at the intra-procedural level. In this setup, the program is analyzed, using the control flow graph (CFG) and program dependence graph (PDG), to find predictive words. Predictive words are events that will occur in sequence in a control-flow path. Then, the monitor at runtime will either receive a single event or a predictive word. This approach does not reduce the instrumentation points, hence does not reduce the overhead of instrumentation, however, it emits predictive words which may produce faster verdicts.

9   Conclusion and Perspectives

We introduce an analysis supporting *residual runtime verification* for parametric properties that can be expressed by finite-state automata. Our approach over-approximates the behavior of the program and analyzes its methods separately relying only on their control-flow graphs to statically identify safe regions. We have demonstrated the effectiveness of our approach in monitoring the bad prefixes of a property, however, our approach can also be used with good prefixes (when monitoring co-safety properties for instance). Our approach is capable of producing overhead optimizations without any dependence on a specific type of static analysis, separating the task of static analysis from the residual analysis and allowing for seamless integration with many RV frameworks. It is fully implemented and integrated within the BISM instrumentation tool, which is the state-of-the-art instrumentation tool for Java programs. We also demonstrated the significant performance benefits at runtime.

Our work lays the foundation for a residual analysis framework that, at its core, does not depend on any specific static analysis technique. Nevertheless, we plan to extend it with plugins that allow the user to easily incorporate static analysis results aiming to reduce over-approximations and increase precision. The user might opt to include static call graph construction and escape analysis for a more precise approximation of parametric traces, also data-flow pointer analysis for better approximations of projected traces. We plan to provide a language that easily integrates the results of such analysis into our residual analysis mainly via refining the safe list of instructions. We also plan to extend our approach to analyze concurrent programs and handle thread-escaping references.

References

1. Ahrendt, W., Beckert, B., Hähnle, R., Rümmer, P., Schmitt, P.H.: Verifying object-oriented programs with key: a tutorial. In: de Boer, F.S., Bonsangue, M.M., Graf, S., de Roever, W.-P. (eds.) FMCO 2006. LNCS, vol. 4709, pp. 70–101. Springer, Heidelberg (2007). https://doi.org/10.1007/978-3-540-74792-5_4

2. Ahrendt, W., Pace, G.J., Schneider, G.: A unified approach for static and runtime verification: framework and applications. In: Margaria, T., Steffen, B. (eds.) ISoLA 2012. LNCS, vol. 7609, pp. 312–326. Springer, Heidelberg (2012). https://doi.org/10.1007/978-3-642-34026-0_24

3. Avgustinov, P., et al.: ABC: an extensible AspectJ compiler. In: Proceedings of the 4th International Conference on Aspect-Oriented Software Development, AOSD 2005, pp. 87–98. Association for Computing Machinery, New York (2005). https://doi.org/10.1145/1052898.1052906

4. Azzopardi, S., Colombo, C., Pace, G.: Clarva: model-based residual verification of java programs. In: Proceedings of the 8th International Conference on Model-Driven Engineering and Software Development, MODELSWARD, pp. 352–359. INSTICC, SciTePress (2020). https://doi.org/10.5220/0008966603520359

5. Barringer, H., Falcone, Y., Havelund, K., Reger, G., Rydeheard, D.: Quantified event automata: towards expressive and efficient runtime monitors. In: Giannakopoulou, D., Méry, D. (eds.) FM 2012. LNCS, vol. 7436, pp. 68–84. Springer, Heidelberg (2012). https://doi.org/10.1007/978-3-642-32759-9_9

6. Bartocci, E., Falcone, Y., Francalanza, A., Reger, G.: Introduction to runtime verification. In: Bartocci, E., Falcone, Y. (eds.) Lectures on Runtime Verification. LNCS, vol. 10457, pp. 1–33. Springer, Cham (2018). https://doi.org/10.1007/978-3-319-75632-5_1

7. Bauer, A., Leucker, M., Schallhart, C.: Runtime verification for LTL and TLTL. ACM Trans. Softw. Eng. Methodol. 20(4), 14:1–14:64 (2011). https://doi.org/10.1145/2000799.2000800

8. Blackburn, S.M., et al.: The DaCapo benchmarks: Java benchmarking development and analysis. SIGPLAN Not. 41(10), 169–190 (2006). https://doi.org/10.1145/1167515.1167488

9. Bodden, E., Lam, P., Hendren, L.: Clara: a framework for partially evaluating finite-state runtime monitors ahead of time. In: Barringer, H., et al. (eds.) RV 2010. LNCS, vol. 6418, pp. 183–197. Springer, Heidelberg (2010). https://doi.org/10.1007/978-3-642-16612-9_15

10. Bodden, E., Lam, P., Hendren, L.J.: Partially evaluating finite-state runtime monitors ahead of time. ACM Trans. Program. Lang. Syst. 34(2), 7:1–7:52 (2012). https://doi.org/10.1145/2220365.2220366

11. Chen, F., Roşu, G.: Parametric trace slicing and monitoring. In: Kowalewski, S., Philippou, A. (eds.) TACAS 2009. LNCS, vol. 5505, pp. 246–261. Springer, Heidelberg (2009). https://doi.org/10.1007/978-3-642-00768-2_23

12. Chimento, J.M., Ahrendt, W., Pace, G.J., Schneider, G.: STARVOORS: a tool for combined static and runtime verification of Java. In: Bartocci, E., Majumdar, R. (eds.) RV 2015. LNCS, vol. 9333, pp. 297–305. Springer, Cham (2015). https://doi.org/10.1007/978-3-319-23820-3_21

13. Chimento, J.M., Ahrendt, W., Schneider, G.: Testing meets static and runtime verification. In: Proceedings of the 6th Conference on Formal Methods in Software Engineering, FormaliSE 2018, pp. 30–39. Association for Computing Machinery, New York (2018). https://doi.org/10.1145/3193992.3194000

14. Choi, J.D., Gupta, M., Serrano, M., Sreedhar, V.C., Midkiff, S.: Escape analysis for Java. SIGPLAN Not. 34(10), 1–19 (1999). https://doi.org/10.1145/320385.320386

15. Dwyer, M.B., Purandare, R.: Residual dynamic typestate analysis exploiting static analysis, p. 124 (2007)

16. Falcone, Y., Fernandez, J., Mounier, L.: What can you verify and enforce at runtime? Int. J. Softw. Tools Technol. Transf. 14(3), 349–382 (2012). https://doi.org/10.1007/s10009-011-0196-8

17. Falcone, Y., Havelund, K., Reger, G.: A tutorial on runtime verification. In: Broy, M., Peled, D.A., Kalus, G. (eds.) Engineering Dependable Software Systems. NATO Science for Peace and Security Series, D: Information and Communication Security, vol. 34, pp. 141–175. IOS Press (2013). https://doi.org/10.3233/978-1-61499-207-3-141

18. Falcone, Y., Krstić, S., Reger, G., Traytel, D.: A taxonomy for classifying runtime verification tools. Int. J. Softw. Tools Technol. Transfer **23**(2), 255–284 (2021). https://doi.org/10.1007/s10009-021-00609-z

19. Havelund, K., Goldberg, A.: Verify your runs. In: Meyer, B., Woodcock, J. (eds.) VSTTE 2005. LNCS, vol. 4171, pp. 374–383. Springer, Heidelberg (2008). https://doi.org/10.1007/978-3-540-69149-5_40

20. Havelund, K., Reger, G., Thoma, D., Zălinescu, E.: Monitoring events that carry data. In: Bartocci, E., Falcone, Y. (eds.) Lectures on Runtime Verification. LNCS, vol. 10457, pp. 61–102. Springer, Cham (2018). https://doi.org/10.1007/978-3-319-75632-5_3

21. Hopcroft, J.E., Motwani, R., Ullman, J.D.: Introduction to Automata Theory, Languages, and Computation, 3rd edn. Addison-Wesley Longman Publishing Co., Inc. (2006)

22. Jakse, R., Falcone, Y., Méhaut, J., Pouget, K.: Interactive runtime verification - when interactive debugging meets runtime verification. In: 28th IEEE International Symposium on Software Reliability Engineering, ISSRE 2017, Toulouse, France, 23–26 October 2017, pp. 182–193. IEEE Computer Society (2017). https://doi.org/10.1109/ISSRE.2017.19

23. Karandikar, P., Niewerth, M., Schnoebelen, P.: On the state complexity of closures and interiors of regular languages with subwords and superwords. Theoret. Comput. Sci. **610**, 91–107 (2016). https://doi.org/10.1016/j.tcs.2015.09.028

24. Kupferman, O., Vardi, M.Y.: Model checking of safety properties. Formal Methods Syst. Des. **19**(3), 291–314 (2001). https://doi.org/10.1023/A:1011254632723

25. Leucker, M.: Sliding between model checking and runtime verification. In: Qadeer, S., Tasiran, S. (eds.) RV 2012. LNCS, vol. 7687, pp. 82–87. Springer, Heidelberg (2013). https://doi.org/10.1007/978-3-642-35632-2_10

26. Leucker, M., Schallhart, C.: A brief account of runtime verification. J. Logic Algebraic Program. **78**(5), 293–303 (2009). https://doi.org/10.1016/j.jlap.2008.08.004

27. Sánchez, C., et al.: A survey of challenges for runtime verification from advanced application domains (beyond software). Formal Methods Syst. Des. **54**(3), 279–335 (2019). https://doi.org/10.1007/s10703-019-00337-w

28. Soueidi, C., Falcone, Y.: Capturing program models with BISM. In: Proceedings of the 37th ACM/SIGAPP Symposium on Applied Computing, SAC 2022, pp. 1857–1861. Association for Computing Machinery, New York (2022). https://doi.org/10.1145/3477314.3507239

29. Soueidi, C., Kassem, A., Falcone, Y.: BISM: Bytecode-Level Instrumentation for Software Monitoring. https://gitlab.inria.fr/monitoring/bism-tool

30. Strom, R.E., Yemini, S.: Typestate: a programming language concept for enhancing software reliability. IEEE Trans. Softw. Eng. **12**(1), 157–171 (1986). https://doi.org/10.1109/TSE.1986.6312929

31. Vallée-Rai, R., Co, P., Gagnon, E., Hendren, L., Lam, P., Sundaresan, V.: Soot - a Java bytecode optimization framework. In: Proceedings of the 1999 Conference of the Centre for Advanced Studies on Collaborative Research, CASCON 1999, p. 13. IBM Press (1999)

32. Wang, C., Chen, Z., Mao, X.: Optimizing Nop-shadows typestate analysis by filtering interferential configurations. In: Legay, A., Bensalem, S. (eds.) RV 2013. LNCS, vol. 8174, pp. 269–284. Springer, Heidelberg (2013). https://doi.org/10.1007/978-3-642-40787-1_16

33. Zhang, X., Leucker, M., Dong, W.: Runtime verification with predictive semantics. In: Goodloe, A.E., Person, S. (eds.) NFM 2012. LNCS, vol. 7226, pp. 418–432. Springer, Heidelberg (2012). https://doi.org/10.1007/978-3-642-28891-3_37

Author Index

Printed in the United States
by Baker & Taylor Publisher Services